ENTHUSIAST IN WIT

ENTHUSIAST IN WIT

————⟨⟨•⟩⟩⟨⟨•⟩⟩————

A Portrait of
John Wilmot, Earl of Rochester
1647–1680

————⟨⟨•⟩⟩⟨⟨•⟩⟩————

by
VIVIAN DE SOLA PINTO

UNIVERSITY OF NEBRASKA PRESS
LINCOLN   1962

Publishers on the Plains

UNP

Copyright © by V. de Sola Pinto 1962
Library of Congress Catalog Number 61–12031
PRINTED IN ENGLAND

To
The University of Nottingham
a kind mother to me
for many years

CONTENTS

vii

PLATES

THERE seem to be four oil paintings of Rochester at present in existence, as well as a drawing by David Loggan, now in the British Museum. Of the four oil paintings, the fine three-quarter length in the Victoria and Albert Museum by Sir Peter Lely, reproduced as Plate 1 in this volume, is probably the earliest. It represents the young Rochester, and may well have been painted when he became a Gentleman of the Bedchamber in 1666/7. Better known is the 'fancy' portrait of the Earl by Jacob Huysmans, of which two versions exist, one at Warwick Castle and one at the National Portrait Gallery; the latter is reproduced as Plate 4. It represents Rochester crowning with laurels his monkey, doubtless the animal referred to in *A Satyr Against Mankind* and in one of his letters to Henry Savile. This picture was probably painted about 1676. A fourth oil painting is a head and shoulders at Hinchinbrooke reproduced in the present author's edition of Rochester's poems in the New Muses' Library. The painting of Lady Rochester (Plate 2), now at Chargot, Somerset, is the only known portrait of the Countess, and is reproduced by kind permission of its present owner, Colonel Sir Edward Malet. The portrait of Rochester's mistress, the famous actress, Elizabeth Barry (Plate 3), is from a picture belonging to Mr. C. H. Hartmann, by whose kind permission it is reproduced. Mr. Hartmann believes it to be an eighteenth-century copy of an original sketch by Kneller which belonged to Horace Walpole and was engraved by C. Knight in 1792. The profile allegorical figure in the right-hand bottom corner of the equestrian portrait of William III at Hampton Court by Kneller is also said by Walpole to be a portrait of Mrs. Barry and may well be related to the other picture. I am indebted to Mr. David Piper of the National Portrait Gallery for information about the pictures of Mrs. Barry. Plates 1 and 4 are reproduced by courtesy respectively of the Victoria and Albert Museum and The National Portrait Gallery.

PREFACE

THE first version of this work was published in 1935 under the title, *Rochester, Portrait of a Restoration Poet*. That book has been out of print for many years. Soon after it was published, I began to find mistakes and deficiencies in it. In the decade following its appearance much new information about Rochester came to light. In April, 1940 my friend Professor J. H. Wilson published in *The Review of English Studies* his important discovery that the old story of Rochester's responsibility for the assault on Dryden in Rose-Alley, Covent Garden, in December 1679, was almost certainly baseless, and in 1941 his edition of the *Rochester-Savile Letters*, containing material of the greatest value for the elucidation of the poet's biography, was published by the Ohio State University Press. In June 1944 an anonymous contributor to *The Times Literary Supplement* drew attention to Phillips MS. 17730, a manuscript book containing a hitherto unpublished account by Rochester's servant Thomas Alcock of the Earl's adventures in the guise of the Italian mountebank Alexander Bendo on Tower Hill.

This manuscript was subsequently acquired by the Library of the University of Nottingham, where I have been able to make use of it in the preparation of the present work. In the early nineteen-fifties I was engaged in the preparation of my edition of Rochester's poems, which was published in the New Muses' Library in 1953, and I learned a great deal about the poet from that work. Rochester, to use a phrase of Burke's, has been 'rolling through my head' for a quarter of a century. The result has been such an extensive revision, rewriting and supplementation of the original text of my study that the book which is now being offered to the public can, I think, fairly claim to be regarded as a new work, and I have, therefore, thought it appropriate to give it a new title, which I have borrowed from the apt description of Rochester by his friend and admirer Sir Francis Fane.

I hope this book will go some way towards satisfying the need which certainly exists at present for a comprehensive and reliable

study of this important English poet, embodying the results of research carried out in this country and in America during the last
quarter of a century. For the valuable help I have received from
friend and colleagues on both sides of the Atlantic I wish to express
my sincere thanks; I am particularly grateful to Professor J. H.
Wilson of the State University, Columbus, Ohio, who has not only
given me much helpful advice and encouragement, but has also
allowed me to make use of his own valuable unpublished notes on
Rochester.

V. DE S. PINTO

University of Nottingham,
July, 1961

LIST OF AUTHORITIES AND ABBREVIATIONS

I. TEXTS OF ROCHESTER'S WRITINGS

MANUSCRIPTS

H.
British Museum Harleian MS. 7003. Album containing autograph letters by Rochester and letters addressed to him.

F.P.
The Famous Pathologist or the Noble Mountebank. MS. book containing account by Thomas Alcock of Rochester's adventures as a mountebank on Tower Hill with a transcript of 'The Noble Mountebanks Bill'. Formerly Phillips MS. 17730, now Nottingham University MS. 1489. This work was published in October 1961 by Sisson and Parker Ltd., as No. 1 of the Nottingham University Miscellany, edited with an Introduction and Notes by V. de S. Pinto.

Port
Album containing autograph poetry and prose by Rochester in the Duke of Portland's Collection in Nottingham University Library.

PRINTED BOOKS

F.L.I.
Familiar Letters Written by the Right Honourable John Late Earl of Rochester and Several Other Persons of Honour and Quality. London: Printed by W. Onley, for Sam Briscoe, 1697.

F.L.II
Familiar Letters : Volume II Containing Thirty Six Letters by the Right Honourable, John, late Earl of Rochester. London: Printed for Sam Briscoe, 1697 (Preface by Charles Gildon).

Hayward
The Collected Works of John Wilmot, Earl of Rochester, edited by John Haywood. The Nonesuch Press, MCMXXVI.

P.
Poems by John Wilmot, Earl of Rochester, edited with an introduction and notes by Vivian de Sola Pinto. London: Routledge and Kegan Paul, 1953.

xi

Thorpe   *Rochester's Poems on Several Occasions*, edited by James Thorpe. Princeton, New Jersey: Princeton University Press, 1950.

V.   *Valentinian : A Tragedy As 'tis Alter'd by the late Earl of Rochester, and Acted at the Theatre Royal London :* Printed for Timothy Goodwin, 1685.

W.   *The Rochester-Savile Letters 1671–1680*, edited by John Harold Wilson. The Ohio State University Press, 1941.

1691   *Poems, &c on Several Occasions: with Valentinian, A Tragedy Written by the Right Honourable John Late Earl of Rochester. London, Printed for Jacob Tonson at the Judge's Head in Chancery-Lane near Fleet-Street*, 1691.

II. BIOGRAPHY ETC.

A.K.L.   *All the King's Ladies, Actresses of the Restoration*, by J. H. Wilson. Chicago: 1958.

Aubrey   *Brief Lives Chiefly of Contemporaries by John Aubrey*, ed. A. Clark. Oxford: 1908 (2 vols.).

Balfour   *Letters Written to a Friend by the Learned and Judicious Sir Andrew Balfour*, M.D. Edinburgh: 1700.

Behn   *The Works of Aphra Behn*, ed. M. Summers. Stratford-on-Avon: 1915 (6 vols.).

B.H.   *Bishop Burnet's History of His Own Time*, ed. The Earls of Dartmouth and Hardwick. Oxford: 1833 (6 vols.).

Blount   *The Miscellaneous Works of Charles Blount Esq.*, Pt. I the Oracle of Reason [London]: 1695.

Boswell   *The Restoration Court Stage (1660–1702)*, by Eleanoure Boswell. Harvard: 1932.

Brooks   *A Bibliography of John Oldham the Restoration Satirist*, by Harold F. Brooks. Reprinted from the Proceedings and Papers of the Oxford Bibliographical Society, Vol. V., Pt. I.

Bryant   *Samuel Pepys the Years of Peril*, by Arthur Bryant. Cambridge: 1935.

B.S.P.   *Some Passages of the Life and Death of the Right Honourable John Earl of Rochester*, by Gilbert Burnet. London: 1680.

B.U.   *Biographie Universelle (Michaud) Ancienne et Moderne.* Paris et Leipzig: 1811–62 (85 vols.).

Chamberlayne   *Angliae Notitia or the Present State of England*, by Edward Chamberlayne. 4th ed., London: 1670.

C.H.E.L.   *The Cambridge History of English Literature*, ed. A. Ward and A. R. Waller. Cambridge: 1908 (14 vols.).

Chesterfield   *The Letters of Philip Dormer Stanhope 4th Earl of Chester-field*, edited with an Introduction by Bonamy Dobrée in six volumes. London and New York: 1932.

C.H.G.R.   *The History of the Great Rebellion and Civil Wars in England*, by Edward Earl of Clarendon, ed. W. D. Macray. Oxford: 1888 (6 vols.).

Cibber   *An Apology for the Life of Mr. Colley Cibber Written by Himself*, ed. R. W. Lowe. London: 1889 (2 vols.).

C.L.   *The Life of Edward Earl of Clarendon Written by Himself*. Oxford: 1857 (2 vols.).

Collinson   *The History and Antiquities of the County of Somerset*, ed. the Rev. J. Collinson. Bath: 1791 (3 vols.).

Coronation   *The Coronation, a Poem*, by Ro. Whitehall. London: 1661.

C.S.P.D.   *The Calendar of State Papers Domestic Series of the Reign of Charles II*, ed. M. A. Green.

C.T.B.   *The Calendar of Treasury Books, 1660–80*, ed. W. A. Shaw.

Curll   *The History of the English Stage From the Restoration to the Present Time by Mr. Thomas Betterton* [by E. Curll]. London: 1741.

Davenant   *The Works of Sir William Davenant Kt*. London: 1673.

Davies   *Dramatic Miscellanies*, by Thomas Davies, a new edition, London: 1785 (3 vols.).

Dennis   *The Critical Works of John Dennis*, ed. E. N. Hooker, Baltimore: 1943 (2 vols.).

D.N.B.   *The Dictionary of National Biography*.

Dryden, ed. Noyes   *The Poetical Works of Dryden. A new edition*, ed. G. R. Noyes. Cambridge, Mass.: 1950.

Dryden, ed. Scott   *The Works of Dryden*, ed. Walter Scott. London: 1808 (18 vols.).

E.A.   *Études Anglaises*. Paris: 1937–.

E.D.   *The Diary of John Evelyn*, ed. E. S. de Beer. Oxford: 1955 (6 vols.).

E.M.   *The English Miscellany*, ed. M. Praz. Rome: 1950–.

E.M.W.   *The Miscellaneous Works of John Evelyn Esq.*, ed. T. Upcott. London: 1825.

E.P.   *Selections from the Correspondence of Arthur Capel Earl of Essex 1675–1677*, ed. C. E. Pike, Camden Society, Third Series, vol. xxiv. London: 1913.

Etherege   *The Dramatic Works of Sir George Etherege*, ed. H. F. B. Brett Smith. Oxford: 1927 (2 vols.).

Fane MS.   Sir Francis Fane's manuscript commonplace book. (Library of Shakespeare's Birthplace, Stratford-upon-Avon.)

F.L.D. *Love in the Dark or the Man of Business. A Comedy*, by Sir Francis Fane, Jr. London: 1675.

Gadbury *Ephemeris or a Diary*, by John Gadbury. London: 1698.

G.E.C. *The Complete Peerage of England, Scotland, Ireland, Great Britain and the United Kingdom by G.E.C.*, ed. Hon. Vicary Gibbs. London: 1910–52.

Gepp. *Adderbury*, by H. J. Gepp. Banbury: 1924.

Gould *The Works of Mr. Robert Gould.* London: 1709 (2 vols.).

G.S.S. *Seventeenth Century Studies*, by E. Gosse. London: 1914.

Hamilton *Antoine Hamilton Memoires du Chevalier de Gramont*, ed. C. E. Engel. Monaco: 1958.

Harris *The Life of Edward Mountagu K.G, First Earl of Sandwich*, by F. R. Harris. London: 1912 (2 vols.).

Hartmann *Charles II and Madame*, by C. H. Hartmann. London: 1934.

Hatton *Correspondence of the Family of Hatton 1601–1704*, ed. E. M. Thompson, Camden Soc. N.S., 22, 23. Westminster: 1878 (2 vols.).

H.B. *Inglesi e Scozzesi All' Universita di Padova*, by H. Browne. Venice: 1921.

Hexastichon *ΕΞΑΣΤΙΧΟΝ ΊΕΡΟΝ*. Oxford: 1677 (Jan. 1677, 8). (Br. Mus. C. 51, d.2.)

Hill *Familiar Letters which passed between Thomas Hill Esq. and Several Eminent and Ingenious Persons.* London: 1767.

H.M.C. *Reports of the Royal Commission on Historical Manuscripts.*

Hobbes *The English Works of Thomas Hobbes of Malmesbury*, ed. Sir W. Molesworth. London: 1889 (11 vols.).

H.R.C. *Remarks and Collections of Thomas Hearne*, ed. C. E. Doble. Oxford: 1885–9 (11 vols.).

H.R.H. *Reliquiae Hearnianae : The Remains of Thomas Hearne*, ed. P. Bliss. London: 1869 (3 vols.).

Isis *Isis, an International Review.* Cambridge, Mass.: 1927–.

J.H.L. *The Journals of the House of Lords.*

Johnson *The Works of Samuel Johnson.* Oxford: 1825 (9 vols.).

Lachère. *Le Procès du Poète Théophile de Viau*, by A. Lechèvre. Paris: 1909 (2 vols.).

Langbaine *An Account of the English Dramatic Poets*, by G. Langbaine. Oxford: 1691.

Longueville *Rochester and Other Literary Rakes of the Court of Charles II.* London: 1902 [by T. Longueville].

L.P.C. *The Princess of Cleve*, by Nat. Lee, Gent. London: 1689.

L.S.D.C. *The Letters, Speeches and Declarations of King Charles II*, ed. A. Bryant. London: 1935.

L.S.E.   *The Letters of St. Évremond*, ed. J. Hayward. London: 1930.

Luttrell   *A Brief Historical Relation of State Affairs from September, 1678 to April, 1711*, by N. Luttrell. Oxford: 1857 (6 vols.).

Malone   *The Critical and Miscellaneous Works of John Dryden with an Account of the Life and Writings of the Author*, by E. Malone. London: 1800.

Marshall   *A Supplement to the History of Woodstock Manor and its Environs*, by the Rev. E. Marshall. Oxford and London: 1874.

Marvell   *The Poems and Letters of Andrew Marvell*, ed. H. M. Margoliouth. Oxford: 1937 (2 vols.).

Monk   *History of Burford*, by W. J. Monk. Burford and London: 1874.

M.O.O.   *Memorials of Old Oxfordshire*, ed. P. H. Ditchfield. London: 1903.

Nicoll   *A History of English Drama 1660–1900*, by Allardyce Nicoll. *Volume I Restoration Drama 1660–1700*, 4th edition. Cambridge: 1952.

Oldham   *The Compositions in Verse and Prose of John Oldham to which are added Memoirs of Life*, by E. Thompson. London: 1770 (3 vols.).

Orrery   *The Dramatic Works of Roger Boyle, Earl of Orrery*, ed. by W. S. Clark. Harvard: 1937 (2 vols.).

Otway   *The Works of Thomas Otway*, ed. J. C. Ghosh. Oxford: 1932 (2 vols.).

Parsons   *A Sermon Preached at the Funeral of the Rt. Honorable John Earl of Rochester*, by R. Parsons. Oxford: 1680.

Pascal   *Pensées de M. Pascal sur la Religion* [ed. E. Perrier]. Paris: 1670.

Pepys   *The Diary of Samuel Pepys edited with Additions* by Henry B. Wheatley. London: 1928 (8 vols.).

P.O.A.S., 1697 *Poems on Affairs of State from the Time of Oliver Cromwell to the Abdication of K. James the Second.* [London]: 1697.

P.O.A.S., 1698 *Poems on Affairs of State : From Oliver Cromwell, to this present time. Part III.* [London]: 1698.

Pope   *The Works of Alexander Pope*, ed. W. Elwin and W. J. Courthope. London: 1882 (10 vols.).

P.Q.   *The Philological Quarterly.* Iowa: 1923–.

Prinz   *John Wilmot Earl of Rochester. His Life and Writings*, by J. Prinz. Leipzig: 1927.

Raby — Folio manuscript book carrying the bookplate of Thomas Wentworth, Baron Raby, in the Department of English Library, Ohio State University, Columbus, Ohio.

R.E.S. — *The Review of English Studies.* London: 1925–.

Rochesteriana — *Rochesteriana being some anecdotes concerning John Wilmot Earl of Rochester*, collected and edited by Johannes Prinz. Leipzig: 1926.

R.W.C. — *The Registers of Wadham College (1613–1871)*, ed. R. B. Gardiner. Oxford: 1889–95.

S.C. — Savile Correspondence. *Letters to and from Henry Savile 1661–1689*, ed. W. D. Cooper, Camden Society, O.S. 71. Westminster: 1858.

Sedley — *The Poetical and Dramatic Works of Sir Charles Sedley*, ed. V. de S. Pinto. London: 1928 (2 vols.).

S.E.M. — *The Empress of Morocco. A Tragedy*, by Elkanah Settle. London: 1673.

Sheffield — *The Works of John Sheffield, Earl of Mulgrove etc.* London: 1723 (2 vols.).

Sibbald — *Memoria Balfouriana Sive Historia Rerum Pro Literis Promovendis R.S.* Edinburgh, 1699. [by Sir Robert Sibbald.]

Sibbes — *Bowels Opened or a Discovery of the Near and Dear Love, Union and Communion between Christ and the Church*, by R. Sibbes. London: 1648.

Smith — *Selected Discourses*, by John Smith. London: 1660.

S.P.D., Chas. II — State Papers, Domestic, Charles II (Public Record Office).

Spingarn — *Critical Essays of the Seventeenth Century*, ed. J. E. Spingarn. Oxford: 1908 (3 vols.).

Spence — *Anecdotes, Observations and Characters of Books and Men*, by the Rev. J. Spence, ed. S. W. Singer. London: 1858.

Temple — *Letters Written by Sir W. Temple Bart. and other Ministers of State.* Published by Jonathan Swift. London: 1700 (2 vols.).

T.L.S. — *The Times Literary Supplement.* London.

T.M.A. — *ΤΕΧΝΗΠΟΛΕΜΟΓΑΜΙΑ or the Marriage of Armes and Arts*, 12 July 1651 [by R. Whitehall]. (Br. Mus. 1077, h.58(2) .)

T.T. — Temi e Testi. Anna Mario Crinò. *Il Popish Plot*. Rome: 1954.

Underwood — *Etherege and the Seventeenth Century Comedy of Manners*, by Dale Underwood. Yale: 1957.

V.M. — *Memoirs of the Verney Family*, compiled by F. P. Verney. London: 1892–4 (4 vols.).

Voltaire   *Lettres Philosophiques de Voltaire*, ed. G. Lanson. Paris: 1924.

Walpole,   *A Catalogue of Royal and Noble Authors of England*, 2nd
C.R.N.A.   edition. London: 1759 [by Horace Walpole].

Walpole,   *The Letters of Horace Walpole Fourth Baron Orford*, ed.
Letters   Mrs. P. Toynbee. Oxford: 1903 (16 vols.).

W.A.O.   *Athenae Oxonienses*, by Anthony à Wood, ed. P. Bliss. London: 1813–20 (3 vols.).

Whitfield   *Beast in View A Study of the Earl of Rochester's Poetry*, by F. Whitfield. Cambridge, Mass.: 1939.

Willey   *The Seventeenth Century Background*, by Basil Willey. London: 1934.

Williams   *Rochester*, by Charles Williams. London: 1935.

W.L.T.   *The Life and Times of Antony à Wood*, ed. A. Clark. Oxford: 1891 (5 vols.).

W.M.   *The Welbeck Miscellany No. 2 A Collection of Poems by Several Hands Never before printed*, 1934 [ed. F. Needham].

              his form had not yet lost
All her Original brightness, nor appear'd
Less than Arch Angel ruind, and th'excess
Of Glory obscur'd: . . .

INTRODUCTION

THE seventeenth century in England was an age of experiment and intellectual adventure. It is the gulf that lies between the firm ground of the Middle Ages, which crumbled beneath the blows of Bacon and his successors, and the firm ground of the Enlightenment established by Newton and Locke at the beginning of the eighteenth century. To day we are in a peculiarly favourable position to understand the men of the seventeenth century. We also feel that we have no solid ground beneath our feet. The mechanico-materialistic universe which seemed to our fathers and grandfathers so impregnable is now crumbling away just as the scholastic-medieval universe was crumbling away in the days of Donne and Browne and Glanville. We too must test all things without the help of a universally believed theory of life and the universe. We too must endeavour to find for ourselves a significance in the strange and incomprehensible world that environs us, and orient our lives without the guidance of an age-long tradition. So we can sympathize with the disillusionment of the contemporaries of Hobbes, their experiments in philosophy and religion, and their restless paradoxical lives. The writers of that age, however, have come down to us for the most part in portraits made by critics and biographers of the eighteenth and nineteenth centuries, and their features have been popularized as they appeared to the minds of men and women who lived in the reigns of the Hanoverian kings and Queen Victoria. It is a task for criticism now to get behind these conventional pictures and to reinterpret the authors of the seventeenth century in the spirit of an age which is, perhaps, more akin to theirs than to that of our Georgian and Victorian forefathers. This task has been notably achieved already with reference to the metaphysical poets by Sir Herbert Grierson and others, who have established Donne in his proper place as one of the most important and interesting of English poets and have revealed the true quality of such writers as Herbert, Vaughan and Marvell. John Wilmot,

Earl of Rochester, has been even more unfortunate than the metaphysical poets. They were neglected or misinterpreted by well-
meaning admirers. Rochester was, if anything, too well known, but
his literary reputation has suffered from the blaze of notoriety that
has surrounded his personality. His poetry never really had a fair
chance, because so much attention was claimed by the mass of tradition and anecdote concerning his life and character. Besides being a
poet, he was a nobleman, a libertine, and a wit. He made many
enemies, and finally he was converted to religion at the end of his
life in a dramatic way that naturally made an appeal to the imaginations of the pious. So his reputation was at the mercy of three
sections of the English public, the Puritans the Bacchanalians and
the Gossips.

The Puritans found ample materials for edification in the admirable
Life and Death of John, Earl of Rochester, written by Gilbert Burnet,
the historian, who was the chief agent in bringing about the poet's
conversion, and in the funeral sermon preached by Robert Parsons,
his mother's chaplain, on the appropriate text from the Gospel of
St. Luke, 'I say unto you, that likewise joy shall be in heaven over
one sinner that repenteth, more than over ninety and nine just persons, which need no repentance.' Both these works passed through
many editions in the eighteenth and nineteenth centuries, and numerous tracts were founded on them with such titles as *The Libertine
Overthrown* (n.d.), *The Two Noble Converts* (1680) and *The Hazard
of a Deathbed-Repentance* (1728).

The Bacchanalians did quite as much harm as the Puritans. Rochester, like most of the aristocratic poets of his age. probably never
authorized the publication of any of his poems. In 1680, the year of
his death, there appeared the first of a long series of dishonest editions of his poetry issued by publishers of very doubtful reputation,
in which pornographic material is given a prominent part, and much
obscene doggerel, which is certainly not by Rochester, is included.
Similar editions continued to appear throughout the eighteenth
century, and there are manuscript commonplace books too, in
which indecent trifles that Rochester may or may not have written
for the amusement of his friends, have been diligently transcribed
for the benefit of generations of sniggerers. The account of Rochester
in Hamilton's *Memoirs of De Gramont*, and the letter concerning his
exploits falsely ascribed to St. Évremond and printed at the head of
some editions of his works have been as useful to the Bacchanalians

as Burnet's memoir and Parsons's sermon have been to the Puritans. And just as the Puritans produced tracts concerning Rochester's repentance, so the Bacchanalians produced pornographic fiction like Captain Alexander Smith's *The School of Venus* (1716), and *The Singular Life, Amatory Adventures and Extraordinary Intrigues of John Wilmot, the renowned Earl of Rochester* (about 1864). They succeeded in perpetuating the conventional portrait of the gay, light-hearted, cynical debauchee which may be placed beside the equally conventional portrait of the noble convert.[1]

Finally there is the tradition of malicious personal gossip, which was already beginning in Rochester's lifetime.[2] The fountainhead of such gossip after his death was probably John Sheffield, Earl of Mulgrave and afterwards Duke of Buckingham. Pope told his friend Spence that 'Lord Rochester was of a very bad turn of mind as well as debauched'.[3] He had this information 'from the Duke of Buckingham and others that knew him'. Sheffield was a bitter personal enemy of Rochester, and the reports that Pope received from him and members of his circle would naturally be prejudiced and unreliable.

So between them the Puritans, the Bacchanalians and the Gossips surrounded Rochester's memory with a kind of haze that distorted the judgments even of the greatest critics. There was also a feeling that there was something dangerous about the man and his opinions, just as there was a feeling in the nineteenth century that there was something dangerous about Byron and Shelley. Had he not mocked at everything that society held most sacred, and even satirized Reason itself? So, even such a great critic as Dr. Johnson cannot do him justice. The whole of Johnson's criticism of Rochester is coloured by the statement that 'he lived worthless and useless, and blazed out his youth and health in lavish voluptuousness, till, at the age of one-and-thirty, he had exhausted the fund of life, and reduced himself to a state of weakness and decay'. And he remarks significantly that Rochester's studies were 'yet more criminal' than his 'course of drunken gaiety, and gross sensuality'.[4] Similarly Sir Edmund Gosse, who wrote a just and admirable appreciation of Rochester's songs, had to compare his Muse to 'a beautiful child

---

[1] For a Victorian view of Rochester see Harrison Ainsworth's *Old St. Paul's* (1841). The exploits attributed to him in this novel are, of course, wholly fictitious. The latest addition to the bacchanalian biographies of Rochester is *Rake Rochester* by Charles Norman, New York, 1954.

[2] See below, p. 166.   [3] Spence, 4.   [4] Johnson, VII, 158.

which has wantonly rolled itself in the mud, and which has grown so
dirty that the ordinary wayfarer would rather pass it hurriedly by,
than do justice to its native charms',[1] and to picture him as a 'petulant
and ferocious rake, whose wasting hold on life only increased his
malevolent licence'.[2]

The time is now ripe for a revaluation of Rochester. The records
of a poet's life can be of great assistance to the reader who wants to
form a just estimate of his works, but imperfect records are often
worse than useless. If we wish to judge Rochester fairly, we must
form our conception of his character not only from the conversations
with Burnet, the sermon of Parsons and the anecdotes preserved by
Hamilton and others, but also from the brilliant Dorimant of Etherege's comedy, the kind, humorous husband, father and friend of
the letters to his wife, his son and Henry Savile, the serious inquirer
into the nature of the soul and the origin of religion revealed in
Charles Blount's correspondence, and the courageous and indomit-
able spirit who never flagged in his quest after the true significance of
life till he was rewarded by the overwhelming religious experience
of June 19th, 1680. But, above all, we must let Rochester speak for
himself in his poetry. There we shall find living with an intensity
which makes all the gossip about his life seem shadowy and irrelevant his great and enduring qualities of passionate sincerity,
intellectual energy, imagination, irony and humour.

[1] G.S.S., 316.   [2] Ibid.

Chapter One

————⟪•⟫⟪•⟫————

FROM DITCHLEY TO PADUA

————⟪•⟫⟪•⟫————

If the traveller from Oxford to Chipping Norton leaves the main
road at a certain point north-west of Woodstock, after passing through
a very beautiful and peaceful part of rural England, he will come to
the stately Park of Ditchley, where among great elms and cedars he
will find a noble Palladian mansion built in 1722 for the Earl of
Litchfield by that excellent architect James Gibbs. This Lord Litchfield was one of the Lees of Ditchley, a descendant of the adopted
son of the famous Sir Henry Lee, Queen Elizabeth's loyal champion
and Ranger of Woodstock Park. Before Gibbs's mansion was built,
there was an older house at Ditchley, the 'low antient timber house
with a pretty bowling greene', which John Evelyn visited on 20
October 1664,[1] when he dined with the fourth Sir Henry Lee, and
looked at his pictures, which he found 'not ill Painted'.

This house is said to have stood about two hundred yards to the
west of the present building on a spot which is now covered by a
fine group of cedars. No trace of the old Ditchley manor house survives. It has vanished as completely as the Tudor and Stuart ladies
and gentlemen who once inhabited it. Not even a picture of it has
been preserved.[2] Fortunately, however, that garrulous antiquary,
Thomas Hearne, visited it on a certain fine June day in 1718,[3] a few
years before it was demolished, and gives a long account in his diary
of the house and its contents. He tells us of its 'Front on the South
. . . very pretty, considering the Method of Building at that time',

---

[1] E.D., III, 382, 383.   [2] M.O.O., 148, 149.   [3] H.R.C., VI, 186–91.

I

its old hall hung with stags' antlers, and poetical descriptions of the hunts of which they were trophies, the 'fine long gallery above stairs, . . . at least 29 Yards in length' with its family pictures, Queen Elizabeth's bedroom, the small size of which astonished him, the chair which Lady Charlotte Fitzroy, the daughter of Charles II had made for her father, and in which he used to go to sleep while she scratched his head, Sir Thomas Wyatt's epitaph, and other curiosities. A very pleasant place this old Ditchley House must have been, not so imposing as Gibbs's great pile, but perhaps more cheerful, full of character and of memories of English history.

During the Civil War, and under the Commonwealth and the Protectorate Ditchley was ruled by a lady with a strong character and a majestic presence. This was Anne St. John, daughter of Sir John St. John, a Wiltshire knight. She had married the son of the second Sir Henry Lee, and after his death in 1640 remained at Ditchley as the guardian of her child. Her second husband, whom she married probably in 1644, was Henry, Viscount Wilmot, the famous cavalier general, who had fought for Charles I since the Bishops' War of 1639, and who was to be one of the chief instruments in effecting the escape of Charles II from the field of Worcester. Perhaps the marriage can be explained by the theory of the attraction of opposites. Both Anne St. John and Henry Wilmot were remarkable persons. The lady was pious, but also a shrewd woman of business who managed her affairs with notable vigour and success.[1] Wilmot is described by Clarendon as haughty, unprincipled, fond of drink and company, but a good soldier and a very witty and amusing companion. It is worth noticing that he seems to have had an intellect capable of looking beyond the merely partisan view of the Civil War. During the campaign in the West in 1644, he is reported to have said that the King was afraid of peace, and to have recommended that the war should be ended by his abdication and the elevation of the Prince of Wales to the throne. It was even believed that he was plotting with Essex to unite the Royalist and Parliamentarian armies and impose peace on both the King and the Parliament. As a result of these rumours he was arrested and deprived of his command on 8 August 1644.[2] Later, when the King's armies had been finally defeated, he retired to France, where he fought a duel with his enemy Lord Digby, on 3 April 1647. Two days before, on 1 April, at

[1] V.M., III, 464–7.   [2] C.H.G.R., VIII, 95.

eleven o'clock in the morning, his only child, John Wilmot, was born at Ditchley. It was an appropriate beginning to a stormy career. Gadbury, a famous seventeenth-century astrologer, cast the horoscope of the child many years later and found that the conjunctions of the heavenly bodies at that time were favourable for 'an inclination to *Poetry*' and 'a large Stock of *Generous* and *Active spirits*'.[1] A student of heredity might have foretold that the mingling of the blood of the mercurial and versatile Wilmots with that of the saturnine and puritanical St. Johns was likely to produce a brilliant, paradoxical and unstable character.

When the little boy was being brought up at the pleasant old house at Ditchley, his father was on the Continent with the exiled cavaliers. After the death of Charles I, Henry Wilmot, whose character was far more congenial to the new king than it had been to the old, was taken into high favour. On 3 April 1649, Charles II made him a gentleman of his bedchamber. He accompanied his master on the unfortunate expedition to Scotland in 1650, and remained with him until the final defeat at Worcester, when his courage, coolness and ingenuity were among the chief factors in effecting the escape of the King. After those thrilling days when the fugitives made their way through a hostile and suspicious England to the Dorset coast, Wilmot passed with Charles into France and became one of the most prominent and energetic members of the exiled Court. On 13 December 1652 he was created Earl of Rochester. He was employed in several diplomatic missions on the Continent and in 1655 he was in England directing Royalist conspiracies against Cromwell's Government. Although there is no evidence that he went to Ditchley, it cannot be doubted that he took the opportunity of going to visit his wife whom he had not seen for many years and his child whom he had never seen at all. It needs no strong effort of imagination to conceive the emotional disturbance that such an encounter would have produced in a sensitive, delicate child of eight. An historical novelist might give a moving picture of the only meeting of the fat, jovial cavalier in disguise with the bright-eyed, intelligent little boy who was to inherit his title. Henry Wilmot's plans were frustrated by Cromwell's efficient intelligence service, and he returned to the Continent. He died at Sluys on 19 February 1657/8 and was buried at Bruges, but his body was afterwards brought to England and

---

[1] Gadbury, xxiii.

reinterred in Spelsbury Church, near his ancestral estate at Adderbury in Oxfordshire.[1]

John Wilmot thus inherited the earldom of Rochester and Adderbury Manor when he was eleven years old. His guardians were his mother and a friendly neighbouring squire, the excellent Sir Ralph Verney of Claydon in Buckinghamshire, a great friend of Lady Rochester.[2] His heritage must have seemed a barren one. The government established in England was that of the Protectorate. The elder Wilmot died a 'malignant', or enemy of the Puritan State, and his estates were forfeited, though his widow asserted her right to retain her jointure lands on the ground that they belonged to a Parliamentary and Puritan family.[3] Moreover, none of the peerages conferred by Charles I or Charles II since the Civil War were recognized at Whitehall, so officially, on the death of his father, the child became not Earl of Rochester, but Viscount Wilmot, the title given by Elizabeth to his grandfather. However, for all good Royalists the son of Henry Wilmot, the King's loyal servant and hero of the escape from Worcester, was Earl of Rochester now and for the rest of his life.

The child was handsome, docile and intelligent. His first tutor was Francis Giffard, a young clergyman, who was twenty-six in the year in which the elder Wilmot died. A graduate of Queen's College, Cambridge, he had been ejected by the Puritans from a Wiltshire living and Lady Rochester had taken him into her house as her chaplain. He was an enthusiastic loyalist and ended his career as a nonjuror. His pupil liked him, and he found young Wilmot 'very virtuous and good natur'd (as he was always) and willing & ready to follow good advice'. The little boy was not robust and his tutor slept in his room 'to prevent any ill accidents'.[4] The days that they spent together walking over the pleasant Ditchley lawns and perhaps playing bowls in the pretty bowling-green, must have been among the happiest in Rochester's life. Lady Rochester decided to supplement Giffard's teaching by regular schooling, and the boy was sent over the Cotswolds to the old grammar school at Burford, which had a considerable reputation in the seventeenth century. John Martin was headmaster at this date, and he had the reputation of being an able teacher. Among former pupils of the school were Dr. Peter Heylyn, the royalist divine, and Marchamont Nedham, Cromwell's

[1] W.L.T., II, 492.　　　[2] V.M., IV, 244.　　　[3] Ibid., III, 276, 277.
[4] H.R.C., III, 263; H.R.H., I, 242.

official journalist. Boys who came 'out of the Country' paid '12d.
entrance and 6d. a quarter'. There were no boarding-houses in those
days and the boys lodged in the little medieval town. The hours seem
terribly long to us now. Morning school started at six o'clock in the
summer and seven in winter and went on till eleven when the boys
went to dinner. They began work again at one o'clock and finished
at four, after which they either went to church or sang psalms and
read a chapter of the Bible at school. Every Sunday they came to the
master's house at eight in the morning, and went with him to church.
Four times a year the master had to exhort them to give thanks to
God, and to recite the names of all the Founders and Benefactors
which were inscribed on a table in the school house, and then they
sang a psalm.[1] Rochester had always been a delicate child, and Giffard
mentions his abnormal tendency to constipation. Nearly two centuries
were to elapse before organized games and physical exercises were to
become part of the curriculum of English schools. The long hours
spent over books at Burford probably did permanent harm to the
child's constitution. Of the effect on his mind we know little. John
Martin must have given him a very good grounding in Latin, and
he was certainly able to read the Latin classics with pleasure throughout his life. Probably he learned a little Greek as well,[2] and the
constant study of the Bible and recitation of the psalms gave him
splendid models of English prose style. Strange thoughts must have
passed through the young Earl's mind as he sang the psalms with
his fellow scholars. Was all this religiosity part of the divine scheme?
Had not the gay, loose-living soldiers of the King, like his father,
scoffed at it? And what kind of just a Deity was it that allowed the
usurper to rule in Whitehall while the true heir to the throne
languished in poverty and exile?

In the winter of 1659–60 his thralldom came to an end, and at an
age when a modern boy enters a public school he went up to the
University. It was on 18 January that he was entered as a 'Fellow
Commoner' or 'Nobleman' at Wadham College, Oxford.[3] This
meant, according to the custom of that aristocratic age, that he wore
a special gown that distinguished him from undergraduates of inferior rank and was a member of the Fellows' common-room where
he could associate with the dons and listen to their conversation.
Dorothy Wadham's foundation was the newest of the Oxford Colleges

---

[1] Monk, 133, 134.   [2] H.R.C., III, 263, cf. B.S.P., 3.   [3] R.W.C., 231.

at this time, as it had been endowed in the reign of James I. It was also the most advanced society in Oxford in intellectual matters a real centre of the English Enlightenment, the scientific and philosophic movement of the seventeenth century. After the Parliamentary Commission had remodelled the University, John Wilkins had been appointed Warden of Wadham in 1648, and it was he more than any other man who had given the college its reputation. At Wilkins's lodgings at Wadham the 'experimentall philosophicall clubbe'[1] which afterwards became the Royal Society, used to meet, and discussed mathematics, physics and mechanics instead of free-will, predestination and Church government. In 1658/9 Cromwell had appointed Wilkins to the Mastership of Trinity College, Cambridge, and he was succeeded at Wadham by Dr. Walter Blandford who was Warden when Rochester entered the college. Rochester's tutor was a Mr. Phineas Bury, 'a gentleman of good parts' and 'a very learned and good natured man'.[2] At the Fellows' table at Wadham the precocious boy must have heard talk that sounded very strange and fascinating after the pietism that prevailed in his mother's house and at Burford Grammar School. Here were men who were far more interested in discussions concerning the properties of matter than the nature of God. Here was a brave new world governed not by a jealous Old Testament Deity but by the infallible laws of mathematics.

In those cold January days when Rochester went into residence at Wadham, Monk's army was on the march to London, and England was full of rumours of great political changes. On the night of 13 February[3] there was great excitement at Oxford when the news arrived that Monk had declared for a free parliament. Bells were ringing throughout the city, and at the gate of the Queen's College a great bonfire was lit, into which rumps and sheeps-tails were thrown to symbolize the contempt of undergraduates for the rump parliament. A rump was even flung into the window of old Dr John Palmer, Warden of All Souls, who was a member of that hated assembly. During that spring outward signs of loyalism began to appear in the University. In April the book of Common-Prayer was being read in chapels, and the Royal Arms were placed again above the schools, while the sign of the King's head reappeared over the inn of that name. On 1 May the old May Day revelry was revived,

[1] Aubrey, II, 301.   [2] B.S.P., 4.   [3] W.L.T., I, 303.

and a maypole set up in Cornmarket Street, 'to vex the Presbyterians and Independents'. On the 10th, Charles II was proclaimed.

The King entered his capital on his birthday, 29 May, and 'the World of England was perfectly mad. They were freed from the chaines of darkness and confusion which the Presbyterians and phanaticks had brought upon them'.[1] Thus Rochester's university career was passed in an atmosphere of turbulence and excitement. The University was reverting with almost ludicrous suddenness to its old loyalist principles, and the sudden change went to the heads of many of its members and led to riotous behaviour. 'Those that hated a tavern or alehouse formerly' now frequented them openly. Others that used 'to bear the face of demure saints' would now 'put forth a wanton (in plaine terms a baudy) expression, and as occasion served a pretty little oath'. May-games, morris-dances and revels were now encouraged instead of forbidden. Young Mr. Robert South, of Christ Church, formerly regarded as one of the chief hopes of the Independent Party and once the favourite of Dr. Owen, the Cromwellian Dean, was now heard to condemn the hypocrisy and dissimulation of his former friends and to attack the Puritans from the pulpit, making fun of their 'wry faces, ill looks, puling tones, etc'. Stage-plays, strictly forbidden in the Puritan University, were acted again, and perhaps the first play that Rochester saw was Cowley's comedy *The Guardian*, acted on 19 July at Newman's Dancing-School, by St. Michael's Church.[2]

The young nobleman's guide through this carnival of Restoration Oxford was a certain Robert Whitehall, a merry, red-faced Fellow of Merton who was renowned for his gargantuan potations of claret.[3] His record was not a shining one. He had once been a Student of Christ Church and had been ejected by the Parliamentary Commissioners. He is said then to have crept into favour with the new rulers of England by acting as a buffoon to Cromwell's friend Ingoldsby,[4] and thus to have obtained the Merton Fellowship which he succeeded in retaining at the Restoration. We are not surprised to learn that Rochester 'soon grew debauch'd'[5] in this man's company. Whitehall is said to have 'doted' on his young friend, and also to have pretended to instruct him in the art of poetry. He was a small poet himself, and in the palmy days of the Protectorate had

[1] Ibid., 317.   [2] Ibid., 322.   [3] Ibid., 144.
[4] D.N.B., s.a. Robert Whitehall.   [5] H.R.C., III, 263.

published verses on the installation of Richard Cromwell as Chancellor of the University.[1] From these lines it appears that he posed as champion of advanced ideas in education, despising 'misty Scotus' and the schoolmen, and praising the study of geography and mathematics. The lad of fourteen must have felt very much of a man as he sat by this Falstaffian figure in the Saracen's Head and other Oxford taverns, and listened to praise of the new learning and ridicule of the canting Puritans:

> As for example; see a Fellow come,
> With Wax enough about his gouty Thumb;
> To make a nodous tumour mend its pace,
> Or Carbuncle spit venome in your Face:
> See and admire this fellow laying down
> His *Awle* and *Stirrup*, is no longer *clowne*:
> But sits upon the *Bench*, and winks and nods,
> As gravely, as if sent us by the *Gods*.
> Or see a learned Farriar, who i' th' morn,
> Was at his lawfull call, his *Drench* and *Horn*:
> His beaten Ginger, and his Diapente,
> Now Leader of a gang of about *Twenty*
> And of these *Nineteen* minds, yet all combine
> Against the *Common foe, Church discipline*:
> 'Tis *Tyranny* cry's One, *unwarrantable*,
> A Second, and a Third *Abominable*;
> A Fourth, what holy Writ can for it plead?
> Why Saucebox, where it doth, thou can'st not *read*;
> Or if ten thousand Texts were urg'd, you'l say,
> The Spirit meant them quite another way.[2]

In these rough verses of Whitehall we can almost hear his slightly drunken voice as he told stories of the days of Cromwell to the son of Henry Wilmot. From a copy of verses sent by Whitehall to the Earl some years later we learn that he used to lend his young friend his Master's gown to protect him from proctorial interference in his night rambles.[3] Nights spent in Oxford taverns (where in Whitehall's words he 'daggled' the borrowed gown among the 'good fellows') must have done even more harm to Rochester's health than the long hours of school at Burford, and to a modern observer there is something pathetic in the spectacle of the slender, bright-cheeked boy becoming 'debauched' at the age of fourteen under

[1] T.M.A.   [2] Coronation, 3.   [3] W.M., 44, 45.

8

Whitehall's expert tuition.[1] It is likely enough that the venereal disease from which he was to suffer throughout his short life was contracted at this time.

The earliest extant verses ascribed to Rochester are some lines sent to the King on his return to England in May, 1660. It was said that these lines were really the work of Whitehall,[2] though there is nothing in them that might not have been composed by a clever boy of thirteen. It is quite likely, however, that Whitehall helped to polish them:

> Virtues Triumphant Shrine! who do'st engage
> At once three Kingdoms in a Pilgrimage;
> Which in extatick duty strive to come
> Out of themselves, as well as from their home:
> Whilst *England* grows one Camp, and *London* is
> It self the Nation, not Metropolis;
> And Loyal *Kent* renews her Arts agen,
> Fencing her ways with moving Groves of Men,
> Forgive this distant homage, which does meet
> Your blest approach on sedentary feet:
> And though my youth, not patient yet to bear
> The weight of Arms, denies me to appear
> In Steel before you; yet great SIR, approve
> My manly wishes, and more vigorous Love;
> In whom a cold Respect were Treason to
> A Father's Ashes, greater than to you;
> Whose one Ambition 'tis for to be known,
> By daring Loyalty, your *Wilmot's* son.[3]

Charles must have smiled when he heard himself called a shrine of virtue, but he can hardly have failed to be touched by the allusion to Rochester's father. There is a straining after conceits typical of the mid-seventeenth century in these boyish verses, but there is a vigour and a perspicuity too (in spite of shaky grammar) in the last couplets, which already presages a new force in English poetry. The other surviving undergraduate verses ascribed to Rochester are a Latin and an English poem on the death of Charles II's sister, the Princess of Orange. Whitehall probably had a hand in these too, and he may have written the Latin elegiacs. The English poem has

[1] H.R.C., III, 263; see Aubrey I, 211 for Rochester's 'faire, cleer, rosie complexion'.
[2] W.A.O., III, 1231. [3] P. 3, 164, 165.

a faint fore-shadowing of Rochester's satiric wit in the lines on seventeenth-century physicians.

> Art's Basilisks, that kill whom e're they see,
> And truly write Bills of Mortality.[1]

The fantastic element in the medicine of the age must have been brought to Rochester's notice by the arrival in Oxford in February, 1660/61 of a certain James Themut, a 'high Dutch' quack from Vienna who lodged at the Saracen and issued a printed broad-sheet in which he set forth his achievements and qualifications. In this engaging document he claims to cure a vast variety of diseases ('by God's help and the strength of Medicine') 'falling sickness, Madness, Phrenzie and Giddiness in the head', as well as 'stinking breath, rotten Teeth, scurvey, or Water-canker'. He could work 'most arti-ficially into all the inward and hidden diseases of Men and Women' which are specified at considerable length and with the utmost frankness. He attracts the simple-minded by a fine display of can-dour and benevolence:

'Nor let anyone suppose what he hath written, to be untruth; for (if any please to visit him) he will make it appear by good certificates and their own experience; his principal aim being to do good to such as are in misery, and not to hide his Candle under a Bushel, but set it on a Candlestick'. The comedy was completed by the disappearance of Themut a month after his arrival with a large quantity of money, which he had induced his patients to pay him in advance. It can hardly be doubted that the future creator of 'Alexander Bendo,' read Dr. Themut's bill with the greatest attention, and he may well have kept a copy of the broadsheet.[2]

On Saturday, 7 September 1661, at half-past four in the after-noon, the great bell of St. Mary's rang for half an hour to summon all the doctors, noblemen and masters to the University Church. When they had assembled, a watchman was sent up the steeple to look out for a coach coming over Shotover Hill. At six o'clock the signal was given that the coach was in sight, and the whole assembly moved down the High Street to Magdalen. At the head of the pro-cession were six bedells and the verger, then the Vice-Chancellor, Richard Baylie, President of St. John's, then smart, dapper Mr.

---

[1] Ibid., 5, 165.
[2] Bodl. MS., Wood's Diaries, Feb. 1660-61; W.L.T., I, 377; for 'Alexander Bendo' see below, pp. 81-89.

South, now Public Orator and well in sight of episcopal honours, then the noblemen (who in that aristocratic age took precedence over the doctors and masters), and finally the doctors in scarlet and the masters in black gowns. Among the noblemen was the Earl of Rochester now a tall, slender boy of fourteen and with him a young Scottish peer, the Earl of Newpurg. At Magdalen the Vice-Chancellor, noblemen and doctors enter the Chapel, while the masters have to be content to line the quadrangle. Meanwhile the great Earl of Clarendon, Lord Chancellor of England, and Chancellor of the University, in whose honour all these preparations have been made, has been met on the Headington road by the Lord Lieutenant of the County with most of the local gentry on horseback, who escort his great gilded coach, drawn by six Flanders mares, to Magdalen gates. There the Vice-Chancellor and the Orator come to the side of the coach and Mr. South makes an 'elegant short speech', on which the great man compliments him and expresses his regret that he should be in such an uncomfortable position 'by reason of the crowd and incivility of the people'. That night the Chancellor slept at the President's lodgings at Magdalen. On Sunday they all had to listen to an indifferent sermon of Dr. William Barker of New College, and then there was a whole round of ceremonial visits. This elaborate welcome given to the Chancellor did not prevent him from publicly chiding Dr. H. Wilkinson of Magdalen Hall because too little attention was paid to the Book of Common-Prayer in his hall, and because he had not only 'factious but debauched schollers'. At nine o'clock on Monday morning Convocation was held in the schools, and thither went the Chancellor and with him Rochester and the Scottish Earl clad in scarlet robes. Here, after a brief oration by the Orator, Clarendon conferred the degree of M.A. on the two young noblemen. He admitted Rochester, we are told, 'very affectionately into the fraternity by a kiss on the left cheek'.[1] The throng of dons, undergraduates and courtiers probably saw little significance in this ceremony. For them it was merely an honour conferred by the great Chancellor on the son of a great loyalist. For us, however, it may appear to be a strange encounter between the representatives of two worlds, the old world of dignity, of stiff ceremonial and of conservative legalism confronting a new world of irreverence, free thought and experiment, the author of *The History*

---

[1] W.L.T., I, 412–14; W.A.O., III, 229.

of the Great Rebellion doing honour to the poet who was to write the lampoons on Charles II and the *Satyr against Mankind.*

Charles II never forgot those who had done him service in the days of adversity, and none who helped him in the escape from Worcester went unrewarded at the Restoration. Henry Wilmot was dead, but his son was living, and the King took a personal interest in the boy from the beginning. In February 1661, while Rochester was still at Oxford, he granted him a pension of £500 a year.[1] He also arranged for the completion of his education by some years of travel on the Continent, and himself appointed a tutor to accompany him on his Grand Tour. The King's choice was an excellent one. It fell on a learned Scottish gentleman, Sir Andrew Balfour, M.D., brother of Sir James Balfour, Lyon King-at-Arms, and a great collector of books and rarities.

In 1661 Sir Andrew Balfour was thirty. A man with the widest interests, a physician, a naturalist, and an enthusiastic student of all kinds of curiosities and antiquities, he was a seventeenth-century 'virtuoso' of the best type with a personal charm that reminds one of Sir Thomas Browne. He had studied at St. Andrews, Oxford, Paris, Montpellier and Padua. In London he had made the acquaintance of the great English physicians, Harvey and Scarborough. He had visited on the Continent before to collect specimens of rare plants and animals as well as to study antiquities. This was not the first occasion on which he had acted as a tutor to a young Englishman. He had made a grand tour with a Yorkshire knight, and on his return had stayed for a time at his house. He had then applied himself particularly to the study of medicine, and had entered the University of Caen, where he graduated as M.D. on 20 September 1661. Soon after, he returned to England, and at the request of Charles II accepted the post of tutor to Rochester.[2]

On 21 November they set out together with Rochester's 'servants and trunks'.[3] Balfour must have been a good travelling-companion, 'a Man of an Excellent Wit, and of a Ripe Judgement, and of a most taking behaviour'.[4] No one could have been better calculated to

---

[1] C.S.P.D., 1660–1, 523; see records of the payment of this pension in C.T.B., 1660–7 244, 253, 372, 699.

[2] D.N.B., s.a. Sir Arthur Balfour, Sibbald, II, 47–54, Sibbald calls the Yorkshire Knight 'D. Watkinsonpelior'.

[3] C.S.P.D., 1661–2, 154.

[4] Balfour, II, ii. The application of the details given in Balfour's book to his travels with Rochester is partly conjectural. Sibbald (II, 54–61) states that Balfour 'cum

wean the young man from the debauched habits that he had contracted at Oxford and develop his mind in healthier directions. We can see the grave Scottish doctor and the handsome vivacious English boy setting out from Southwark to Rye 'on Sadle Horses for 12s a man'; and staying there at the Mermaid Inn until 'there be Passingers enough'. They cross on the packet boat to Dieppe and there lodge at the inn called *A la Bastile* where the son of the host speaks English. After looking at the shop called *Au Roy de la Chine* that sells '*Ivory, Horn* and *Tortoisshell*, for *Combs, Boxes, Dialls*, and a Thousand other conceats', they hire horses and ride on to Rouen where they lodge at a house with the good Protestant sign of *Au Bon Pasteur*. They admire the bridge of boats, and climb the steeple of the Cathedral where they have a fine view of the old city and can see the giant bell called St. George of Amboise. They visit the Palace of the Parliament and compare its great hall with Westminster Hall. They continue their journey to Paris by means of an arrangement called 'the messenger' by which for a payment of thirteen or fourteen francs each they can have horse, lodging and diet for the journey with six pounds of luggage. At Pontoise, where they eat their last meal, each gentleman in the party gives the conductor a tip of thirteen sous. At Paris they lodge with a Mr. Hues at the Rue de la Bouchery in the Faubourg St. Germain. Sir Andrew is a good guide to the sights of the city. He takes his pupil to the Luxembourg Palace and Gardens where they meet Monsieur Marchant, the great naturalist, and to the King's Garden, where Balfour has a firm friendship with the gardener from whom he can obtain rare plants and seeds. At the King's Library they see the 'Books of Miniature done by *Monsieur Robert*' esteemed by Balfour to be 'the best curiosity of that kind in the World'. They go to the Jesuits' College and there Rochester is able to inspect 'the 3 *Systems* of the World, according to the severall *Hypotheses* of *Copernicus, Tycho*

---

illustrissimo *Comite* circulium Galliae et Italiae perfecit' and that they visited Milan, Florence, Pisa, Bologna, Venice, Padua, Vicenza, Rome and Naples. He mentions that Balfour met Lesley and Pendrick at Rome, and that, when he was at Naples on this occasion, he climbed Vesuvius. He also tells us that he formed a friendship (*Familiaritatem . . . contraxit*) with Dr. Walter Pope when he was in Rome. From one of Hill's *Familiar Letters* (see below, p. 20, note 1) we know that Pope was in Rome in February, 1663 (i.e. 1663/4). It would, therefore, appear that Balfour and his pupil visited Rome before they went to Venice, where Pope saw Rochester on 1 October 1664. In view of these corroborations, it seems extremely likely that the rest of the itinerary given in Balfour's book is, in fact, that of his tour with Rochester.

Brache and *Ptolomeus*, represented in Motion'. Perhaps the young Earl attends Monsieur Barlet's course in Chemistry, of which Sir Andrew thinks very highly, paying ten crowns for the course and two for the text-book. They spend much time looking at the numerous bookshops in the Rue St. Jacques, at the Palais Royal, and especially in the Place de la Sorbonne, where 'French Books, as *Romances* &c.', are sold. Monsieur Marchant takes them to a mathematical instrument maker '*dans l'Isle du Palais*' where 'Microscops of al sorts' can be obtained, and the Earl can have his portrait painted by Monsieur Ferdinand, the fashionable artist. They make many pleasant excursions in the neighbourhood of Paris, one to '*Versaile*, A House begun by the late King, but finished by the present . . . a most delicate fine place.' At St. Denys they inspect with due Protestant scepticism such relics as 'One of the Nails that fix'd our *Saviour's* Bodie to the Cross', one of the 'Potts wherein our Saviour changed the water into wine', and the lantern that was carried before *Judas* when he betrayed our Saviour.[1]

From Paris they pass on in a leisurely manner on a tour through France, and, though Balfour thinks that 'out of Paris there is litle thing either to be seen or learned "in all France"', he is nevertheless, a mine of information concerning the natural history and antiquities of the French provinces, and has a pretty taste in the wines of the country. They saunter from one pleasant old French town to another, admiring 'the Civilitie of the People . . . the Sweetness of the Air, and Puritie of the French Language' at Blois, the silk manufactures of Tours, where 'Tiffenes', 'Brocarts' and 'Tabbies' are made, and the Protestant University at Saumur, where they are welcomed by two Englishmen, Messrs. Doule and Gray. They work their way southward to Provence and Languedoc, taking care to draw money 'from *Paris.* to *Lions*, either by Bill of Exchange or letter of Credit, upon some honest substantiall Merchant'. At Lyons they lodge at the inn '*Aux-Trois-Rois*'. There Sir Andrew rejoices to find excellent bookshops which have 'great traffick with all *Germany*, *Switzerland* and *Italy*'. He pays particular attention to Rochester's literary interests and never fails to point out places associated with the great names of European literature. Thus, when they are in Provence, he arranges a pilgrimage to Vaucluse, and there, by the famous spring, he shows his pupil two ruined castles in one of which 'did

[1] Balfour, 7–14.

14

sometimes live that Noble Philosopher and Poet *Franciscus Petrarca*' and in the other '*Donna Laura*, his Mistress, in the praise of whose beautie and vertue he composed his most excellent *Triumfe d'Amore*; a Monument that hath outlasted her familie, in which her Memorie is like to live as long as Wit and Learning continues in reputation.' At Marseilles Sir Andrew is careful to point out the Cathedral which was said to have been originally a Greek temple of Diana, but Rochester is perhaps more interested in the famous perfumeries where he can buy scents and sweet powders and gloves perfumed with frangipani to take back to England. At Montpellier Sir Andrew is delighted to have the chance of renewing acquaintance with his old friends at the University. They continue their tour to Toulouse, Montauban and so to Bordeaux where to the joy of the good Sir Andrew they are regaled with fat ortolans and real Graves, 'the best Wine about *Bourdeaux*'.[1]

As an old traveller, Sir Andrew advises that they should go to Italy in the late autumn after the heat of the summer is over, when they can become more easily acclimatized. They take a 'Felluck', or felucca, from Cannes to Genoa, paying eleven or twelve crowns, and providing themselves with health certificates which have to be presented at Italian ports. The Italian authorities are suspicious, too, of 'secret weapons' and 'prohibited books', 'yet', Balfour adds slyly, 'there are wayes enough to convey Books, or any other thing . . . from any Sea-port, without any Danger'. From Cannes they coast along the Riviera by Monaco and Nice admiring 'the little smal Villages, as it were in the Clefts of the Hills', and the olive-trees planted 'where one would think nothing but crows could venture to Big'. So they reach Genoa, and there Sir Andrew tells his pupil of the great trade of the Genoese and quotes the proverb: '*Cento per Cento e Niente, Cento Cinquanto per Cento e quelcha cosa, du Cento per Cento e quadagnio Honesto.*' They walk down *la Strada Nova*, a street of marble palaces, which must have made the towns of Stuart England seem pitifully mean and cramped to the young Englishman. From Genoa they pass to Tuscany, and Sir Andrew is delighted with the 'Physical Garden' of Pisa which he finds to be even better than that of Padua. At Lucca he remarks that 'The Humour of the people is Chearful and very Civil. . . . Men and Women converse freely amongst themselves, or with Strangers. They use

[1] Ibid., 19–71.

Balls & Dancing much after the *French* fashion.' It is in this pleasant light-hearted seventeenth-century Italy that Rochester's education was completed. At Florence they are hospitably received by an Englishman, Dr. Kirton, 'a very civill and obligeing Gentleman . . . low in stature and prettie ancient', and they spend many days inspecting the palaces, the churches, the paintings and sculpture . . . 'an infinite number of Masterpieces', Sir Andrew, who is no ascetic, draws the attention of his pupil not only to the masterpieces of Michael Angelo, but also to the excellent Florentine wines: 'as the Red *Florence* Wine, which is counted the best for ordinar Drinking, being stomachical and without sweetness, the White *Florence* Wine, which is sweet, *Verdea*, which is delicious small Sweet white wine; *Monte Pulciano*, White and Red, both very good Wines'. It is pleasant to think of the genial Scottish doctor and his brilliant young pupil drinking these delightful wines as they sit in the shade of the Florentine trees.'[1]

They go from Florence to Rome by way of Siena, not forgetting to call at Montefiascone by the way in order to taste 'a most Delicious Kind of *Muscatello* Wine'. At Rome they lodge in the English Pension *Alla Villa di Londra*, and Balfour hastens to call on two great friends of his, among the Englishmen living in the city, Signor Roberto Pendrick and Signor don Guilelmo Lesly, the Chaplain to Cardinal Barberino, whom he admires so much that he calls him *deliciae humani generis*. We can follow tutor and pupil in their walks round churches, palaces, gardens, and ruins. At the Farnese Palace they admire Caracci's frescoes, and the famous antique bull at the Palazzo Medici, 'a most beautiful statue of *Venus* of *Grecian* Antiquitie', and at the Pamphilio Palace they take much pleasure in Bernini's great fountain with its 'four great delicate Marble Statues, representing the foure great Rivers of the World'. On summer evenings this fountain is stopped up and then the water overflows the street and people come in the evening in their coaches, 'and drive softly up and down the water to take the fresco, which is one of the greatest *Gusto's* in Rome', Sir Andrew declares, breaking into a curious Anglo-Italian in his enthusiasm. They visit the Castle of St. Angelo, the foundling hospital of St. Spirito, and the Capitol. Rochester hears a history of the walls of Rome, and the unique quality of the architecture of the Pantheon is explained to him. At

[1] Ibid., 82–109.

the Coliseum the botanist in Sir Andrew overcomes the antiquary, and he remarks characteristically that 'there is good herberizing in it'; and at the Baths of Caracalla, through whose 'flowery glades and thickets'[1] Shelley was to wander over a century and a half later, Rochester is bidden to admire an extremely rare 'kind of capillary called Hemionitis'. So they pass by a bewildering succession of bridges, triumphal arches, obelisks and catacombs concerning each one of which Sir Andrew gives historical information, and they buy great folios adorned with engravings for the young Earl to take back to his Oxfordshire home.

Sir Andrew knows all about the best things to eat at Rome—melons, cucumbers, tunny, sturgeon, 'porcepics', quails and ortolans —and, as usual he is an authority on the wines, 'Galliardi, Greco, Muscatello, di Sangosa, Lagrima &c.' He warns his pupil against Italian water and advises as 'the best remedy to Drink none at all'. Perhaps it was in Sir Andrew's company that Rochester acquired that talent for drinking large quantities of wine for which he was afterwards famous.

Expeditions are made into the country round Rome, to Tivoli, where the unromantic Sir Andrew dismisses the famous waterfall with the remark that 'it makes a horrid noise', and to the Villa Frascati, where his mechanical mind is moved to admiration by the hydraulic devices that made a centaur wind his horn and Apollo and the Muses play various instruments.[2]

One of the most prominent and widely discussed figures in Italy at the time of Rochester's visit was the Neapolitan poet-painter Salvator Rosa, who was forty-seven in 1662 and at the height of his powers. He was living in Rome then with his mistress Lucrezia Paolino and was patronized by princes and cardinals. He had not only won fame by his powerful and arresting paintings but was also known as the author of brilliant, outspoken satiric poems which had not been published but which the author used to read to gatherings of his friends. There are passages in these satires that bear some resemblance to passages in Rochester's satiric poems and it is possible that the young Englishman may have been present at some of the meetings at Rosa's house when he read his poems, or alternatively that he may have read them in manuscript copies. It is a curious fact that in a letter to his friend G. B. Ricciardi dated

[1] See Preface to *Prometheus Unbound*.   [2] Balfour, 112–50.

1662 and written in Rome Rosa speaks of certain verses on Nothing (versi del Niente) that Ricciardi had sent him. These verses seem to have disappeared, but it is possible that they may have given the young English poet hints for his famous poem on the same subject.[1]

From Rome they continue their journey southward to Naples, and they are reminded that Christendom is still beset by enemies, when at Teracina they find only 'a pittiful *Inn* without the town' when 'there is no manner of Furniture, but Wood to make Fire: it not being secure for anybody to live in it, because of the Turks that often Land here, and take what they can meet with'. They ride along the Appian Way and marvel at the 'vast Expense to make a way of that Length, and Breadth so well paved with Quadrangular Stones, that even to this Day (altho' it be of common & frequent Passage) continueth intire as if it were newly done', and near Capua Sir Andrew tells his pupil that great legend of the Renascence, how here 'in the Reign of *Alexander* VI . . . the Body of a Delicate Young Woman, was found altogether intire in a Marble Chest. She was of incomparable beautie having her long Flaxen Hair drawn together upon her Head with a Circle of Gold. The Body did almost Swim in a mervellous kind of Liquour and had a burning Lamp at the feet there of, which the Air, coming in at the opening of the Sepulchre, did instantly extinguish. The Body (as did appear by the Letters graven upon the place) had lyen there thirteen Hundred Years. Some have been of Opinion that it was the body of *Tulliola*, the dearly beloved Daughter of *Cicero*. It was presented in its integrity to the Conservators of *Rome*, and for some Days kept in the Capitol as a singular curiosity; but *Pope Alexander* coming to understand it, caused it to be thrown into the *Tyber*.'

At Naples Sir Andrew dilates on the history of the ancient Parthenope and Cumae, and dwells lovingly on 'the sweetness of the Air, & delicacy of the country' and on the 'many Emperours and *Roman Senators* who being wearied with the Wars, and weightiness of Government did repair to this place, that they might live pleasantly & Peaceably and give themselves to the study of Letters'. Now Naples is a Spanish possession and the travellers are surprised at the readiness with which 'so many brave and valourous Men' submit to a foreign yoke. The great churches of Naples are visited and the two sceptical Protestants listen to the stories of the miraculous crucifix

[1] See 'Rochester and Salvator Rosa' by V. de S. Pinto in E.M. no. 7.

which said to St. Thomas Aquinas 'Bene scripsisti de me Thoma' and the phial of the blood of St. Gennaro which boils when brought near his head. But Rochester is probably more interested in the house of pleasure that belonged to Sannazaro, the great Neapolitan poet, and the bookshops. When he was lying on his death-bed seventeen years later he remembered with gratitude how the good Sir Andrew 'engaged him by many Tricks . . . to delight in Books and Reading'. Together they visit the tombs of Virgil and Sannazaro, the Grotto dei Cani, Pozzuoli, the lake of Avernus, the Cave of the Sibyl and Baiae, where they see 'that delicat Pleasant Field called the *Elizium*, so much renouned by Virgil in the 6*th* Book of the *Aeneids*'. 'The most delicious Place in the whole world' Sir Andrew calls it, and in the early March day when they visit it, it is 'not only green but cover'd with *Anemonies* and other Flowers.' They climb Vesuvius and Sir Andrew gives his pupil much scientific information about volcanoes. He also remembers to take him to a village about midway to the city and to make him 'Taste of those excellent Wines, that grow upon the fertile places of the Hill and particularly of *Lachryma Christi*, otherwise called *Lagrima di Soma* . . . a gross bodied Red Wine, strong and sweet to the taste, and very pleasant.' Often Sir Andrew goes 'herborising' in the country round Naples, finding many varieties of 'Narcissus's, many Colours of single *Anemones*' and other flowers and plants. And while he is thus occupied, human nature being what it is, we can suppose that his pupil entertained himself with the company of the dark-eyed beauties for whom Naples was renowned.[1]

In April they returned to Rome and journeyed northward in the spring by way of Loretto where Sir Andrew is less interested in the legend of the Casa Sancta and other 'pieces of devotion' than in its noble and well-stocked wine cellar and its great tun 'out of which they draw 3 or 4 sorts of Wine, some red, some white'. From Loretto they go to Ancona and Rimini and thence to Bologna where there are more churches and bookshops to be seen, and then Sir Andrew has to show his pupil the Rubicon and the pillar with the inscription recording Caesar's crossing. At Ferrara they looked reverently on to the 'Sepulchre & Epitaph of the famous Poet *Ariosto*', and from there they take the canal-boat to Venice where they are welcomed by the excellent English Consul Giles Jones, and perhaps lodge in his house.[2]

[1] Balfour, 154-95.   [2] Ibid., 198-215.

FROM DITCHLEY TO PADUA

It is probable that they spent the summer at Venice. They were certainly there on 1 October 1664, when they were seen by Dr. Walter Pope, a Fellow of Rochester's college, a distinguished scientist and a friend of Sir Andrew Balfour, whom he had met at Rome. Among other Englishmen who were at Venice at the time were Roger Palmer, Earl of Castlemaine, who had been with the Venetian forces in Candia, Edward and Robert Russell, the two sons of the Duke of Bedford, and Slingsby Bethel, the republican, who was to achieve notoriety later as 'Shimei' in Dryden's 'Absalom and Achitophel'.[1]

Seventeenth-century Venice, though no longer the great commercial and naval power that it had been in the previous century, was still the great European city of pleasure and art, holding a position similar to that of Paris in the modern world. There Sir Andrew and his pupil 'swim in a gondola' in the Grand Canal, marvel at St. Mark's and its treasures, and are fascinated by the cosmopolitan crowd on the Piazza di San Marco: 'People of many Nations with different habits,' as Sir Andrew writes, reminding us that the drab uniformity of modern dress was still far away in 1664. At Venice, Sir Andrew unbends somewhat, and enjoys what he calls 'the great Divertisement' which 'is to go in Gondols upon the great Canale, where towards the Evening, one may see Five or six hundred Gondols touring up and down, full of Ladies and Gentlemen, & severalls of them with musick, both vocal and instrumental; which is one of the greatest Gustos imaginable'. Again we may well suppose that Rochester's amusements at Venice were not always so decorous as those recommended by Sir Andrew, and we may remember that the city was famous in the seventeenth century for its beautiful courtesans.[2]

From Venice, at the end of October 1664, they went to the neighbouring university city of Padua, and there on the 26th, Rochester was actually enrolled as a student in the 'English Nation'.[3] There were always a number of English and Scottish students at this university, and at this time the Professor of Logic was a Scottish Doctor Cadenhead, an old friend and fellow student of Sir Andrew. The two young Russells followed Rochester to Padua and entered the University on 8 December. The students had a bad reputation for turbulence, and what Sir Andrew Balfour calls 'a beastly custom

[1] Hill, 55; J. Isaacs, in R.E.S., Jan, 1927, 75, 76; Sibbald, II, 57.
[2] Balfour, 216–27. [3] H.B., 164.

20

of carrieing Arms in the Night', and attacking persons who incurred their displeasure.[1] Rochester's later escapades in England may owe something to the example of these riotous Italian students. It is likely that he spent the winter of 1664/5 at Padua, and travelled home with his tutor in the early spring. They pass by Verona and Lake Garda, where at Desenzano, Rochester may have remembered Catullus, but where Sir Andrew was chiefly interested in the wonderfully good fish, such as '*Pykes*, *Pearches*, red and white Trouts', and the delicious wine at the 'Ostelria'. At Milan they are impressed by the size and magnificence of the Cathedral, but regret that 'the design is Gothick'. They pass through Turin to Mont Cenis, where they cross the Alps, and are surprised to find themselves 'in the middle Region of the Air', with clouds beneath them. They have to leave their horses and take mules and then dismount from them and be wheeled by guides in 'a kind of Barrow' over the highest part of the Pass. In 'a constant deluge of Rain' they travel to Chambéry, visiting on the way the monastery of the Grand Chartreuse where they are hospitably received by the monks and are shown paintings representing the sufferings of English Catholics under Henry VIII and Elizabeth.[2] They return by Grenoble to Lyons and from thence to Paris, where the young Earl is entrusted by Henriette, Duchess of Orléans, the sister of Charles II, with a letter to her brother. The letter was delivered by him to the King at Whitehall on Christmas day, 1664.

That Christmas the chief subject of conversation at the English court was the appearance of a comet in the night sky above London on several nights during December. Charles II, in his reply to his sister's letter delivered by Rochester, describes it as 'no ordinary starr',[3] words which are perhaps an even more apt description of the new arrival at Whitehall than of the comet.

It is pleasant to find that Rochester was so grateful to Sir Andrew Balfour for his 'great Fidelity and Care of him'[4] that he insisted on making him stay with him as his guest for some time after their return.[5]

---

[1] Balfour, 230.   [2] Ibid., 236–64.   [3] Hartmann, 135.   [4] B.S.P., 5.
[5] Sibbald, II, 54.

Chapter Two

———— «◈»«◈» ————

THE CLIMATE OF OPINION

———— «◈»«◈» ————

Vast *Bodies* of *Philosophy*
I oft have seen and read,
But all are *Bodies Dead*,
Or *Bodies* by *Art fashioned*;
I never yet the *Living Soul* could see
But in thy *Books* and *Thee*.
'Tis only *God* can know
Whether the fair *Idea* thou dost show
Agree intirely with his *own* or no.
This I dare boldly tell,
'Tis so *like Truth*, 'twill serve our turn as well.
                    Cowley, *Ode to Mr. Hobs.*
The Court . . . not only debauched him; but made him a
perfect *Hobbist.*
                    Anthony à Wood on Rochester.

WHEN Rochester was three years old, Thomas Hobbes, of
Malmesbury, formerly secretary to the great Francis Bacon, published a little book called *A Treatize on Human Nature*, and in the
following year (1651) his famous *Leviathan* appeared. Rochester
read Hobbes's books with enthusiasm in his early youth and accepted
his philosophy wholeheartedly.[1] It was indeed a way of thinking
that was likely to make a peculiar appeal to a young man with a
strong intelligence and an inquiring mind in the middle of the
seventeenth century. For hundreds of years Europe had been under
the domination of certain beliefs and a certain morality, the products

———

[1] W.A.O., III, 229; Parsons, 26.

of the Christian religious tradition and of that scholastic philosophy which had grafted on to it elements from ancient Greek thought. This body of beliefs had received some rude shocks since the latter part of the fifteenth century. The discoveries of Columbus and the astronomers had revealed an earth and a universe wholly unlike the cosmology associated with the Christian tradition. Rochester had probably seen models of the new and old systems of astronomy side by side at the Jesuit's College at Paris,[1] a sight well calculated to disturb the religious ideas of a young man in 1662. In England, Bacon had spoken with contempt of the finespun arguments of scholasticism and had recommended the pursuit of 'the pure knowledge of Nature' and experimental science. In France, Descartes had tried to make an entirely fresh start in philosophy by banishing all preconceived ideas and reconstructing his view of the universe on what appeared to be the firm basis of the fact of his own existence. Scattered all over Western Europe there was a small but growing quantity of minds to which the old philosophies and religious dogmas seemed like dingy antiquated curtains shutting out the pure light of truth. But the old beliefs with the old pictorial way of thinking of religion still remained unchallenged for the great majority.

Virtue was inseparably associated with these beliefs, and virtue in the seventeenth century was a positive force of almost terrifying intensity. It hung over children, especially, like a cloud, and, when they were amenable to its influence, utterly dehumanized them. Of little Richard Evelyn, the son of John Evelyn, the diarist, we read that 'Never did this child lye in bed (by his good will) longer then six or seven, winter or summer; and the first thing he did (being up) was to say his French prayers, and our Church Catechism; after breakfast that short Latine prayer, which having encountred at the beginning of our Lillie's Grammar, he had learned by heart . . . wonderful was it to observe the chapters which himselfe would choose, and the psalmes and verses that he would apply upon occasions, and as in particular he did to some that were sick . . . bidding them to consider the sufferings of Christ, how bitter they were, and how willingly he endured them.'[2]

We can form a fair conception of the quality of this tremendous background of religiosity which overshadowed the lives of young

---

[1] Balfour, 10, 11.   [2] E.M.W., 109.

people in the middle of the seventeenth century from a collection of Dutch engravings published by Rochester's old Oxford acquaintance Robert Whitehall in January 1677/8 for the benefit of some young men of noble birth, and particularly for Rochester's own son, the little Charles, Viscount Wilmot, who was then seven years old. Whitehall acquired twelve sets of Dutch engravings, each forming a complete series illustrating the whole of the Bible story, and for each of them he wrote a 'hexastich' or poem of six lines. He had the twelve sets of engravings pasted in twelve folio volumes and the verses printed underneath the pictures, thus creating one of the rarest books of the seventeenth century.[1] These Dutch pictures are a curious record of the way in which the more naïve minds of the seventeenth century visualized the Bible story. Some of them must have provided the profane occasions for mirth rather than for pious contemplation. The creation of Eve for instance is depicted as taking place before a remarkable assembly of animals, including a very fat elephant, a turkey, a peacock, several dogs, an ostrich, and a curious kind of camel. Abihu and Nadab expire amid solid-looking flames and rolling clouds of smoke. Jael, with an engaging smile, stands at the door of her house and welcomes Sisera. Solomon on a throne decorated with a number of fat lions, which look like French poodles, receives a kneeling Queen of Sheba, who is obviously a stout Dutch matron in her Sunday clothes. An entirely naked Job argues with his friends, while his house burns in the distance and a little black-winged Satan flutters happily overhead. A fat cherub flies down from heaven to touch the lips of a heavily bearded Isaiah with a piece of burning coal held between a large pair of iron pincers. A whale with a magnificent curly tail spews forth the patient Jonah on to a beach tastefully decorated with large sea-shells and marine flora. The Virgin is in a homely Dutch room with a work-basket and scissors at her feet, when the angel, carrying a large part of a rose-tree in his hand, flies in to greet her, and at the 'Great Assize' on the Last Day, a Saviour seated on a globe in the midst of the heavens with a fat cherub blowing a trumpet at His feet, contemplates with a fatuous expression the dead rising from the graves, the damned sinking into hell-fire, and the blest rising to join the company of the saints seated on woolly clouds. The religion that these pictures represent has lost all its freshness and charm. It is a stale

---

[1] W.A.O., IV, 176; Hexastichon.

and musty thing that could have no attraction for a cultivated and original mind. Its counterpart in England may be found in the writings of the more popular divines whose books were the 'best sellers' of the seventeenth-century bookshops. Such a writer is Richard Sibbes, the Puritan master of Catherine's Hall, Cambridge, to whose works Rochester alludes contemptuously in his *Satyr Against Mankind*.[1] Probably Sibbes's numerous devotional books were favourites of Rochester's pious and simple-minded mother. The title of one of them may well have been the occasion of much ribald laughter among the undergraduates of Wadham. It is 'Bowels Opened or a Discovery of the Near and Dear Love, *Union* and *Communion* between Christ and the Church'. '*Let us*',[2] writes Sibbes in this book, '*inure our selves to beare the yoake of Religion from our youth*, which will make it easie afterwards. It were an excellent thing, if those who are young (in the prime of their yeares) would inure themselves to the exercise of religion, this would make it easie unto them, to read the word of God, to open their spirits unto him in Prayer. It may please God hereby (though they be negligent herein) yet they may be called to Religion. But for an old man there is much worke to doe to reade, to get anything into his braine, when his memory is pestered with other things, and corrupt nature in him is armed with a world of excuses, that might have been prevented by a timely and seasonable training up in a course of Religion. Prophane young persons know not what they do when they put off Religion. Have they excuses now? They will have many more hereafter, when Satan and corruption will bee much stronger. O let them beare the yoake of Religion, that is, inure themselves to duties that become Christians, which may facilitate and make it easie and plyable, that it may not be harsh to our nature. If a man doe not heare, pray and read, he can never have Faith, Grace, Knowledge, Mortification of corruption (wherein Religion stands) but because these lead to duties that are hard to nature, and harsh, it is wisdome to inure young ones thereto betimes . . .' Such teaching as this presents none of the beauty of the religious life, none of the 'sweet reasonableness' of Christianity. It stresses its 'hardness to nature' and harshness. It makes it appear as a galling yoke, a mortification of the flesh. It is

---

[1] P., 120, 217.

[2] Sibbes, 204, 205. Basil Blackwell advertised in his Catalogue 655 (1957) a copy of *The Principles of the Christian Religion* by James Usher (7th ed., 1679) carrying the arms of Anne Rochester.

true that there were other teachers like Jeremy Taylor and the Cambridge Platonists whose doctrine was far more in accordance with the new ways of thinking, but they were few and far between, and it is quite likely that the young Rochester never came into contract with their writings. For him and for other 'prophane young persons', traditional Christianity, as represented for instance in such pictures as those collected by Whitehall, or in the works of such authors as Richard Sibbes, must have seemed to be an ugly and oppressive device of priests and old people purposely designed to hide the truth away from inquiring minds and to keep them in subjection.

On the other hand they saw Hobbes with a bold, firm hand dragging down the whole cumbrous fabric and revealing what we recognize now to be only a different aspect of reality, but what must have seemed to his ardent young disciples in the seventeenth century the whole truth at last. Hobbes had a wonderfully clear and neat mind, and a genius for simplification. For him 'the *universe*, that is, the whole mass of things that are, is corporeal, that is to say, body; and hath the dimensions of magnitude, namely, length, breadth, and depth: . . . and that which is not body, is no part of the universe; and because the universe is all, that which is no part of it, is *nothing*, and consequently *no where*.'[1] In other words, Hobbes revived materialism, which had been regarded as both a pernicious heresy and an exploded doctrine since the introduction of Christianity. Unlike previous philosophers he was not interested in speculating on the origin of things. He was certain that they existed, and that they were 'material', and that was enough; he did not perceive that in assuming uncritically the existence of 'body or matter' he was committing exactly the same fault as his opponents, who similarly assumed the existence of God and the Soul.[2] For Hobbes there was nothing in the world but matter and motion, and the primary fact in human nature for him was what he calls 'sense'. 'Sense' is the result of the action of matter in motion on living bodies, which for Hobbes is simply the impact of one mass of atoms on another. There was no such thing as 'soul', or 'spirit', or 'mind'. These were mere words invented by ancient thinkers in order to keep men in subjection, 'empty names', used to frighten people 'as men fright birds from the corn with an empty doublet, a hat, and a crooked stick'.[3]

[1] Hobbes, III, 672 (*Leviathan*, IV, 46).   [2] Cf. Willey, 94, 95.
[3] Hobbes, III, 674.

Thought and perception are purely mechanical processes and can be accounted for by purely material causes:

'*Conceptions* and *apparitions* are nothing *really*, but *motion* in some internal substance of the *head*, which motion *not* stopping there, but proceeding to the *heart*, must of necessity either *help* or *hinder* the motion which is called *vital*; when it *helpeth*, it is called *delight, contentment* or *pleasure*, which is really nothing but motion about the heart, as conception is but motion in the head . . . and the same delight, with reference to the object, is called *love*: but when such motion *weakeneth*, or hindereth the vital motion, then it is called pain; and in relation to that which causeth it hatred.'[1] Imagination is explained simply as '*decaying sense*',[2] by which term means that it consists merely of the remains of the impressions made on the human body by other 'bodies' or pieces of matter: 'As standing water put into motion by the stroke of a *stone*, or a blast of wind, doth *not presently* give over moving as soon as the stone settleth: so *neither* doth the *effect* cease which the object hath wrought upon the *brain*, so soon as ever by turning aside of the organs the *object ceaseth* to work; that is to say, though the *sense* be *past*, the *image* or *conception* remaineth; but more obscure while we are *awake*, because some object or other continually *plieth* and soliciteth our eyes, and ears, *keeping* the mind in a stronger motion, whereby the *weaker* doth not easily *appear*. And this obscure conception is what we call *phantasy* or *imagination*.'[3] To the Romantic poets of a later age, 'imagination' was glorified because it was 'obscure', dim and shadowy. Thomas Campbell found that 'distance lends enchantment to the view'. But Hobbes (like Descartes) disliked anything that was misty or confused, and for him 'enchantment' would have been a term of contempt, not of praise. Dreams, indeed, he had to admit, though the result of 'imagination', were often as clear as real sense impressions received in waking life, but he explained that fact away by pointing out that in sleep the senses cease to operate, and therefore no longer interfere with the mechanical process of the 'decaying sense' by imposing new perceptions on the brain.

Hobbes's philosophy, though it is disguised under orthodox phraseology in some places, is in effect a reasoned attack on the ways of thinking that had been accepted in Western Europe for centuries. The existence of 'soul' or 'spirit', as a supernatural, even a

[1] Ibid., IV, 31 (*Human Nature*, VII).   [2] Ibid., III, 4 (*Leviathan*, I, 2).
[3] Ibid., IV, 9 (*Human Nature*, III).

divine substance was the keystone of the whole vast edifice of Christian doctrine from St. Augustine onwards. The entire fabric or orthodox traditional morality depended upon it. Certain actions were right because they were the commands of God (Who was a Spirit) given directly to Moses on Sinai or through the mouth of Christ, or indirectly by means of the inspiration of the prophets and the apostles. Similarly other actions were wrong because they had been forbidden by what in seventeenth-century language were called the Divine Decrees. Another view was the Platonic opinion that right was right because it benefited the immortal and incorporeal soul, and wrong was wrong because it harmed it.

But Hobbes taught that 'good' and 'evil' were mere convenient names with no permanent meaning and with no divine authority behind them. 'Every man, for his own part calleth that which *pleaseth*, and is delightful to himself, *good*; and that *evil* which *displeaseth* him; insomuch that while every man *differeth* from another in *constitution*, they differ also from one another concerning the common distinction of good and evil. Nor is there any such thing as absolute goodness considered without relation; for even the goodness which we apprehend in God Almighty, is *his goodness to us*.'[1]

'But whatsoever is the object of any man's appetite or desire, that is it which he for his part calleth *good*: and the object of his hate and aversion, *evil*; and of his contempt, *vile* and *inconsiderable*. For these words of good, evil and contemptible, are ever used with relation to the person that useth them, there being nothing simply and absolutely so; nor any common rule of good or evil, to be taken from the nature of the objects themselves.'[2] Such words must have seemed to young men like Rochester to shatter the whole of the dark cloud of connotation that surrounded such words as 'sin' and 'evil'. The thunders of Sinai were bogies to frighten children with. Men would no longer be afraid of things; he would be able to explain them by means of mathematics, and would feel himself superior to them.

No passage in Hobbes's works can have been more eagerly studied by his young disciple than that which describes 'Pleasure and Displeasure' in the chapter of *Leviathan* called 'Of the Passions'.

'Of pleasures or delights some arise from the sense of an object present; and those may be called *pleasure of sense*; *the word 'sensual'*,

[1] Ibid., IV, 32 (*Human Nature*, VII).   [2] Ibid., III, 41 (*Leviathan*, I, 6).

as it is used by those only that condemn them, having no place till there be laws. Of this kind are all onerations and exonerations of the body, as also all that is pleasant in the *sight, hearing, smell, taste,* or *touch.* Others arise from the expectation that proceeds from foresight of the end, or consequence of things; whether those things in the sense please or displease.'[1]

'Those who condemn' the pleasures of sense are the priests and teachers who have a vested interest in illusions inherited from the ages of monkery and superstition, the 'kingdom of darkness' as Hobbes contemptuously calls them.

Hobbes's object, as Basil Willey has shown in his excellent study of his philosophy[2] is to a large extent a 'suasive' one. He wants to give a philosophic basis to his theory of the necessity of a strong central government. But his young readers cared little for his political theory. They found in such passages as that which I have italicized in the foregoing extract, a reasoned defence of sensuality. It is true that Hobbes had gone on to argue that laws were necessary to put an end to the 'state of nature' when man was governed only by his desires, but his philosophy implies the notion that sensuality is the natural state of man and that laws are merely man-made conveniences necessary for the preservation of society. Rochester with that logical directness which was characteristic of his mind tried the experiment of putting the 'state of nature' to the text of practice.

The Restoration was a great experimental age. While the virtuosi of the Royal Society were experimenting in physics and mechanics and biology and the men of religion like Bunyan and George Fox were experimenting with the saintly life, Rochester made the experiment of living the complete life of pleasure. As a poet he was unconsciously seeking for a significant emotion which could be the material of his art. Hobbes's philosophy at first glance does not seem to be favourable to poetry. It revealed a universe of colourless, tasteless, soundless atoms, arranged in abstract mathematical patterns. But this was not the aspect of it that appeared to his young disciples at first. What appealed to them was its boldness and originality, its contrast with traditional inhibitions, and the justification which it offered for their own sensuality. Rochester found significant emotion for a while in the very freshness of the materialist philosophy and in the defiance of traditional morality to which it

---

[1] Ibid., III, 42, 43. [2] Willey, 93, 94.

logically led. In a characteristic poem probably written not long
after his return from his travels, he deliberately reverses the sentiment of Lovelace's famous cavalier song:

> I could not love thee, dear, so much,
>   Lov'd I not honour more.

Lovelace's poem has been called 'The Cavalier to his Mistress';
Rochester's poem might be entitled 'The Libertine to his Mistress';

> How perfect Cloris, & how free
> Would these enjoyments prouve,
> But you wth formall jealousy
> Are still tormenting Love.
>
> Lett us (since witt instructs us how)
> Raise pleasure to the topp,
> If Rivall bottle you'l allow
> I'le suffer rivall fopp,
>
> Ther's not a brisk insipid sparke
> That flutter [s] in the Towne
> But wth y^r wanton eyes you marke
> Him out to be y^r owne.
>
> Nor ever thinke it worthe y^r care
> How empty or how dull
> The heads of y^r admirers are
> Soe that their purse[1] bee full
>
> All this you freely may confess
> Yet wee'll not disagree
> For did you love you [r] pleasures less
> You were not fitt for mee.
>
> While I my passion to persue
> Am whole nights taking in
> The Lusty juice of Grapes, take you
> The juice of Lusty Men—
>
> Upbraide mee not that I designe
> Tricks to delude y^r charmes
> When running after mirth and wine
> I leave y^r Longing Armes.

> For wine (whose power alone can raise
> Our thoughts soe farr above)
> Affords Idea's fitt to praise
> What we think fit to Love.[1]

Rochester's mind was essentially serious. His experiment in living the life of pleasure was carried out with the whole force of his character. But very soon he began to feel that it was unsatisfactory, and that there was some part of human nature that it failed to satisfy. In the song called 'The Fall', he contrasts the 'state of nature' before the introduction of 'law' in the sense of Hobbes, with the incapability of man to find complete pleasure in the life of the senses now:

> How blest was the Created State
>   Of Man and Woman, e're they fell,
> Compared to our unhappy Fate,
>   We need not fear another Hell!
>
> Naked, beneath cool Shades, they lay,
>   Enjoyment waited on Desire:
> Each Member did their Wills obey,
>   Nor could a Wish set Pleasure higher.
>
> But we, poor Slaves to Hope and Fear,
>   Are never of our Joys secure:
> They lessen still as they draw near,
>   And none but dull Delights endure.[2]

The author of these lines is disappointed with the temporary and insecure quality of sensual pleasure in the world as it is now. This disappointment was to grow until it turned to bitterness and the mood of satire. But for a while the life of pleasure, led in elegant and cultivated surroundings, and sometimes, as we shall see, coloured with tenderness and genuine affection, afforded the poet, if not the high spiritual emotion which the inner necessity of his nature really demanded, at any rate, as a kind of substitute, moments of exquisite aesthetic satisfaction which produced some of the loveliest lyrics of the age.

[1] P., 167, 168.   [2] Ibid., 23.

Chapter Three

————⟪◆⟫⟪◆⟫————

VERY ACCEPTABLE IN A COURT

————⟪◆⟫⟪◆⟫————

I

THE England to which Rochester returned at Christmas, 1664, was very different from the gloomy, Puritanical country of his boyhood. The centre of this new England of the Restoration was 'the town', or the fashionable West End of London, which was just beginning to assume the social position that it retained for two and a half centuries. We must picture a West End in which the green fields of Middlesex come down as far as Piccadilly and border the gardens of the houses on the north side of Holborn. This 'town' consisted of a narrow fringe of houses straggling along the north bank of the river round the great curve from the ancient city of London with its medieval wooden tenements, its narrow, tortuous streets and its great Gothic cathedral still crowning Ludgate Hill to Westminster Abbey and Westminister Hall, and the old St. Stephen's Chapel where the House of Commons met. Between Westminster and Charing Cross was the real social and political centre of Restoration England, the Court of King Charles II in the great rambling collection of buildings called Whitehall Palace. For half a mile it stretched along the Thames with its classic banqueting hall built by Inigo Jones, its little octagonal cockpit used as a court theatre, and its innumerable apartments, gardens and galleries. Here was the great Stone Gallery, open to all comers and always full of a throng of fine ladies and gentlemen, politicians, chaplains, soldiers, lackeys and gaping country cousins. To the west of the Stone Gallery was the great Privy Garden with its famous sundial, and to the east,

32

looking over the river were the royal apartments where the King lived with his dark, squat little Portuguese queen, his lords and gentlemen of the bedchamber and a bevy of fair and merry maids of honour. It was a court full of gaiety, colour and music. Charles II, now a man of thirty-five, tall, swarthy, witty and amorous, with an immense appetite for pleasure and a hatred for stiffness and formality, was the incarnate spirit of the place. His trumpeters and kettledrummers marched through the park in scarlet and gold, his courtiers and mistresses rustled through the galleries of Whitehall in the superb silks and satins that we can still see in Lely's portraits, and his palace was the home of political and amorous intrigue and of the arts. Paintings by the great Flemish and Italian masters hung on its walls and in its chambers and galleries flutes, oboes and violins were for ever discoursing the airs of Henry Lawes, of Purcell, of Lully and of Grabut.

Beyond Whitehall to the west was St. James's Park with its green trees and shady walks and King Charles's famous artificial lake where his collection of exotic birds swam round the Duck Island of which the King formally appointed St. Évremond, the genial old French philosopher, Governor. To the north-west was the old Charing Cross standing at the cross-roads where King Street, Westminster, met Suffolk Street, St. Martin's Lane and the Strand. Beyond it was the half-ruined Savoy Palace and the old mansions of the great noblemen with their gardens sloping down to the broad unembanked river, and on the other side of the Strand, Covent Garden and Drury Lane, with the new Bohemia of theatres, taverns and coffee-houses. Here were 'idle places and lanes' full 'of abundance of loose women' standing at the doors. Here were the 'brisk blades', or 'town gallants', with their great white periwigs, who lolled on the benches of the new modish playhouses and listened to Mr. Betterton and the pretty, pert actresses speaking the verses of Mr. Dryden and the prose of Mr. Etherege. Further east still was Whetstone Park, where Mother Creswell and her like sold strong waters and fresh-faced wenches to all who had guineas to buy them with.

Into this world of beauty and squalor, of colour and music and splendour and vice, Rochester was launched at the age of eighteen, when he must have been one of the most handsome and accomplished young men in Europe.

He was a Graceful and well shaped Person, tall and well-made, if not a little too slender: He was exactly well bred, and what by a modest behaviour natural to him, what by a Civility become almost as natural, his Conversation was easie and obliging. He had a strange Vivacity of thought, and vigour of expression: His Wit had a subtilty and sublimity both, that were scarce imitable.[1]

This was a notable addition to the group of witty young courtiers in whose company the pleasure-loving King loved to pass his time, much to the disgust of the staid and formal Clarendon and other noblemen of the old school. They were called the 'merry gang' at the Court, and included the wealthy and volatile Duke of Buckingham, the 'generous, good-natured' Lord Buckhurst, the merry, blackeyed, Kentish knight Sir Charles Sedley, Harry Killigrew, a member of the famous Cornish cavalier family, George Etherege, whose comedy *Love in a Tub* had given him a great reputation among the wits, and Henry Savile, a plump and jovial young Yorkshireman, who is described by Clarendon, as 'a young Man of Wit and incredible Confidence and Presumption'. This gay company soon began to think of the young Earl of Rochester as their leader. With them he dined at the Rose and the Bear, and Chatelain's 'French house', bought gloves and scents in the shops in the New Exchange, lounged in the Mulberry Garden, supped with the King at Lady Castlemaine's lodgings, drove in the park and danced at Whitehall. Max Beerbohm has written that a dandy has always been the leader of English Society. Rochester was the first and greatest of the English dandies. He had something more than a good taste in clothes, in wines and in women; he had a natural fineness of mind, 'a peculiar brightness' of wit 'to which none could ever arrive'.[2] Here in real life was the pattern of the modern fine gentleman, the brilliant 'wild gallant' whom the dramatists had already been trying to put on the stage. 'No wonder a young man so made, and so improved, was very acceptable in a Court.'[3]

The winter of 1664/5 had been a very severe one. There was 'bitter cold, frost and snow' up till the end of February, and among the icy winds of the North Sea, English and Dutch ships were beginning the hostilities that led to the Second Dutch War. At Court people were talking of the mad freaks of the maids of honour, and especially of Miss Price and Miss Jennings, who had dressed themselves like orange-wenches, and gone out to sell oranges but had met first Harry Killigrew and then the old libertine Lord Brouncker,

---

[1] B.S.P., 6, 7.   [2] B.H., I, 485.   [3] B.S.P., 8.

and had returned home discomforted after a squabble with some 'blackguard boys' who had tried to steal their oranges.[1] Lady Castlemaine was still the reigning mistress, but her empire had long been threatened by the 'innocent raw girl' Frances Stewart, on whom the King 'doted', and with whom he was always dallying in the galleries and chambers of Whitehall.

One day as Rochester was coming out of the Palace, Lady Castlemaine alighted from the 'grand chariot' in which Pepys saw her lolling on her back in the Park. The rogue attempted to snatch a kiss, but the lady with a sudden blow sent him reeling backwards. He recovered himself in an instant, and spoke the following lines which he composed on the spot:

> By Heavens 'twas bravely done,
> First to attempt the Chariot of the Sun
> And then to fall like *Phaeton*.[2]

On another occasion he encountered a very different figure at the entrance to Whitehall. This was the learned Dr. Isaac Barrow, one of the royal chaplains, famous as a preacher, theologian and mathematician. Barrow, if we may believe his biographer, was not an impressive figure being 'low of stature, lean and a pale complexion' and his dress was notorious for its slovenliness. Rochester must have been astonished at the quick wit of this shabby little parson, by whom he was, for once, outmanoeuvred in repartee. Bowing low, the Earl accosted him thus ironically: 'Doctor, I am yours to the shoe-tie.' Bowing still lower, Barrow answered, 'My lord, I am yours to the ground.' Rochester: 'Doctor, I am yours to the centre.' Barrow: 'My lord, I am yours to the antipodes.' Rochester (scorning to be foiled by a musty old piece of divinity, as he termed him): 'Doctor, I am yours to the lowest pit of hell.' Barrow (turning on his heel): 'There, my lord, I leave you.'[3]

In the spring of 1665 there came to court a foppish old cavalier called Lord Hawley, a Somersetshire gentleman, who had been granted a barony by Charles I and had the reputation of a 'Court-Buffoon'. With him was his pretty granddaughter, Elizabeth Malet, daughter of a Sir John Malet of Enmore who had died before the Restoration.[4] Her mother had taken as a second husband Sir John Warre, Knight, Sheriff of Somersetshire and M.P., a formidable

---

[1] Pepys, IV, 336; Hamilton, 283–5.   [2] P., 148.   [3] D.N.B., s.a. Isaac Barrow.
[4] Collinson, II, 496.

and ambitious person. Elizabeth was an heiress and the King thought she would be a good match for Rochester. He chose a wife for his young friend with as shrewd a judgment as he had chosen a tutor. Elizabeth was a beauty with delicately chiselled features and fine eyes, and she was 'worth, and will be at her mother's death (who keeps but a little from her), £2,500 per annum',[1] a great fortune in the seventeenth century. She was also witty and highly intelligent. Naturally she had many suitors. Among them were Lord William Herbert, heir to the Earl of Pembroke, Lord Hinchinbrooke, son of Pepys's Earl of Sandwich, Lord John Butler, a younger son of the great Duke of Ormonde, and a certain Sir Francis Popham. The King, we are told spoke often to the lady for Rochester 'but with no successe'.[2] Her haughty purse-proud relatives were doubtless horrified at the notion of her throwing herself (and her fortune) away on a young man of barely eighteen with no property except the little manor of Adderbury, no money except his pension from the King and no prospects.[3]

The rebuff with which Rochester's advances were received seems to have awakened in him the wild, reckless spirit that manifested itself several times during his life. He resolved to try a method that was not uncommon in the seventeenth century and carry the lady off by force. On Friday, 26 May 1665, Elizabeth Malet went to sup with the King's favourite, Mrs Frances Stewart, at her lodgings in Whitehall. Late that night Lord Hawley fetched her in his coach, and when they reached Charing Cross they were stopped by a party of armed men, some mounted and some on foot. The young lady was seized and placed in another coach-and-six, where two women were provided to receive her. She then disappeared into the night.[4]

Her relatives appealed to the King at once, and he acted with great promptness and vigour. On Saturday morning a proclamation was issued calling on 'all Sherriffs, Mayors, Officers of the Reave, and other his Majesty's men and loving subjects whom it may concern' to search for 'all persons who shall appear guilty of the Misdemeanour . . . and having found to apprehend & in Safe Custody to detain' them 'until further Order'.[5] On Sunday it was known that

---

[1] Pepys, IV, 393.   [2] Ibid., IV, 393; VI, 75.
[3] See J. H. Wilson on 'Rochester's Marriage' in R.E.S., 19, 401. My account of the whole affair in the following pages is indebted to this article.
[4] Pepys, IV, 393.
[5] C.S.P.D., 1664–5, 389; S.P.D., Chas. II Ent. BK., 22, 153.

Rochester had been captured at Uxbridge, but that Miss Malet was not yet found. Soon after she seems to have been restored to her relations. From the very imperfect accounts of the affair that we have, it would appear that Rochester did not attempt to force his company on the lady, but was following her, perhaps on horseback. His design may have been to take her to his Oxfordshire home and woo her there. There is a curious scrap of verse in his handwriting preserved at Welbeck Abbey, which possibly alludes to this abduction:

Sab: Lost.

Blac	
Page	
Coach	Shee yeilds, she yeilds, Pale Envy said Amen
Will	The first of woemen to the Last of men
Ja.	Just soe those frailer beings Angells fell
Post:	
Gill.	Ther's no midway (it seemes) twix't heav'n & hell,
Gard:	Was it y^r end in making her, to show
But:	Things must bee rais'd soe high to fall soe low?
Uphols:	Since her nor Angells their owne worth secures
Cooke	Looke to it gods! the next turne must bee y^{rs}
Doll	You who in careles scorn Laught att the wayes
C.K.	
I.B.	Of Humble Love & call'd 'em rude Essayes
Sar:	Could you submitt to Lett this Heavy thing
Fr.:	Artless & wittless, noe way merriting[1]
H.M.	
D.M.	

It may be conjectured that the list of abbreviated names represents the members of Rochester's household who formed the party that seized Miss Malet, and that 'Gill' and 'Doll' were the two women who were provided to look after her.

Rochester was brought back from Uxbridge to the Tower, where he was imprisoned for his 'high Misdemeanour', and there he was seen one day by a learned, eccentric Wiltshire gentleman called John Aubrey. From his prison the young Earl addressed a contrite petition to the King, which

Sheweth
That noe misfortune on earth can bee so sensible to y^r Peticõner as ye losse of y^r Ma^{ttes} favour.

[1] P., 61.

That Inadvertency, Ignorance in ye Law, and Passion were ye occasions of his offence.

That had hee reflected on ye fatall consequence of incurring y^r Maties displeasure, he would rather have chosen death ten thousand times then done it.

That y^r Peticõner in all humility & sence of his fault casts himself at y^r Maties feet, beseeching you to pardon his first error, & not suffer one offence to bee his Ruine

And hee most humbly prayes that y^r Ma^ty would be pleased to restore him once more to y^r favour, & that he may kisse you hand.[1]

It was not likely that Charles would turn a deaf ear to such an appeal as this, and on 19 June an order was sent to the Lieutenant of the Tower authorizing him to discharge his prisoner on condition that he gave 'good & sufficient security' and promised 'to render himself to one of his Majesty's Principal Secretaries of State' on the first day of the next Michaelmas Term.[2]

While Rochester was in prison the first great battle of the Dutch War had been fought and won by the Duke of York's fleet off Lowestoft. Many courtiers were with the Duke, and among them, Charles Berkeley, Earl of Falmouth, the King's dearest friend had been killed. Here was a clear way for Rochester to regain the King's favour and perhaps that of Elizabeth Malet as well. He volunteered for service with the fleet, which had refitted at Lowestoft and Harwich after the battle, and was now putting to sea under the command of Pepys's patron the old Cromwellian Admiral Edward Montagu, now Lord Sandwich. On 6 July Rochester set out with a note from the King to the Admiral 'to recommend this bearer my Ld. Rochester to your care, who desires to go a volontere with you', and on the 17th the Admiral wrote[3] from the Yorkshire coast, near Flamborough Head, to tell his master that Rochester had come aboard. In the same letter, Sandwich reports that the whole fleet is under sail and bound for the coast of Norway. The object of this expedition was to capture the immensely wealthy Dutch East India Fleet which was reported to be in those waters. When the coast of Norway was reached it was learnt that the Dutch ships had taken refuge in Bergen Harbour, and, as the approach was impracticable for large ships, Sir Thomas Teddiman was sent with twenty frigates

[1] C.S.P.D., 1664–5, 389; S.P.D., Chas. II, CXXII, 55.
[2] C.S.P.D., 1664–5, 435; S.P.D., Chas. II, Ent. BK. 22, 178.
[3] C.S.P.D., 1664–5, 478.

to go in and take the rich prizes. Rochester volunteered for service with Teddiman's squadron and took part in the action on board the flagship the *Revenge*, where he is said to have shown 'as brave and as resolute a Courage as was possible'.[1] The story of the negotiations with the Danish Governor, the impatience of the English and their disastrous attack on the Dutch ships and Danish forts is well known to readers of naval history, but the letter that Rochester wrote to his mother describing the action is not so well known. Its easy, un-unaffected style, combining courtly deference with a charming familiarity and its fine, sensitive handwriting, make it a notable expression of the spirit of the young Rochester in his prime before he became disillusioned and embittered.

> From the Coast of Norway amongst the rocks.
> Aboard the Revenge, August th 3^d.

Madam,

I hope it will not bee hard for your La^{sp} to believe that it hath binn want of opportunity & noe neglect in mee the not writing to your La^{sp} all this while. I know noe body hath more reason to express theire duty to you, than I have, & certainly I will never bee so imprudent as to omitt the occasions of doing it. there have been many things past since I writt last to your La^{sp} wee have had many reports of de Ruyter & the Eastindia fleete but none true till towards the 26 of the last month wee had certaine intelligence then of 30 saile in Bergen in Norway a haven belonging to the King of Denmarke But the Port was found to bee so little that it was impossible for the greate ships to gett in, soe that my Lord Sandwich ordered 20 saile of fourth & fifth rate frigottes to goe in and take them. They were commanded by Sr Thomas Teddeman one of the vice Admiralls, it was not fit for mee to see any occasion of service to the King without offering my self, so I desired & obtained leave of my Ld Sandwich to goe with them & accordingly wee sett saile at six o clock at night and the next day wee made the haven Cruchfort (on this side of the towne 15 leagues) not without much hazard of ship wrack, for (besides the danger of Rocks wch according to the seamen's judgment was greater than ever was seene by any of them) wee found the Harbour where twenty shipps were to anchor not bigg enough for seven, soe that in a moment wee were all together one upon another ready to dash in pieces having nothing but bare Rocks to save ourselves, in case wee had binn lost; but it was gods great mercy wee gott cleere & only that, for wee had no humane probability of safety; there we lay all

---

[1] B.S.P., 9.

night and by twelve a clock next day gott of and sailed to Bergen full of hopes and expectation, having allready shared amongst us the rich lading of the Eastindia merchants some for diamonds some for spices others for rich silkes & I for shirts and gould wch I had most neede of, but reckoning without our Hoast wee were faine to reckon twice, however we came bravely into the Harbour in the midst of the towne and Castle and there Anchored close by the Dutch men, wee had immediately a message from the Governour full of civility & offers of service, wch was returned by us Mr. Mountegue being the messenger, that night wee had 7 or ten more wch signified nothing, but mere empty delayes, it grewe darke & we were faine to ly still untill morning, all the night the Dutch carried above 200 pieces of Cannon into the Danish Castells & forts, and wee were by morne drawne into a very faire halfe moone ready for both towne & ships, wee received severall messages from breake of day untill fower of clock much like those of the over night, intending nothing but delay that they might fortifie themselves the more, wch being perceived we delayed noe more, but just upon the stroke of five wee lett flye our fighting coulours & immediately fired upon the shipps, who answered us immediately & were seconded by the Castles & forts of the towne, upon wch wee shott at all and in a short time beat from one of their greatest forts some three or fower thousand men that were placed wth small shott upon us; but the Castles were not to bee [fought dow]ne, for besides the strength of theire walls they had so many of the Dutch Guns (with theire owne) wch played in the hulls & Deckes of our shipps, that in 3 howers time wee lost 200 men & six Captaines our Cables were cut & we were driven out by the winde, wch was soe directly against us that wee could not use our fireships wch otherwise had infallybly done our business, soe we came off having beate the towne all to pieces without losing one shipp, we now lie off a little still expecting a wind that wee may send in fire-shipps to make an end of the rest, Mr. Mountegue & Thom^s Windhams brother were both killed with one shott just by mee, but God Almyghty was pleased to preserve mee from any kind of hurt, Madam I have bin tedious but begg your Las^{sp} pardon who am

Your most obedient son
Rochester.

I have binn as good a husband as I could, but in spight of my teeth have binn faine to borrow mony.[1]

Rochester was still with the fleet in the autumn of 1665. On 12 September he was sent by Sandwich with a despatch to the King, and he himself gave a personal account to Charles of the action on 9 September when a number of Dutch ships were taken, though the main fleet escaped into the Texel. Sandwich writes enthusiastically of the young volunteer's conduct. He describes him as 'Brave, Industrious, & of parts fitt to be very usefull in yᵣ Maᵗᵗᵉˢ service.' The King replied on the 16th acknowledging Sandwich's letter, and also the verbal message from the Admiral delivered by Rochester.[1]

During those days spent on the decks and in the cabins of the great wooden sailing ships amid 'masts, stormes, short victualls, adverse winds', Rochester's mind was occupied with other things besides naval affairs and thoughts of Oxfordshire and Whitehall. He was asking himself questions which were to present themselves to his mind often during the rest of his short life. What was death? What was the relation between soul and body? Could the soul survive the body? What reliance was to be placed on the promises of religion concerning a 'future state'. Were Lucretius and Mr. Hobbes right and was there nothing in the world but assemblages of atoms thrown together in geometrical patterns by chance or design? Here, where men were daily facing death, was a chance to make an experiment, and it was characteristic of the man and of his age that he should try to clear up the question of immortality by experiment, just as members of the Royal Society were using the same method to clear up problems that had puzzled wise heads for centuries. The story of Rochester's experiment can best be told in Burnet's words:

> When he went to Sea in the Year 1665, there happened to be in the same Ship with him Mr. *Mountague*, and another Gentleman of Quality, these two, the former especially, seemed perswaded that they should never return into *England*. Mr. *Mountague* said, He was sure of it: the other was not so positive. The Earl of *Rochester*, and the last of these, entred into a formal Engagement, not without Ceremonies of Religion, that if either of them died, he should appear, and give the other notice of the future State, if there was any. But Mr. *Mountague* would not enter into the Bond. When the day came that they thought to have taken the *Dutch*-Fleet in the Port of *Bergen*, Mr. *Mountague*, though he had such a strong Presage in his Mind of his approaching death, yet he generously staid all the while in the place of greatest danger: The other Gentleman signalized his Courage in a most undaunted manner, till near the end of the Action, when he fell on a sudden into such a trembling, that he could scarce stand: and Mr. *Mountague* going to him to hold him up, as they were in each others Arms, a Cannon Ball killed him outright, and carried away Mr. *Mountague's* Belly, so that he died within an Hour after.

[1] C.S.P.D., 1664-5, 562; S.P.D. Chas II, CXXXII, 83.

41

Rochester's two comrades were Edward Montagu, a son not of the Admiral but of Lord Montagu of Boughton, and a certain Mr. Windham. The result of the experiment was negative, the spirit of Windham never returned to tell his friend news of the other world, and Rochester told Burnet that this 'was a great snare to him, during the rest of his life'. Still, he was somewhat shaken in his materialism by the presentiment felt so strongly by Montagu, and to a less extent by Windham, and justified by their death. This seemed to show that spirit was something distinct from body after all, and also that 'the Soul either by a natural sagacity, or some secret Notice communicated to it, had a sort of Divination',[1] and therefore could hardly be due to the merely mechanical action of a concourse of atoms.

The next summer Rochester tore himself away again from a court where, in spite of the plague that was raging in London, all was gaiety and pleasuring, and the Maids of Honour were astonishing the town with their new doublets, periwigs and hats which gave them a piquant masculine appearance.[2] Without giving any warning to his friends or relations he slipped away from Whitehall and went on board Sir Edward Spragge's ship on 31 May, the day before the opening of the sanguinary Four Days' Battle in the Channel between the English fleet under Monk and Rupert, and the Dutch under Van Tromp and De Ruyter. Rochester was in the thick of the fighting and was one of the few volunteers in Spragge's ship that were not killed. During the battle Spragge wanted to send a message to one of the other captains, and Rochester volunteered to take it. He went in a small boat under heavy fire, delivered his message and returned to his ship, 'which was much commended by all that saw it'.[3]

A German biographer of Rochester has expressed surprise because he did not continue to serve in the wars after this distinguished beginning.[4] It seems to the present writer not only natural that he should have left off fighting after he had satisfied his desire for experience of a hard and dangerous life, but also likely that the strong antipathy to war and militarism expressed in his poems and letters is not unconnected with the shock given to a sensitive mind by such a spectacle as the carrying away of Mr. Montagu's belly by a cannon-ball, and similar horrors witnessed during the battles in the North Sea and the Channel.

---

[1] B.S.P., 17, 18.   [2] Pepys, V, 305.   [3] B.S.P., 11.   [4] Prinz, 36, 37.

1. John Wilmot, Earl of Rochester (by Sir Peter Lely).

2. The Countess of Rochester.

Charles II was apparently so pleased with Rochester's service in the navy that he made him a free gift of £750 on 31 October,[1] and so, perhaps, cleared off the debts mentioned in the Earl's letter to his mother from Bergen.

By 15 November Rochester was back at Court and dancing in a grand ball in honour of the Queen's birthday where Mrs. Stewart appeared 'in black and white lace, and her head and shoulders dressed with dyamonds', and the King in a 'rich vest of some rich silke and silver trimming'. The other members of the company included the Duke of York, Prince Rupert, Monmouth, Buckingham, Lord Ossory, and among the ladies, the Queen, the Duchesses of York and Monmouth and the wife of the Swedish Ambassador. Fat, meddlesome Mr. Pepys watched the proceedings with great pleasure from an uneasy position in the loft over the ballroom.[2]

After Rochester's imprisonment in the Tower strong efforts were made by Lord and Lady Sandwich to obtain Elizabeth Malet's hand for their son, Lord Hinchinbrooke. In June 1665 Lady Sandwich told Pepys that 'my Lord Rochester is now declaredly out of hopes of Mrs. Mallett, and now she is to receive notice in a day or two how the King stands inclined to giving leave for my Lord Hinchinbrooke to look after her, and that being done to bring it to an end shortly'.[3] Lord Hawley and Sir John Warre were certainly pressing her to marry a man of substantial means. They knew that, when she married, her considerable property would pass out of their hands, but, if she married into a wealthy family, they could hope to drive a hard bargain and keep part of the spoils for themselves.[4] Elizabeth, probably after Rochester's attempt to abduct her, gave her word to her guardians that she would not marry without their consent;[5] but she found, apparently, that she did not care for any of the suitors they approved, though she was quite willing to amuse herself with them. She drank Butler's health 'in a pretty big glasse halfe full of Clarett . . . more than ever shee did in her life'.[6] and made a proposal, probably in jest, for an elopement, which shocked the conventional Lord Hinchinbrooke, who, we are told by Pepys, was not 'fully pleased with the liberty and vanity of her carriage'. On 26 August 1666 she definitely broke with him, declaring

[1] C.S.P.D., 1665-6, 35.   [2] Pepys, VI, 61-3.   [3] Pepys, IV, 400.
[4] J. H. Wilson, op. cit., R.E.S., 19, 401.   [5] Harris, II, 176.
[6] Ibid., letter from Harry Nicholls to the Duke of Ormonde.

E

'her affections were settled', no doubt on my Lord Rochester.[1] In November 1666 she was gaily passing her suitors in review: Lord Herbert 'would have had her', Hinchinbrooke was 'indifferent to have her', Butler 'might not have her', Rochester 'would have forced her', and Popham 'would kiss her breach to have her'.

Finally, after months of temporizing, Elizabeth seems to have considered herself absolved from her promise to her guardians. She now understood their motives and saw that they were ' "ready to make a prey of her": her timber was cut down, her estate was lessened'.[2] Rochester whose tongue 'would tempt the Angels to a second fall',[3] appeared now in the light of a deliverer, and she was married to him on 29 January 1666/7[4] without the consent of her guardians. The King, however, gave his approval to the match and is said to have been 'very well satisfyed' with it. Rochester's mother, the old dowager countess, was anxious about Elizabeth's estate and wrote to her old friend Sir Ralph Verney asking for his help: 'We are in some care to get the estate, they [Elizabeth's family] are come to desire to parties with friends, but I want a knowing friend in business, such a won as Sir Ralph Verney.'[5] It is clear that the Warres were fighting hard to keep their hands on as much of the property as possible.

Pepys saw Lord and Lady Rochester together in the pit of the Duke's Playhouse six days after their marriage[6] at a performance of a play called *Heraclius*, and he notices how the new Countess smiled to Lord John Butler, her old suitor, when he came into the theatre. In March Rochester was appointed a Gentleman of the King's Bedchamber,[7] and probably about the same time his wife was made Groom of the Stole to the Duchess of York.[8] A gentleman of the bedchamber received a salary of £1,000 a year. His duties involved personal attendance on the King for a week in every quarter when he had to lie on a pallet-bed in the royal bedchamber, and in the absence of the Groom of the Stole, help the King in his toilet. When the King ate in private, and the official cup-bearers, carvers and servers were not on duty, the gentleman of the bedchamber supplied their

---

[1] Pepys, V, 219, 387.   [2] Harris, II, 176.   [3] Etherege, II, 237.
[4] H.M.C., Le Fleming Papers, 22.   [5] Williams, 39.   [6] Pepys, VI, 153.
[7] C.S.P.D., 1666–7, 560; Chamberlayne, 259. The increase in Rochester's pension from the original £500 to the £1,000 due to him as Gentleman of the Bedchamber did not apparently take place without some difficulty. His 'docquet' for the increased annuity did not pass the Treasury till 18 Nov. 1667. See C.T.B., 1667–8, 116, 121.
[8] Chamberlayne, 331.

place. Among Rochester's colleagues were his friends Buckingham and Buckhurst, and the King must have found a good deal more entertainment when these members of 'the merry gang' were on duty than when he had to submit to the ministrations of the solemn Duke of Newcastle or the ugly, shifty Scotsman, Lauderdale.[1]

In June, Rochester received a commission as Captain in Prince Rupert's regiment of horseguards, and in July he was summoned to the House of Lords, although he was still a minor.[2] It was his twenty-first year, and life had been very good to him. He was a nobleman at one of the most brilliant courts in Europe, and he was high in the favour of his King. He was a poet, and a wit, and he had married a beauty and an heiress. If the world consisted only of matter, as Mr. Hobbes had proved to his satisfaction, it was a very pleasant world. There was colour and music at Whitehall, and there was brilliant talk with Etherege, Buckhurst, Sedley, Wycherley and Shadwell at the Rose and the Bear. There was abundant outdoor sport, hunting and hawking in the green English countryside. There was racing at Newmarket and Epsom, as well as nearer home on Burford Downs and at Woodstock Park. Why should not Lord Rochester enjoy himself without thinking too much, like the other gay, free-living English gentlemen of his age secure in their wealth and their traditional social position? But it happened that Lord Rochester was rather different from the other English gentlemen. There was something growing up in his mind that made him less and less inclined to be content with the easy solutions of the problem of life. Ten years later he was to look back and see himself at twenty as a 'gay glitt'ring Fool . . . with all his noise, his tawdrey Cloaths and Loves'.[3]

Robert Whitehall did not forget his young friend now that he was a brilliant courtier. Probably he was not a little proud of his connection with one of the great men at Whitehall. On 1 January 1666/7, he sent him his portrait from Oxford with a copy of witty verses:

> MY LORD:
> Ou[r] picture we have sent,
> An Embleme of approaching Lent;
> But that red[d] letter in each cheeke
> Speaks Holyday, not Ember-weeke:
> So incorporeall, so aery

[1] Ibid., 257–9.
[2] C.S.P.D., 1667, 179, 183, 339, 450; H.M.C., 8th Rep., App., 111b. [3] P., 124.

This Christmas t'will be t'ane for Fairy.
Hang it or burne it, choose you which
Yet now I think it on't tis no witch,
Nor Conjurer, for (to its grace)
You'[1] find it ha's no Bacon face:
And though orbicular the frame
It bears a more Majestick name. . . .[1]

II

Much of Rochester's lyrical poetry probably belongs to the period
immediately before and after his marriage. The young Earl and
Countess both wrote verse and it appears that they often lived together in that imaginary world of rococo pastoral that made a
strong appeal to poetic minds at that period all over Europe. The
pastoral convention, which had appeared to the eyes of the great
men of the Renaissance charged with imaginative splendour, had
undergone a curious transformation by the second half of the
seventeenth century. The shepherds and shepherdesses had lost
their grandeur and had become small, dainty, elegant figures. When
Spenser called Ralegh 'Shepherd of the Ocean', the word 'Shepherd' was filled with high poetic meaning. It connoted a man who
was an inhabitant of an ideal world transcending everyday existence.
Milton's *Lycidas* is perhaps the last poem in which the pastoral convention has this lofty significance. For the new generation that was
writing poetry in the years that followed the Restoration the pastoral
implied an imaginary existence in a non-moral world of delicate
grace, elegance and charm, the world of the *Astrée* of Honoré
D'Urfé. The transition is from the shepherds of Virgil and Milton
to the *bergeries* of Watteau and Fragonard. This rococo pastoral, as we
may call it to distinguish from the classical and Renaissance pastoral,
could very easily become silly. It had become silly by the time that
Congreve's Lady Wishfort wanted to 'retire to deserts and solitudes,
and feed harmless sheep by groves and purling streams', and when
Pope wrote his exquisite parody of it in 'A Song by a Person of
Quality':

Flutt'ring spread thy purple pinions,
    Gentle *Cupid*, o'er my Heart;
I a Slave in thy Dominions;
    Nature must give way to Art.

[1] Portland MS. printed in W.M., No. 2, 44, 45.

> Mild *Arcadians*, ever blooming,
>   Nightly nodding o'er your Flocks,
> See my weary Days consuming,
>   All beneath yon flow'ry Rocks.[1]

But in the reign of Charles II the rococo pastoral was not silly. It was in some degree the symbol of an ideal kind of life, not indeed a lofty ideal like that of Spenser or Milton, but the truly poetic ideal of a delicate, courtly existence removed from everyday life and everyday morality. The typical poet of this Utopia of gallantry was Rochester's friend Sir Charles Sedley. He felt all the charm of the rococo pastoral and did not trouble to think about it too much. At their worst his poems are utterly insipid; at their best they are like paintings on a fan, all delicate *nuances*:

> Ah, *Chloris!* that I now could sit
>   As unconcern'd, as when
> Your infant beauty cou'd beget
>   No pleasure, nor no pain.
>
> When I the Dawn us'd to admire,
>   And prais'd the coming day;
> I little thought the growing fire
>   Must take my Rest away. . . .[2]

Rochester is a much greater poet than Sedley. He can think as well as feel. The words which Pater applies to the art of Watteau describe the difference between the two poets excellently:

> Antony Watteau paints that delicate life of Paris so excellently, with so much spirit, partly because, after all, he looks down upon it or despises it. . . .
> Those coquetries, those vain and perishable graces, can be rendered so perfectly only through an intimate understanding of them. . . . Hence that discontent with himself which keeps pace with his fame. . . .
> It is altogether different with Jean-Baptiste. He approaches that life, and all its pretty nothingness, from a level no higher than its own.[3]

If we substitute 'Rochester' for 'Antony Watteau', 'Whitehall' for 'Paris', and 'Sedley' for 'Jean-Baptiste', we have an accurate description of the quality of the two Court poets of the Restoration.

---

[1] Pope, IV, 489. [2] Sedley, I, 147.
[3] *Imaginary Portraits* by Walter Pater, Library Ed., 1910, 26.

John Wilmot and Elizabeth Malet, then, saw themselves sometimes as the impassioned shepherd and the scornful shepherdess of the rococo Arcadia:

A SONG

Give me leave to rail at you,
I ask nothing but my due;
To call you false, and then to say
You shall not keep my Heart a Day:
But alas! against my Will,
I must be your Captive still.
Ah! be kinder then; for I
Cannot change, and would not die.

Kindness has resistless Charms,
All besides but weakly move;
Fiercest Anger it disarms,
And clips the Wings of flying Love.
Beauty does the Heart invade,
Kindness only can persuade;
It gilds the Lover's servile Chain,
And makes the Slaves grow pleas'd again.[1]

THE ANSWER

Nothing ades to Loves fond fire
More than scorn and cold disdain
I to cherish your desire
Kindness used but twas in vain
You insulted on your Slave
To be mine you soon refused
Hope not then the power to have
Which ingloriously you used.

Think not Thersis I will ere
By my Love my Empire loose
You growe Constant through despare
Kindness you would soon abuse
Though you still possess my hart
Scorn and rigor I must fain
There remains noe other Art
Your Love (fond fugitive) to gain.[2]

[1] P., 30.   [2] Ibid., 31, 171–3.

A manuscript copy of the second of these two poems survives in Lady Rochester's handwriting and it is probably her own composition. The two lyrics form a record of a delicate, courtly technique of love-making which contrasts curiously with the coarse libertinism with which gossip has commonly associated Rochester's name. Beside them may be placed the following superb compliment in the manner of the earlier seventeenth century, preserved in Rochester's autograph among the Duke of Portland's manuscripts now in Nottingham University Library.

> 'Twas a dispute 'twixt heav'n & Earth
> Which had produc't the Nobler birth
> For Heav'n, Appear'd Cynthya wth all her Trayne
> Till You came forth
> More glorious & more Worth,
> Than Shee with all those trembling imps of Light
> With which This envious Queene of night
> Had Proudly deck't her Conquer'd selfe in Vaine.
>
> I must have perrish't in that first surprize
> Had I beheld y[r] Eyes
> Love like Appollo when he would inspire
> Some holy brest; laide all his gloryes by.
> Els the God cloath'd in heavenly fire
> Would have possest too powerfully
> And making of his Preist A sacrifice
> Had soe return'd unhallow'd to the Skyes.[1]

This poem has something of the rapture of the Elizabethans. It is more like the work of a contemporary of Ralegh and Campion than a contemporary of Dryden. When Rochester applies himself seriously to the rococo pastoral he can bring this artificial form to life by sheer imaginative intensity just as Watteau did in another medium. Take, for example, this little erotic picture which Watteau might have painted against a background of great, sombre trees and silvery sky:

A Song

> As *Chloris* full of harmless Thoughts
> Beneath a Willow lay,
> Kind Love a youthful Shepherd brought,
> To pass the Time away.

---

[1] Ibid., 37, 175.

She blusht to be encounter'd so,
    And chid the amorous Swain:
But as she strove to rise and go,
    He pull'd her down again.

A sudden Passion seiz'd her Heart,
    In spight of her Disdain;
She found a Pulse in ev'ry Part,
    And Love in ev'ry Vein.

Ah! Youth! (said she) what Charms are these,
    That conquer and surprize?
Ah! let me—for unless you please,
    I have no Power to rise.

She fainting spoke, and trembling lay,
    For fear he should comply:
Her lovely Eyes her Heart betray,
    And give her tongue the Lye.

Thus she who Princes had deny'd
    With all their Pomp and Train;
Was in the lucky Minute try'd,
    And yielded to a Swain.[1]

Poetry like this is half-way between Herrick and Carew and Prior and Gay. It has the imaginative power and tenderness of the older poets combined with the perspicuity and grace of the Augustans. The following dialogue suggests statuary rather than painting. It might be a group by Bernini:

A SONG

Nymph:
Injurious Charmer of my vanquisht Heart
    Canst thou feel Love, and yet no Pity know?
Since of my self from thee I cannot part,
    Invent some gentle Way to let me go.

For what with Joy thou didst obtain,
    And I with more did give;
In time will make thee false and vain,
    And me unfit to live.

[1] Ibid., 29, 30.

Shepherd:
Frail Angel, that thou wouldst leave a Heart forlorn
With vain Pretence falshood therein might lye;
Seek not to cast wild shadows o'er your scorn.
You cannot sooner change, than I can dye.
To tedious Life I'll never fall,
Thrown from thy dear lov'd Breast;
He merits not to live at all,
Who cares to live unblest.

Chorus:
Then let our flaming Hearts be joyn'd;
While in that sacred fire.
E'er thou prove false, or I unkind,
Together both expire.[1]

It is curious to notice in these poems that such words as 'Charmer'
and 'Swain', which were to become completely frigid in the
eighteenth century, are kindled, perhaps for the last time, into
poetic life.

Rochester could play the game of the rococo pastoral splendidly,
when he cared to abandon himself to it, but he could also 'understand and despise' it, and then he uses it ironically and foreshadows
the art of Congreve and Pope:

A SONG

Phillis, be gentler, I advise,
Make up for time mis-spent,
When Beauty on its Death-bed lyes,
'Tis high time to repent.

Such is the Malice of your Fate,
That makes you old too soon;
Your Pleasure ever comes too late,
How early e'er begun.

Think what a wretched Thing is she,
Whose Stars contrive, in spight;
The Morning of her Love should be
Her fading Beauty's Night.

[1] Ibid., 36, 37, 171.

Then if, to make your Ruin more,
   You'll peevishly be coy,
Die with the Scandal of a Whore,
   And never know the Joy.[1]

Another ironic song is more brutal. It is a parody of 'heroic' and classical subject-matter which reminds the modern reader at once of the anti-romanticism of the twentieth century:

GRECIAN KINDNESS

The utmost Grace the *Greeks* could shew,
   When to the *Trojans* they grew kind,
Was with their Arms to let 'em go,
   And leave the lingring wives behind.
They beat the Men, and burnt the Town,
Then all the Baggage was their own.

Then the kind Deity of Wine
   Kiss'd the soft wanton God of Love;
This clapp'd his Wings, that press'd his Vine;
   And their best Pow'rs united move.
While each brave *Greek* embrac'd his Punk,
Lull'd her asleep, and then grew drunk.[2]

'It may almost be said,' wrote Synge in 1908, 'that before verse can be human again it must learn to be brutal.' These words can be applied to the age when seventeenth-century romanticism was dying as well as to that which saw the collapse of the romanticism of the Victorian age.

A group of Rochester's lyrics is distinguished from the rest by its note of genuine and intense passion. We know nothing of the circumstances in which these poems were written. They may have been addressed to Mrs. Barry or some other mistress of Rochester, but it is more likely that they were inspired by Elizabeth Malet. A number of his letters to his wife have survived and they are full of exquisite tenderness and humour. Their tone is exactly that of the best love-songs and I believe that the letters and the songs are addressed to the same person. In these poems Rochester is not merely one of the mob of gentlemen who wrote with ease; he is one of the great love poets of the world, worthy to rank with Catullus and with Burns. He is also one of the few really great English song

---

[1] Ibid., 21.   [2] Ibid., 16.

writers, who can give to language that peculiar freshness and crystal-line clarity that Campion achieved occasionally at the end of the sixteenth century, and Bridges at the end of the nineteenth:

A SONG

While on those lovely Looks I gaze,
　　To see a Wretch pursuing;
In Raptures of a bless'd Amaze,
　　His pleasing Happy Ruin:
'Tis not for Pity that I move:
　　His Fates is too aspiring,
Whose Heart, broke with a Load of Love,
　　Dies wishing and admiring.

But if this Murder you'd forego,
　　Your Slave from Death removing;
Let me your Art of Charming know,
　　Or learn you mine of Loving.
But whether Life, or Death, betide,
　　In Love 'tis equal Measure:
The Victor lives with empty Pride;
　　The Vanquish'd die with Pleasure.[1]

The first stanza of this song is almost perfect: the second is not quite so good, and there is a touch of the Augustan straining after anti-thesis at the end. Here is Rochester's best love-song, an 'entire and perfect Chrysolite':

A SONG

My dear Mistress has a Heart
　　Soft as those kind Looks she gave me;
When with Love's resistless Art,
　　And her Eyes, she did Enslave me.
But her Constancy's so weak,
　　She's so wild, and apt to wander;
That my jealous Heart wou'd break,
　　Should we live one Day asunder.

Melting Joys about her move,
　　Killing Pleasures, wounding Blisses;
She can dress her Eyes in Love,
　　And her Lips can arm with Kisses.

[1] Ibid., 25

53

Angels listen when she speaks,
  She's my Delight, all Mankinds Wonder:
But my jealous Heart would break,
  Should we live one Day asunder.[1]

This is the kind of poetry that Landor called 'diaphanous'. The words of Tennyson on the songs of Burns might well be applied to it: 'in shape . . . the perfection of the berry, in light the radiance of the dewdrop'. There is no better commentary on these songs than the little notes scribbled by Rochester to his wife:

> I kiss my deare wife a thousand times, as farr as imagination & wish will give mee leave, thinke upon mee as long as it is pleasant & convenient to you to doe soe & afterwards forgett me, for though I would faine make you the Author & foundation of my happiness yet would I not bee the cause of your constraint & disturbance, for I love not my selfe soe much as I doe you, neither doe I value my own satisfaction equally as I doe yours.[2]

. . . . .

> Ile hould you six to fower I Love you wth all my heart, if I would bett wth other people I'me sure I could gett two to one, but because my passion is not soe extensive to reach to every body, I am not in paine to satisfye many, it will content mee if you beleive mee & love mee.[3]

One of the most touching and characteristic of the love-poems is almost certainly addressed to Lady Rochester. It is the expression of a complex mood in which the poet at once regrets his infidelities and at the same time finds in them a contrast that increases his appreciation of the only love that can bring him happiness.

A Song

Absent from thee I languish still;
  Then ask me not, When I return?
The straying Fool 'twill plainly kill,
  To wish all Day, all Night to mourn.

Dear: from thine Arms then let me flie,
  That my fantastick Mind may prove
The Torments it deserves to try,
  That tears my fix'd Heart from my Love.

---

[1] Ibid., 35.   [2] H., 224; Prinz., 264.   [3] H., 226; Prinz, 265.

54

When wearied with a world of Woe
To thy safe Bosom I retire,
Where Love, and Peace, and Truth does flow,
May I contented there expire.

Lest once more wand'ring from that Heav'n,
I fall on some base Heart unblest;
Faithless to thee, false, unforgiven,
And lose my everlasting Rest.[1]

This song may remind the reader of some of Donne's best love-poems. It has the same passionate fusion of thought and sentiment, a fusion which appears here perhaps for the last time in English lyric poetry for over a century. Observe also the humour which is mingled with the tenderness of this poetry. Rochester can find amusement in the disparity between 'the straying Fool' who brings torments on himself, and the Glory of the 'Love and Peace and Truth' which are awaiting him. Again we may illustrate the poem by a fragment from one of the letters:

'Tis not an easy thing to bee intirely happy, But to be kind is very easy, and that is the greatest measure of happiness. I say nott this to putt you in mind of being kind to me; you have practis'd that soe long, that I have a joyfull confidence you will never forgett it, but to shew that I myself have a sence of what the methods of my Life seeme soe utterly to contradict.[2]

At such times as these Rochester found for a while that significant emotion for which his spirit craved, and there is a curious piece of evidence that the exaltation which he experienced sometimes in his love-making was in reality closely akin to that religious 'enthusiasm', which at that time he would certainly have derided. Francis Quarles, the old 'metaphysical' religious poet, may well have been a favourite of old Lady Rochester, and Rochester probably knew his *Emblemes* (first published in 1635) from his boyhood. There is a fine poem in that book suggested by the words of the Book of Job: 'Wherefore hidest thou thy face, and holdest me for thy enemie?' Rochester certainly studied this poem very carefully for he reproduced its metre and also certain characteristics of its style in some of his own poems. What is stranger still is that, on one occasion, by means of a few deft changes, he appears to have altered this

[1] P., 18, 19.   [2] H., 212.

impassioned address to God into an equally impassioned address to his mistress. Much moral indignation has been displayed by critics in connection with this act, and Rochester has been accused of plagiarism and irreverence. The charge of plagiarism is entirely beside the point. Rochester never intended his *pastiche* for publication, and he had a perfect right to try private experiments on a piece of contemporary verse. What is really interesting to the serious student of Rochester is that here he finds in the language of religious experience an idiom that suits him perfectly. His adaptation of Quarles's poem must be read in the light of the religious experience that he himself was to undergo at the end of his life. He may have adapted the lines in a light-hearted spirit, but the unconscious part of his mind was finding in them the kind of emotion for which it was craving. His clever modifications in themselves show how thoroughly he entered into the spirit of Quarles's work. There is no more interesting proof of the closeness of much religious emotion in the seventeenth century to the emotion of sexual love. The following lines may be called 'Variations on a Theme of Francis Quarles', and the reader may compare them with the fine poem in *The Divine Emblemes*.

To His Mistress

Why do'st thou shade thy lovely face? O why
Does that Eclipsing hand of thine deny
The Sun-shine of the Sun's enlivening eye?

Without thy light what light remains in me?
Thou art my Life; my way, my Light's in Thee;
I Live, I move, and by thy beams I see.

Thou art my Life—if thou but turn away,
My Life's a thousand Deaths, thou art my way—
Without Thee (*Love*) I travel not but Stray.

My Light thou art, without thy Glorious sight
My Eyes are Darkned with Eternal night;
My Love Thou art, my way, my Life, my light.

Thou art my way I wander if thou fly,
Thou art my light, if hid, how blind am I,
Thou art my Life if thou withdraw'st I Die.

My Eyes are dark and blind, I cannot see.
To whom or whether should my darkness flee
But to that Light, And who's that light but Thee?

If that be all, Shine forth and draw thou nigher,
Let me be bold and Dye for my desire;
A *Phenix* likes to Perish in the Fire.

If my Puft Life be out, give leave to [tine]
My shameless Snuff at the bright Lamp of thine.
Ah! what's thy Light the less for lighting mine?

If I have lost my Path, dear Lover, say,
Shall I still wander in a Doubtful way,
Love shall a Lamb of *Israel's* Sheepfold Stray?

My Path is lost, my wand'ring Steps does [*sic*] stray,
I cannot go, nor safely Stay;
Whom should I seek but Thee my Path, my Way?

And yet thou turn'st thy Face away and flyest me!
And yet I sue for Grace and thou deniest me!
Speak, art thou angry, Love, or try'st me?

Display those Heavenly Lamps, or tell me why
Thou Shad'st thy Face, perhaps no Eye
Can view their Flames and not drop down and Die.

Thou art the Pilgrim's Path, the Blind-Man's eye,
The Dead Man's Life on thee my hopes rely:
If I but them remove, I e'er I Die [*sic*].

Dissolve thy Sun-Beams, close thy Wings and Stay!
See See how I am blind, and Dead and Stray.
. . . O thou that art my Life, my Light, my way!

Then work thy will! If Passion bid me flee,
My Reason shall obey, my Wings shall be
Stre[t]ched out no further then from me to thee![1]

Besides a number of minor alterations, it is interesting to notice
that, wherever Quarles wrote 'my God' or 'Lord', Rochester has

---

[1] P., 132, 220. Punctuation has been inserted.

substituted 'my Love' or 'Love' or 'Lover'. The fine concluding stanza is taken from another poem by Quarles in the same metre.

At certain moments it would seem that Rochester, through the very intensity of his passion, reached out to the world of the spirit, and found the ecstasy that annihilates space and time. Much of the profound unhappiness of his satiric poems is probably due to the memory of this 'felicity and glory', and the desire to regain it. Only on his death-bed was he to achieve an experience of equal significance. Sometimes he would dream that such moments might be enjoyed without reference to the past or the future, that he could isolate them from the follies and impertinences of the life of court and tavern and theatre, that he could live only in those moments of exquisite satisfaction. This dream is the subject of his greatest lyric:

LOVE AND LIFE

All my past Life is mine no more,
 The flying Hours are gone:
Like transitory Dreams giv'n o'er,
Whose Images are kept in store
 By Memory alone.

The Time that is to come is not;
 How can it then be mine?
The present Moments all my lot;
And that, as fast as it is got,
 Phillis, is only thine.

Then talk not of Inconstancy,
 False Hearts and broken Vows;
If I, by Miracle can be
This live-long Minute true to thee
 'Tis all that Heav'n allows.[1]

Here we have an expression of the Epicurean ideal of a life lived for momentary pleasure. This ideal, however, is seen not from the viewpoint of the greedy sensualist, but from that of the spiritual explorer who wants to escape from time and to find an experience that will transcend all ordinary experiences. The beauty of the poem is largely due to the fact that the poet is really aware that his lovely phrase, 'flying hours', is full of sadness, and the hedonistic philosophy only

[1] Ibid., 24.

3. Elizabeth Barry.

4. John Wilmot, Earl of Rochester (attributed to Jacob Huysmans).

a dream. The effect is mournful rather than joyous. It makes us feel that the delicious present which we should like to isolate and to enjoy cannot really be isolated, and is at once fading into the past and melting into the future.

The poet of 'Love and Life' is hungry for the freedom from the tyranny of time and space that the pleasures of the senses could only give him for a fleeting instant. He was bound to turn to religion as soon as he was convinced that it was spiritual experience and not merely a system of antiquated inhibitions.

Chapter Four

————⟪◆⟫⟪◆⟫————

THE UTOPIA OF GALLANTRY

————⟪◆⟫⟪◆⟫————

Often on some frolic, when as a mountebank or merchant, or as companion to the King, he seemed to be borne on the wings of enjoyment, his face would cloud over: and once at a debauch, when all his wit, his spirit, his abundant grace were more intoxicating than the wine, and he seemed himself to be Pan or the young Bacchus, he clasped my arm till the fingers wounded me, and whispered passionately into my ear: 'It isn't that: it isn't there.'—Bonamy Dobrée, *Rochester, A Conversation.*

Some of the best of Rochester's poetry was perhaps lived rather than written, and this kind of poetry, like the music of dead singers and the acting of dead players, can only be dimly guessed at by posterity. All that survives of it now is a mass of fragmentary reminiscence and legend, some of which is obviously apocryphal (like the eighteenth-century accounts of his amours in *The School of Venus*, by Captain Alexander Smith), but much also certainly authentic in essentials, if not always in detail. His life was the fine flower of that non-moral aristocratic society of the Restoration which the writers of comedy tried repeatedly to put on the stage in the reign of Charles II. To appreciate it properly we must not apply to it the standards of practical morality. We must regard it as Charles Lamb regarded 'the Artificial Comedy of the Last Century' and see it as 'the Utopia of gallantry, where pleasure is duty, and the manners perfect freedom', a brilliant experiment in the art of living: Rochester was the leader of this society not only because he was handsome and witty, but because he had a peculiar charm of manner, a genius for intimacy that none of his companions could rival. 'Never', writes one of his admirers,[1] 'was his Talk thought too much or his Visit too long; enjoyment did but increase Appetite, and the more men had of his Company, the less willing they were to part with it. He had a Wit that cou'd make even his Spleen and his ill-humour pleasant to his Friends, and the publick chiding of his Servants, which wou'd have been Ill-breeding and intolerable in any other man, became not only civil and inoffensive, but agreeable and entertaining in him.' Two of his friends, George Etherege and Anthony Hamilton, themselves courtiers, wits and artists, have left portraits of him as he was, perhaps, in the first few years after he came to court. He is the Dorimant of Etherege's *The Man of Mode*,[2] and no picture of Rochester is more convincing than that given by his friend in the first scene of the comedy.[3]

It is late in the morning and we are in Rochester's dressing-room, where preparations for his toilet have been laid out by his valet. He enters in gown and slippers repeating verses from Waller's lines *Upon a War with Spain and a Fight at Sea*:

> *Now for some Ages had the pride of* Spain
> *Made the Sun shine on half the World in vain.*

He has a letter in his hand. It is a billet-doux to a mistress of whom he is tired, and he is laughing at himself for the trouble that he has taken for writing 'this dull insipid thing' 'in cold blood after the heat of the business is over'. He calls for Handy, his valet, who appears and is bidden to fetch a footman to take the letter:

HANDY: None of 'em are come yet.

ROCHESTER: Dogs! Will they ever lie snoring a Bed till Noon?

HANDY: 'Tis all one, Sir: if they're up, you indulge 'em so, that they 're ever poaching after Whores all the Morning.

ROCHESTER: . . . What Vermin are those Chattering without?

HANDY: Foggy *Nan* the Orange Woman, and swearing *Tom* the Shoemaker.

ROCHESTER: Go; call in that over-grown Jade with the Flasket of Guts before her, fruit is refreshing in a Morning.

As Handy goes out, Rochester's mind goes back to Waller, and he murmurs another couplet to himself:

[1] Robert Wolseley, see V. Sig. A 3.   [2] Dennis, II, 248.
[3] Etherege, II, 189–200.

It is not that I love you less
Than when before your feet I lay.

Foggy Nan, the fat Orange Woman comes waddling in with her basket of fruit, and Rochester greets her elegantly:

ROCHESTER: How now, double Tripe, what news do you bring?

OR. WOM.: News! Here's the best Fruit has come to Town t'year, Gad I was up before Four a Clock this Morning, and bought all the Choice i' the Market.

ROCHESTER: The nasty refuse of your Shop.

OR WOM.: You need not make mouths at it, I assure you 'tis all cull'd ware.

ROCHESTER: The Citizens buy better on a Holiday in their walk to *Totnam*.

OR. WOM.: Good or bad, 'tis all one, I never knew you commend any thing; Lord, wou'd the Ladies had heard you talk of 'em as I have done. . . .

Soon, while the Orange Woman is telling Rochester of a handsome young gentlewoman 'lately come to Town with her Mother', who is 'so taken' with him, Sedley appears and joins in the sport of teasing the old woman. When she leaves them, Handy returns with the shoemaker and a footman, who is scolded by Rochester in a way that reminds us of what we have heard concerning the 'publick chiding' of his servants. Then he turns to the shoemaker.

ROCHESTER: How now you drunken Sot?

SHOOM.: 'Zbud, you have no reason to talk, I have not had a bottle of Sack of yours in my Belly this Fortnight.

SEDLEY: The *Orange Woman* says, your Neighbours take notice what a Heathen you are, and design to inform the Bishop, and have you burn'd for an Atheist.

SHOOM: Damn her, Dunghill: if her Husband does not remove her, she stinks so, the Parish intend to indite her for a Nusance.

SEDLEY: I advise you like a Friend, reform your Life; you have brought the envy of the World upon you, by living above your self. Whoring and Swearing are Vices too gentile for a Shoomaker.

SHOOM.: 'Zbud, I think you men of quality will grow as unreasonable as the Women; you wou'd ingross the sins o' the Nation; poor Folks can no sooner be wicked, but th'are rail'd at by their Betters.

ROCHESTER: Sirrah, I'le have you stand i' the Pillory for this Libel.

SHOOM.: Some of you deserve it, I'm sure, there are so many of 'em, that our Journeymen now adays instead of harmless Ballads, sing nothing but your damn'd Lampoons.

ROCHESTER: Our Lampoons, you Rogue?

SHOOM.: Nay, Good Master, why shou'd not you write your own Commentaries as well as *Caesar*?

SEDLEY: The Raskal's read I perceive.

SHOOM.: You know the old Proverb, Ale and History.

ROCHESTER: Draw on my Shooes, Sirrah.

SHOOM.: Here's a Shooe!

ROCHESTER: Sits with more wrinkles than there are in an Angry Bullies Forehead.

SHOOM.: 'Zbud as smooth as your Mistresses skin does upon her: so strike your foot in home. 'Zbud, if 'ere a Monsieur of 'em make more fashionable Ware, I'le be content to have my Ears whip'd off with my own Paring Knife.

SEDLEY: And served up in a Ragoust, instead of Coxcombs to a Company of French Shoomakers for a Collation.

SHOOM.: Hold, hold, damn 'em Catterpillars, let 'em feed upon Cabbidge. Come, Master, your health this Morning! next my Heart now!

So the shoemaker goes off with a half-crown to drink the Earl's health, and another young courtier, Buckhurst or Etherege, comes in to take Rochester and Sedley out to dine. Rochester is now dressed and Handy is 'fiddling about him' arranging his clothes. He brushes the valet aside impatiently:

HANDY: You love to have your Cloaths hang just, Sir.

ROCHESTER: I love to be well dress'd Sir: and think it no scandal to my understanding.

When the servant is dismissed, Rochester turns to his friends with a significant remark: 'That a man's excellency should lie in neatly tying of a Ribbond, or a Crevat!' The speaker of these words has the mind not of a fop but of a philosopher. He lives the life of the world of fashion and thoroughly enjoys it, but he can see through it and beyond it, and can laugh at its absurdities.

In one of his poems, freely adapted from the Greek of Anacreon, Rochester has succeeded in expressing perfectly the spirit of this gay and elegant yet 'easy' and informal society. It is a poem about drinking and it puts us in mind of Burnet's remarks about the debauchery into which Rochester was drawn again by his friends at Court after he had almost completely given it up on his return from Italy, when he 'hated nothing more'.

But falling into Company that loved these Excesses, he was, though not without difficulty, and by many Steps brought back to it again. And the natural Heat of his fancy being inflamed by Wine, made him so extravagantly pleasant, that many, to be more diverted by that humor, studied to engage him deeper and deeper in Intemperance: which at length did so entirely subdue him; that, as he told me, for five years together he was continually Drunk; not all the while under the visible effect of it, but his blood was so inflamed, that he was not in all that time cool enough to be perfectly Master of himself. . . .[1]

Still, for Rochester, drinking was not always mere 'debauchery': sometimes it was an aesthetic experience, and once, at any rate, it gave him a moment of significant emotion which produced a little masterpiece:

Upon Drinking in a Bowl

Vulcan contrive me such a Cup
　As *Nestor* us'd of old:
Shew all thy Skill to trim it up;
　Damask it round with Gold.

Make it so large that, fill'd with Sack
　Up to the swelling Brim,
Vast Toasts, on the delicious Lake,
　Like Ships at Sea, may swim.

Engrave not Battel on his Cheek;
　With War I've nought to do:
I'm none of those that took *Mastrick*,
　Nor *Yarmouth* Leaguer knew.

Let it no Name of Planets tell,
　Fixt Stars or Constellations:
For I am no Sir *Sindrophel*,
　Nor none of his Relations.

But carve thereon a spreading Vine;
　Then add two lovely Boys:
Their limbs in amorous Folds intwine,
　The Type of future Joys.

[1] B.S.P., ii, 12.

> *Cupid* and *Bacchus* my Saints are;
> May Drink and Love still reign:
> With Wine I wash away my Cares,
> And then to Love again.[1]

This song has a classic elegance and grace that has rarely been excelled in English, and is, perhaps, superior to its Greek original. Notice the clearness and sparkling ease of the language, the exquisite 'Damask' of the first stanza, the humour of the 'delicious Lake' in the second, the proper names of the third and fourth, the 'spreading Vine', emblem of fertility appropriately linked to the 'two lovely boys' in the fifth, and the triumphant juxtaposition of *Cupid* and *Bacchus* and the *Saints* in the last. In proportion to its size and intention this Song is as perfect a record of the 'Utopia of Gallantry' as *The Way of the World* itself.

Anthony Hamilton shows Rochester as the central figure in an anecdote concerning one of the numerous intrigues that were always being enacted between the galleries and apartments of Whitehall and the Mall. He is introduced here as not only one of the most handsome and attractive figures at Court, but also a very formidable person, who inspires terror because of his mordant wit and his love of satire. Very soon after he came to Court he seems to have made himself feared as well as admired and loved. There was something terrible in his anger that amazed and frightened the butterflies of Whitehall. This brilliant young nobleman and poet could behave sometimes like a volcano and burst into unexpected eruption. Very soon after his arrival at Court he seems to have quarrelled with a Miss Goditha Price, one of the Duchess of York's Maids of Honour, because she divulged a secret love-affair in which he was engaged. 'Thus', writes Hamilton, 'she drew on herself the most dangerous enemy in the world. No man ever wrote with more charm, more delicacy and more fluency. But in satire his pen was merciless.'[2] The Court was soon filled with lampoons on poor Goditha. Satirical ditties in which her name was freely used were in everyone's hand and on everyone's tongue. Poetry could be a terrible weapon in the reign of Charles II. Another of the Duchess's Maids of Honour was a pretty but rather empty-headed girl called Anne Temple. Hamilton describes her as a brunette with 'a good figure, fine teeth, languishing eyes, fresh complexion, an agreeable smile and an intelligent air' which was

[1] P., 28, 29. [2] Hamilton, 248.

deceptive. Actually, he declares, 'she was simple-minded, vain, credulous, suspicious, a coquette and a prude, very self-satisfied, and very silly'.[1] Rochester flattered her subtly by telling her that 'if heaven had given him a mind susceptible to beauty, he would never have been able to escape from her, but since, thank God, he was only captivated by intelligence, he could enjoy the most delightful intimacy in the world, without fearing any untoward consequences'. He followed up this attack by presenting her with poems in praise of her beauty, in which all rivals were represented as overcome by her charms; and thus her empty little head was turned.[2]

Anne Temple had another admirer, a rather masculine and not very young Maid of Honour called Mary Hobart, daughter of a Norfolk baronet. Miss Hobart, according to Hamilton, had 'a fine shape, something very determined in her manner', 'much wit', little discretion and 'an ill-regulated imagination'. 'Her heart', he continues, 'was tender; but only, it was said, with regard to the fair sex.'[3] She bore a grudge against Rochester, because he had taken away from her a pretty girl called Sarah, who was niece to the 'governess' or 'mother of the maids'. Miss Hobart was charged by the Duchess to protect Anne Temple from Rochester, and she undertook the task with alacrity. Anne had a childish taste for sweets, and Miss Hobart gratified it by giving her access to the Duchess's cabinet which was 'stored with sweetmeats and all kinds of syrups'. One summer day, after a hot ride on horseback, the younger girl was induced to go into her friend's room which adjoined the Duchess's bathrooms, of which Miss Hobart had charge. There she was persuaded to take off her riding-habit and sit in a loose dress in the bathroom while she was regaled with sweets, and there Miss Hobart gave her much sage advice. This advice consisted of warnings against the baseness and perfidy of the courtiers, together with a bitter attack on Sir Charles Lyttleton, Henry Sidney and Rochester.

Lord Rochester is undoubtedly the man who has the most wit and the least honour in England. He is only dangerous to our sex, but so dangerous is he that there is no woman who listens to him three times that does not lose her reputation. He always has good luck; a woman cannot escape him since he can enjoy her in his writings if he cannot have her in any other way, and in the age in which we live, it is very much the same thing in the eyes of the public. However there is nothing more dangerous than the insinuating ways by which he gets possession of

[1] Ibid., 252, 253. [2] Ibid., 255, 256. [3] Ibid., 249, 250.

your confidence. He enters into all your tastes and your feelings, and makes you believe everything he says, though not a single word is sincere. I am willing to wager that, from the way in which he has spoken to you, you believe him the most honourable and sincere man in the world? I really do not know what is his object in the attentions that he is paying to you. It is not that you are not made to deserve any amount of courtship; but when he has succeeded in turning your head, he will not know what to do with the loveliest creature in the whole court: for it is a long time since his debauches, with the help of all the lowest street walkers in town, have brought him to order.

She concluded her harangue by producing the copy of scurrilous verses formerly made by Rochester to satirize Miss Price. Miss Hobart had been good enough to substitute Miss Temple's name for that of the original victim, and she pretended that Rochester had written the poem expressly to defame the girl whom he had been courting. Anne Temple was so angry and humiliated that she burst into tears, and Miss Hobart advised her never to speak to Rochester again. The whole conversation was heard by Rochester's little friend Sarah, who had been washing in one of the Duchess's baths, and had just had time to draw the curtains and get into a bath full of cold water, where she stayed heroically during the whole interview. The girl had a wonderful memory, and perhaps Rochester had already begun to train her for the stage. When he came to her garret, she told him every word that had passed between Miss Temple and Miss Hobart. She was rather nervous, however, on her own account. Was Rochester really in love with Miss Temple? His answer was superb: 'Can you doubt it, since that oracle of sincerity has affirmed it? But then you know that I am not capable of profiting by my perfidy even though Miss Temple complied with my wishes; since my debauches and the street walkers have brought me to order long ago.' Sarah's mind, we are told, was then set at ease. She concluded that the former part of Rochester's speech was untrue, as she knew by experience that the latter was.[1]

The same evening Rochester attended the Duchess's Court, where Miss Temple was looking very beautiful indeed, and was complimented on her appearance. She astonished everyone, however, by making ironical remarks about herself, saying that everyone knew that she was a monster, and that though they might compliment her in public, their fine words were all hypocrisy. She was

[1] Ibid., 262-6.

convinced that the supposed lampoon on her by Rochester was in everyone's hands. Her encounter with Rochester himself must be told in Hamilton's own words:

> When Lord Rochester arrived, she blushed at first, then turned pale, started forward as though to approach him, drew back, pulled her gloves one after the other right up to her elbow—and after having opened and shut her fan violently three times, she waited for him to greet her in his usual way. When he began to do so, the lady made a half turn to the right and showed him her back. Rochester only smiled, and wanting her anger to become still more marked, he walked round her and then took up a position in front of her face. 'Madam,' he said then, 'there is nothing that could be more creditable than to shine as you do, after such a tiring day. Fancy enduring a ride of three hours and then Miss Hobart on top of it, without being prostrate: that is what I call a fine constitution!'

Anne Temple was so enraged and astonished that she could only glare at him with eyes like 'fireballs', while Miss Hobart drew her away in alarm, for she had heard Rochester's words, and did not understand how he could have gained his information. Rochester retired in silence leaving his victim choking with rage.[1]

The last episode of the story is like a scene from a play by Etherege or Wycherley. The faithful Sarah had given Rochester the interesting information that Miss Hobart and Miss Temple had made up their minds to exchange clothes and to walk out in the Mall at nine o'clock with great scarves and masks. Nine o'clock comes, the fashionable hour in summer when courtiers, fine ladies, bullies, and women of the town paraded under the trees in the Mall. Rochester and his friend Harry Killigrew are there looking for the two masked girls. They soon find them, as the company is thin that evening. Miss Temple, mad with rage at the sight of Rochester, instead of retreating, insists on taking her friend up to the two gentlemen in order to vent her anger on the man by whom she believed that she had been betrayed. Miss Hobart only consents to accompany her on condition that she promises not to speak a word in answer to Rochester whatever he may say to her. Just as Anne Temple has made this promise they are accosted by the two young men. Rochester goes at once to Miss Hobart pretending to take her for her friend, and Miss Temple, much to her annoyance, is left

---

[1] Ibid., 266, 267.

with Killigrew, who addresses her as Miss Hobart, and pretends to give her the disinterested advice of a candid friend. He reproves her for blackening the character of Rochester, whom he declares to be one of the most honourable men at Court, and surprises her by reproaching the supposed Miss Hobart with the use that she made of the lampoon originally directed against Miss Price. He warns her severely against pursuing her designs on Miss Temple, and informs her that he knows all about her conversation with that lady, which was overheard by a maid of hers whom she has dismissed. He alludes to her attack on Sir Charles Lyttleton and tells her that he has heard of it and has sworn to be revenged. Although he has a grave appearance, he is one of the most passionate men living. He is going to complain to the Duchess and if he cannot get satisfaction, will pass his sword through the body of the slanderer. The final advice of the candid friend is that Miss Hobart should do her best to make amends by reconciling Miss Temple and Rochester, whose intentions are the most honourable and who would never have looked at her if he had not meant to make her his wife. Anne Temple listened to this discourse in utter amazement, but kept her word and made no reply. Indeed she was too stupefied to answer. When Miss Hobart and Rochester came up to them she was still speechless. Without a word to her friend she ran back to her room at Whitehall, and began stripping off Miss Hobart's clothes in a furious passion, lest she should be contaminated by them. Meanwhile Miss Hobart, amazed at her friend's conduct, determined to follow her and obtain an explanation. She slipped softly into her room, and as Anne was changing her linen came up behind her and embraced her. When Anne Temple saw in whose arms she was, all that Killigrew had said came back to her mind, and she seemed to see in Miss Hobart's eyes the eagerness of a satyr. Shaking her off, she began to scream with terror. Sarah's aunt, the 'mother of the maids' and her niece, came running into the room. It was nearly midnight, and they found Miss Temple undressed and pushing Miss Hobart back in horror. The duenna lectured Miss Hobart severely for frightening and disturbing another Maid of Honour, and ordered her out of the room. The whole story with many embellishments was soon being told all over the Court, and Miss Hobart's reputation received much injury. The Duchess supported her, however, scolded Miss Temple for her credulity, and dismissed the 'mother of the maids' and her niece. Miss Temple would have liked to make some amends to

Rochester, but this was out of her power for he had been banished from the Court.

Ever since he came to court, he had never failed to be banished from it at least once a year; for whenever a word was on the tip of his tongue or at the end of his pen he let it fly without the least regard for consequences. The ministers, the mistresses, often even the Master himself were the victims. If he had not had to do with one of the best natured monarchs in the world, the first of these offences would have been his last one.[1]

Hamilton's anecdote probably refers to events that took place in 1665 or 1666 when Rochester first came to Court. The girl called 'Sarah' may possibly be Sarah Cooke, who became an actress in the King's Company. After her dismissal by the Duchess, Rochester took her to the country and trained her himself for the stage. She is said by Hamilton to have become one of the prettiest, but one of the worst actresses in the kingdom.[2]

[1] Ibid., 267-3.

[2] Ibid., 274. Gordon Goodwin in his edition of *The Memoirs of Count Grammont* (1903) was apparently the first to identify Hamilton's 'Sara' with the actress Sarah Cooke, who spoke two of the Prologues to Rochester's *Valentinian* when it was produced in 1684. (See V. Sigg. C2, C3.) Professor J. H. Wilson has pointed out to me that there are considerable difficulties in accepting this identification. Sarah Cooke was certainly an actress in the King's Company and Hamilton expressly states that Rochester 'ne laissa pas de la faire recevoir dans la troupe du roi'. On the other hand the first recorded appearance of Sarah Cooke was in a play by Leanerd called *Country Innocence* in the spring of 1677. Her career on the stage seems to have been quite successful. She created fourteen rôles, most of them lead or second lead and spoke two new prologues and two new epilogues. From a letter of Dryden's it appears he thought her suitable for the rôle of Octavia in *All for Love* (see A.K.L., 131). Etherege in a letter to his friend Jephson dated 27 Feb., 1688, having learned from him that Mrs. Cooke was seriously ill, probably from consumption resulting from syphilis, wrote: 'Sarah Cooke was always fitter for a player than a Mrs., and it is properer that her lungs should be wasted on the stage than that she should die of a disease too gallant for her.' (Etherege, *Letterbook* ed. Rosenfeld, 1928, p. 337.) The difficulties in the way of identifying 'Sara' with Sarah Cooke can, then, be summarized as follows. First, the events described by Hamilton probably took place in 1665 or 1666. If 'Sara' was Sarah Cooke, what was she doing in the eleven or twelve years before her first recorded appearance on the stage? Secondly, the fact that she had a fairly successful stage career does not tally well with Hamilton's statement that she was 'la plus jolie, mais la plus mauvaise comédienne du royaume'. Thirdly, the passage in Etherege's letter suggests that she was far from being 'the prettiest actress in the kingdom'. None of these difficulties seems to me quite insuperable. We cannot expect a high degree of accuracy from Hamilton, who was, after all, writing a semi-fictional work. His phrase describing Sara may be a mere epigrammatic flourish. It is possible, also, that Rochester may have kept in touch with 'Sara' for a number of years and only succeeded in launching her on the stage in 1677. The fact that Sarah Cooke was chosen to speak a Prologue to *Valentinian* suggests that she had some personal connection with Rochester.

Charles II certainly 'loved Rochester's company for the diversion it afforded'[1] and allowed him remarkable freedoms. At an entertainment given to the Dutch ambassador on the night of 16 February 1668/9, there was heavy drinking after dinner and we are told that company was 'pretty merry'. The next day Pepys heard that among those present were 'that worthy fellow my lord of Rochester', and Tom Killigrew, the dramatist, manager of the King's company of players, self-appointed King's jester and father of Rochester's friend Harry Killigrew. According to Pepys, Tom's 'mirth and raillery' offended Rochester so much that he gave him 'a box on the ear in the King's presence'. This was a serious offence in the seventeenth century, and, if blood had been drawn, Rochester would have been liable to the medieval penalty of losing his hand. The incident, Pepys heard, gave 'much offence to people . . . at Court, to see how cheap the King makes himself, and the more, for that the King hath not only passed by the thing, and pardoned it to Rochester already'. Pepys was shocked to see with his own eyes on the morning of 17 February how, 'The King did publickly walk up and down, and Rochester I saw with him as free as ever, to the King's everlasting shame, to have so idle a rogue as his companion.'[2]

This incident reminds us of Burnet's statement about Rochester that 'the natural heat of his fancy, being inflamed by Wine made him so extravagantly pleasant. . . . This led him to say and do many wild and unaccountable things.'[3] As a result of this offence he was banished from the Court and 'upon more sober advice' went to France in March but first 'he did most solemnly ask pardon' of his friend Harry Killigrew 'for the affront he offered his father'.[4] He seems to have set out for Paris on 12 March 1668/9, and he carried with him a letter from Charles II to the King's beloved sister, 'Madame' (the Duchess of Orléans). 'This bearer, my Lord Rochester,' Charles writes 'has a mind to make a little journey to Paris, and would not kiss your hands without a letter from me; pray use him as one I have a very good opinion of. You will not find him to want wit, and did behave himself in all the Dutch war as well as anybody, as a volunteer.'[5] The Duchess took Rochester to present him to Louis XIV, but that monarch had heard of the boxing of Killigrew's ears, and refused to receive him, saying 'that those that

[1] B.H., I, 486.   [2] Pepys, VIII, 231, 232.   [3] B.S.P., 12.
[4] H.M.C. 7th Rep. App., 531, T. Henshaw to Sir R. Paston.
[5] L.S.D.C., 231, 232.

struck in King's presences should have noe countenance from him, nor those that the King his good brother of England frowned on should have favour'.[1] As Charles had forgiven Rochester and indeed 'countenanced' him, these words of Louis were a rebuke to 'his good brother of England' no less than to Charles's scapegrace favourite.

Early in July 1669, Rochester was with Lord William Cavendish, the Duke of Devonshire's eldest son, who had served with him in the Dutch War of 1665, and other English gentlemen at the Opera in Paris, when Cavendish was attacked by several drunken French officers, and was only saved by being thrown off the stage, where he was standing, into the pit by a servant of Montagu, the English Ambassador. The part which Rochester took in the affair is not clearly recorded. Louis XIV was very angry with the officers who had attacked the English. He apologized to Montagu and had the offenders imprisoned. Cavendish and Rochester, however, pleaded generously on their behalf and they were pardoned.[2] On 15 July, Montagu wrote to Arlington pleading for Rochester's recall and testifying to the discreet way in which he had lived at Paris. 'If hereafter he continues to live as discreetly as he has done ever since he was here, he has other good qualities enough . . . to make himself acceptable wherever he comes.'[3]

In the summer of 1670 Rochester was living in Lincoln's Inn Fields, 'the house next to the Dukes Playhouse in Portugall row'.[4] He was certainly leading a wild, dissipated life at this time. We get a glimpse of this life from the earliest of the extant letters addressed to him by his friend Henry Savile, with whom he had clearly been corresponding for some time.[5] The letter is dated 26 January 1670/1. Savile is in London and Rochester is apparently at Adderbury with his family. Savile regrets that he was unable to be at the christening of Rochester's son, the little Lord Wilmot, which had taken place on 2 January. He goes on to speak of a quarrel between the Ballers and the Farmers. The Ballers, as we know from Pepys, were a set of fast 'young blades' at court who met at the establishment of the well-known procuress 'my Lady' Bennett. According to

[1] Fane MS., f.323.
[2] Grove, 31, 32; H.M.C. Buccleuch Papers at Montague House, I, 429, 430; Temple, II, 70, 71.
[3] H.M.C., Buccleuch Papers, I, 430.   [4] H., 204, 205; Prinz, 258.
[5] W., 31, 78, 79.

Pepys[1] they used to dance naked with Mother Bennett's 'ladies' 'and all the roguish things in the world'. The Farmers were the persons to whom, at the period, the customs were 'farmed', and they can be equated with modern customs house officials. The Farmers seem to have seized a box of the phallic leather instruments called 'dildoes', which the Ballers were attempting to import into the country. In spite of the efforts of Sedley and Savile, who made two journeys into the city to try to save these artificial phalluses, the Farmers 'prompted by ye villainous instigation of theire wives voted them prohibited goods soe that they were burnt without mercy'.

Samuel Butler probably refers to this affair in his poem *Dildoides* which is dated 1672 in a manuscript copy:

> Such a sad Tale prepare to hear,
> As claims from either Sex a Tear,
> Twelve Dildos (means for the Support
> Of aged Letchers of the Court)
> Were lately burnt by impious Hand
> Of Trading Rascals of the Land,
> Who envying their curious Frame
> Exposed those Priapuse's to the Flame.[2]

According to Savile, Rochester carried one of these instruments with him into the country. The Earl, we learn from Savile's letter, had been 'chosen generall' of the Ballers in their war against the Farmers and there was to be no peace 'till they grant us our wine and our Ds custom free'. Savile also sends his friend news of Lord Vaughan, the son of the Earl of Carbery, a member of the same fast set, described by Pepys as 'one of the lewdest fellows of the age, worse than Sir Charles Sidly'.[3]

Rochester's usual way of giving offence at Court was by his satires and lampoons which he seems to have taken an impish delight in circulating in manuscript copies. Burnet writes that

> he laid out his Wit very freely in *Libels* and *Satyrs* in which he had a peculiar Talent of mixing his Wit with his Malice, and fitting both with such apt words, that Men were tempted to be pleased with them: from thence his Composures came to be easily known, for few had such a way of tempering these together as he had.[4]

According to the same authority he employed a footman who 'knew all the Court' to act as his spy; and obtain materials for his satiric poems.

[1] Pepys, VIII, 32.   [2] Raby, 3.   [3] Pepys, VII, 187.   [4] B.S.P., 14.

He furnished him with a red coat and a musket as a centinel, and kept him all the winter long every night at the doors of such ladies as he believed might be in intrigues. In the court a centinel is little minded, and is believed to be posted by a captain of the guards to hinder a combat: so this man saw who walked about and visited at forbidden hours. By this means lord Rochester made many discoveries. And when he was well furnished with materials, he used to retire to the country for a month or two to write libels.[1]

The character of Charles II interested Rochester particularly, perhaps because, like his own, it was full of paradoxes. The contrast between the old view of the monarch hedged by 'divinity' and the actual person of the 'sauntering', good-natured, pleasure-loving Charles Stuart, was a never-failing source of ironic amusement to the poet. His most famous character-sketch of the King is the quatrain of which several different versions survive. That preserved by Hearne, who was a friend of Rochester's old tutor Giffard, is probably authentic. According to this authority, Rochester composed these lines 'on occasion of his majestie's saying, he would leave every one to his liberty in talking, when himself was in company, and would not take what was said at all amiss'.

> We have a pritty witty king
> Whose word no man relys on:
> He never said a foolish thing,
> And never did a wise one.

Charles's good-humoured reply is said to have been that what Rochester had observed was easily explained. He was responsible for his words, but his ministers for his actions. Another example of clever, impromptu rhyming was the stanza composed by Rochester at the King's request when he saw the royal brothers in company with the handsome but foolish Monmouth, Fraizer, the King's Scottish physician, and an ugly fellow called Laurendine.

> Here's *Monmouth* the witty
> *Laurendine* the pritty,
> And *Frazier* the great physitian;
> But as for the rest,
> Take *York* for a jest,
> And yourself for a great politician.[2]

---

[1] B.H., I, 486.   [2] P., 39, 176, 177; H.R.H., I, 119, 120.

But such extempore rhymes as these are mild compared with some of the longer lampoons on the King which have come down to us under Rochester's name. They reproach him in the coarsest and bitterest terms for his idleness and sensuality. These lampoons belong to the old, hard-hitting kind of satire, the satire of Cleveland and of Andrew Marvell, who said of Rochester that he 'was the best English satyrist and had the right veine'.[1] But Rochester's lampoons have none of the conceits or curiously elaborated thought of the satirists of the school of Donne. Their characteristics are a terrible directness and a brutal energy.

In the very coarse lines beginning 'In the Isle of Great Britain', there is a portrait of the King which is worth all the elaborate descriptions of the historians, and is only rivalled by the prose Character by Halifax:

> The easiest Prince and best bred Man alive:
> Him no ambition seeks to move Renown,
> Like the *French* Fool to wander up and down,
> Starving his Subjects, hazarding his Crown.
>
> .   .   .   .
>
> Restless he rolls about from Whore to Whore,
> A Merry Monarch scandalous and Poor.[2]

This is possibly the poem of which Burnet relates the well-known story that 'once being drunk he intended to give the King a libel he had Writ on some ladies: but by a mistake he gave him one written on himself'.[3]

There is a mixture of irony, contempt and genuine affection in these lines of which only Rochester was capable. But the most comprehensive and brilliant of the satires on the King is the famous *History of Insipids* (1676). When Rochester wrote this poem he seems to have had running through his head a skit on the Royal Society called 'Ballad of Gresham's Colledge' probably written by Joseph Glanville about 1663. A couple of stanzas will illustrate the rhythm and style of this amusing performance:

> They Colledg, Gresham, shall hereafter
> Be the whole world's Universitie,
> Oxford and Cambridge are our laughter;

---

[1] Aubrey, II, 304.
[2] P., 136, 137. See also 'Rochester's "Scepter Lampoon" on Charles II' by D. Vieth in P.Q., 1958.
[3] B.H., I, 486.

Their learning is but Pedantry.
These new Collegiates do assure us
Aristotle's an Asse to Epicurus.

By demonstrative Philosophy
They playnly prove all things are bodyes,
And those that talke of Qualitie
They count them all to be meer Noddyes.
Nature in all her works they trace
And make her playne as nose in face.[1]

This poem, which was probably going the rounds at the time that
Rochester first appeared at Court, seems to have affected him in
much the same way as that in which Byron was affected by J. H.
Frere's *Whistlecraft*. Just as Byron took the metre and style of
Frere's poem and used it with immensely powerful effect in *A
Vision of Judgment*, so Rochester took Glanville's dancing stanza
and technique of clattering rhymes and used them in a poem which
is a kind of ironical panorama of the reign of Charles II. He seizes
on some of the principal defects in the King's policy with the acute-
ness of a very keen observer of the political scene:

Chaste, pious, prudent *Charles* the Second,
    The Miracle of thy Restauration
May like to that of *Quails* be reckon'd
    Rain'd on the *Israelitick* Nation:
The wisht for Blessing from Heav'n sent
Became their Curse and Punishment.

The Vertues in thee Charles inherent,
    Altho' thy countenance be an odd piece,
Proves thee as true a God's vicegerent
    As ere was *Harry* with the Codpiece:
For Chastity and pious Deeds
His grandsire *Harry*, Charles exceeds.

.   .   .   .   .

Never was such a Faiths Defender
    He like a politick prince, and pious,
Gives Liberty to Conscience tender,
    And doth to no Religion tye us.
Jews, Christians, Turks, Papists he'll please us
With *Moses, Mahomet*, or *Jesus*.

[1] *Isis*, XVIII, 1932; B.M. Add. MS. 34, 217, 30v–21v.

In all Affairs of Church or State,
   He very zealous is, and able,
Devout at Prayers and sits up late
   At the Cabal and Council Table.
His very Dog at Counsel Board,
Sits grave and wise, as any Lord.

.   .   .   .   .

His Father's foes he doth reward
   Preserving those that cut off's Head:
Old Cavaliers the Crown's best Guard,
   He lets them starve for want of Bread.
Never was any King endow'd
With so much Grace and Gratitude.

Blood, that wears Treason in his Face,
   Villain compleat, in Parson's Gown,
How much is he at Court in Grace
   For stealing *Ormond* and the Crown?
Since loyalty do's no Man good,
Let's steal the King and out-do *Blood*.

A Parliament of Knaves and Sots,
   Members by Name, you must not mention,
He keeps in Pay, and buys their Votes,
   Here with a Place, there with a Pension.
When to give Mony, he can't cologue 'um
He doth with Scorn prorogue, prorogue 'um.

But they long since, by too much giving,
   Undid, betray'd, and sold the Nation:
Making their Memberships a Living,
   Better than e're was Sequestration.
God give thee *Charles* a Resolution
To damn the Knaves by Dissolution.

Fame is not grounded on Success
   Tho' Victories were *Caesars* glory,
Lost battels made not *Pompey* less,
   But left them stiled great in Story.
Malitious Fate doth oft devise
To beat the Brave, and fool the Wise.

Charles in the first *Dutch* War stood fair
   To have been Sovereign of the Deep;
When *Opdam* blew up in the Air,
   Had not his Highness gone to sleep.
Our Fleet slacked Sails, fearing his waking,
The *Dutch* had else been in sad taking.

.   .   .   .   .

Mists, Storms, short Victuals, adverse Winds,
   And once the Navies wise Division,
Defeated Charles his best Designs,
   Till he became his Foes derision.
And he had *swinged* the Dutch at *Chatham*,
Had he had Ships but to come at 'um.

.   .   .   .   .

But *Charles* what could thy Policy be,
   To run so many sad Disasters
To join thy fleet with false *d'Etrees*,
   To make the *French* of *Holland* Masters,
Was't *Carewell*, brother *James*, or *Teague*,
That made thee break the Triple League?

Could *Robin Vyner* have foreseen
   The glorious Triumphs of his Master,
The Wool-Church statue Gold had been,
   Which now is made of Alabaster:
But wise men think had it been Wood,
T'were for a Bankrupt *King* too good.

.   .   .   .   .

By the Lord Mayor and his grave Coxcombs,
   Free-man of *London* Charles is made;
Then to *Whitehall* a Rich Gold Box comes,
   Which was bestow'd on the *French* Jade.
But wonder not it should be so, Sirs,
When Monarchs rank themselves with Grocers.

Cringe, scrape no more, ye City Fopps,
   Leave off your Feasting and fine Speeches,
Beat up your Drums, shut up your Shops,
   The Courtiers then will kiss your Breeches.
Arm'd, tell the Popish Duke that rules,
You're Free-born Subjects, not *French* Mules.

New upstarts, Pimps, Bastards, Whores,
   That Locust like devour the Land.
By shutting up the Exchequer Doors,
   When thither our Mony was trapan'd
Have rend'red *Charles* his Restauration,
But a small Blessing to the Nation.

Then, *Charles*, beware of thy Brother *York*,
   Who to thy Government gives Law;
If once we fall the old Sport,
   You must again both to *Breda*:
Where Spight of all that would restore you,
Grown wise by wrongs, we shall abhor you.

If of all Christian Blood the Guilt
   Cry loud for Vengeance unto Heaven;
The Sea by treacherous *Lewis* spilt,
   Can never be by God forgiven.
Worse Scourge unto his subjects, Lord,
Than Pestilence, Famine, Fire or Sword.

That false, rapacious Wolf of *France*,
   The Scourge of Europe and its Curse,
Who at his Subjects Cry, does dance,
   And study how to make them worse.
To say such Kings, Lord, rule by thee
Were most prodigious Blasphemy.

Such know no Law but their own Lust,
   Their Subjects Substance, and their Blood,
They count it Tribute due and just,
   Still spent, and spilt, for subjects good,
If such kings are by God appointed,
The *Devil* may be the *Lords* Anointed.[1]

.   .   .   .   .

Yet, in spite of the lampoons, Charles could never do without
Rochester's company for long, and he often apparently used to go to
supper with him at his lodgings in an informal way.[2]

---

[1] P., 107–13 (selected stanzas). A copy of this poem under the title 'The Chronicle' is
recorded in C.S.P.D., 1676–7, 97, 98 under the date 3 May 1676, where it is described as
'presented to the board by Mr. Secretary Williamson' together with another set of satirical
verses called *The Busse*, with 'sundry depositions' as a 'seditious and traitorous libel'.
[2] H.M.C., 7th Rep., App., 469, W. Fall to Sir R. Verney.

We have a glimpse of Rochester taking part in a wild frolic that succeeded one of these festive gatherings. It was an occasion when neither the King nor Harry Savile was present, as they were both at sea in the yacht *Greyhound*. The scene was the Great Privy Garden at Whitehall, where the learned Jesuit Franciscus Linus had constructed an elaborate set of 'dialls' or chronometers for the scientifically-minded King. It was probably in the early morning of 25 June 1675 that Rochester, Buckhurst, Fleetwood Shepherd and some others came reeling into the garden after a debauch. The great 'Pyramidical Dial' looked like a huge phallus pointing to the heavens. This image suggested to the Earl a witty piece of metaphysical ribaldry 'What', he cried, 'doest thou stand here to — time?' Then, according to Aubrey 'dash they fell to worke', and the glass spheres with the expensive mechanism which they enclosed were soon smashed to atoms.[1]

It is likely that Rochester deliberately courted the King's anger sometimes in order to have an excuse for leaving Whitehall. He loved nothing so much as adventure, and variety was as necessary for him as meat and drink. There are several stories concerning his exploits during his periods of exile from Court.

Hamilton in the eleventh chapter of the *Mémoires de Gramont*, describes some of his exploits during his periods of exile from the Court.[2] According to this authority on one occasion Rochester, in order to be near at hand, in case the King might recall him,

went to live in the district which is called the City, the part of the town inhabited by substantial burgesses and rich merchants, where politeness, indeed, is not so prevalent as at Court, but where pleasure, luxury and profusion abound in a society which is less unstable and more sincere than that of the courtiers. His plan, at first, was simply to be initiated into the mysteries of these fortunate beings. For this purpose he changed his name and dress, so as to gain admission to their entertainments and partake of their pleasures, and, as soon as an opportunity arose, those of their fair spouses. As he was able to adapt himself to every mentality, it was remarkable how soon he insinuated himself into the good graces of the coarse but wealthy merchants and those of their more delicate, magnificent and tender helpmates. He soon gained admittance to all their parties and junketings. When he was in the company of their husbands, he joined them in declaiming against the follies and weaknesses of the government, and, when he was with the wives, he railed with them at the vices of the Court, and denounced the

[1] Aubrey, II, 34; W., 12 n.   [2] Hamilton, 281–3.

King's mistresses; he would declare that it was at the expense of the poor that this cursed extravagance was maintained; that the City beauties were equal to those at the other end of the town, and that, nevertheless, a decent husband in the City was quite satisfied with one woman. Then, to outbid them in their jeremiads, he would declare that he could not understand why fire had not descended from heaven on to Whitehall as a punishment for tolerating such wretches as Rochester, Killigrew and Sydney [perhaps a mistake for Sedley], who were impudent enough to assert that all the City merchants were cuckolds and all their wives painted harridans. Talk of this kind made him very popular in City gatherings till he became quite bored with the guzzling at their banquets and the cloying attentions of his merchant friends. However, instead of moving closer to the Court, he plunged into the most remote corners of the City. There changing once more his dress and name, he adopted a new role, causing bills to be distributed announcing the recent arrival of a German doctor endowed with miraculous secrets and infallible remedies. The secrets consisted of divining what was past and foretelling what was to come with the help of astrology. The chief virtue of the remedies was to bring rapid relief to young women for all kinds of maladies that might afflict them or accidents to which their sex is prone through excessive charity to their neighbours or excessive indulgence to themselves.

At first his practice, being confined to the neighbourhood, was not considerable but his reputation soon spread to the other end of the town and soon there came flocking to him servant girls of the Court and waiting maids of ladies of quality, who, when they related the marvels performed by the new German doctor, were soon followed by their mistresses.

Among works of a light and witty kind, none were ever so full of charm and fire as those of Lord Rochester; and of all his works the most ingenious and diverting is an account of the various adventures that befell him when he practised medicine and astrology in the City of London.

This passage appears in the *Mémoires de Gramont* shortly after the account of the adventures of Miss Hobart and Miss Temple and therefore might be supposed to refer to events taking place in 1665 or 1666. Hamilton, however, was an artist rather than a historian, and he appears to have telescoped events separated by a number of years. Rochester's escape from the Court into the City society may well have taken place soon after the Hobart-Temple affair. The second story describing his adventures in the guise of a quack doctor in the City almost certainly refers to a much later escapade as it is surely unthinkable that Rochester should have played the same trick on two separate occasions. Burnet briefly refers to this exploit in the following passage[1] in his well-known book on Rochester published just after the poet's death in 1680. After mentioning that Rochester's reading included 'Books of Physick: which the ill state of health he was fallen into made more necessary for himself', he suggests that this kind of reading 'qualifi'd him for an odd adventure which I shall just but mention. Being under an unlucky Accident, which oblige'd him to keep out of the way; He disguised himself, so that his nearest Friends could not have known him, and set up in *Tower-street* for an *Italian Mountebank*, where he had a Stage, and practised Physick for some Weeks not without success'. Tonson's edition of Rochester's *Poems on Several Occasions* published in 1691, eleven years after Burnet's book, includes 'Alexander Bendo's Bill', a version of the witty advertisement which Rochester caused to be distributed in the character of the Italian quack Alexander Bendo. Hamilton speaks of the 'doctor' as a German, but he was an old man when he wrote the *Mémoires de Gramont* and his memory may well have played him false in this detail. 'Dr Bendo' in his bill states that he is 'in his twenty ninth year' and that he travelled abroad when he was fifteen. Rochester here, I am convinced, was telling the truth about himself. He was born in 1647 and was abroad on his travels in 1662. The Alexander Bendo incident can therefore be dated somewhere in the period 1675–6. This period has been described by Professor Wilson as 'the winter of Rochester's discontent',[2] when he was in disgrace at Court on several occasions. The Bendo frolic could have occurred after the smashing of the King's dials in the Priory Garden in June, 1675, an offence which might well have led to banishment or in the early autumn of that year when we know that Rochester had got himself into trouble for offending the King's haughty mistress, Louise de Kéroualle, Duchess of Portsmouth[3] or, finally, the summer of 1676, when it is clear from a letter of Henry Savile to Rochester dated 15 August 1676[4] that the Earl was estranged from the King. A reference to 'your Chymicall knowledge' in this letter may well be an allusion to 'Dr. Bendo'. An ingenious critic[5] has suggested that Dryden's misquotation of Juvenal's 'ad Aethiopem cygnum' in his Preface to *All for Love*,[6]

---

[1] B.S.P., 27. [2] W., 12. [3] Ibid., 35. [4] Ibid., 42, 43.
[5] F. L. Huntley in P.Q., XVIII (1939), 281, 282. [6] Dryden, ed. Scott, V, 318.

when he is certainly referring to Rochester, may be a sly hit at 'the Sign of the Black Swan' mentioned at the end of Alexander Bendo's Bill. *All for Love* was produced in December 1677 and published early in 1678. If the conjecture about 'ad Aethiopem cygnum' is correct, Dryden is likely to be referring to an event which happened fairly recently and was still the talk of the Town. The fullest and most authentic account of the affair (which unfortunately assigns no date to it) has only come to light in recent years. It is contained in a manuscript book[1] made by Thomas Alcock, formerly a servant of Rochester, as a New Year's present for his eldest daughter, Lady Anne Baynton in 1687. Lady Baynton had asked Alcock for a copy of the original broadside of Bendo's Bill. In response to this request he had a copy made of the single bill which still remained in his possession and prefixed to it a most amusing account of the frolic, in which he himself had taken part. According to Alcock, 'to avoid an apparent Storm that threatened the Continual Sunshine he had always breathed in' Rochester disappeared from Court and it was rumoured that he had gone to France. Actually he only went as far as Tower Hill, where he 'took Asylum and Shelter under the disguise of an Italian Mountebank, and vouchsafed the appellative of Doctor Alexander Bendo'. Attended by Alcock, he took lodgings in Tower Street at the house of a Goldsmith and engaged a number of assistants including a merry andrew, an indispensable part of the equipment of a seventeenth-century mountebank, who set up his stage at Crosset Fryers, and by means of his 'Apes Faces' directed passersby to the Doctor's lodgings.

'Dr. Bendo' was an imposing figure in 'an old overgrown Green Gown which he religiously wore in Memory of Rabelais his Master put on at the reception of his Doctor's Degree, at Montpellier, lyned through with exotick furrs of divers colours, an Antique Cap, a great Reverend Beard, and a Magnificent false Medal sett round with glittering Pearl, rubies, and Diamonds of the same Cognation, hung about his Neck in a Massy Gold like Chaine of Princes mettle, which the King of Cyprus (you must know) had given him for doing a Signal Cure upon his Darling Daughter, the Princess Aloephangina, who was painted in a Banner; and hung up at his Elboe.' The 'green gown' was doubtless a relic of Rochester's old tutor Sir Andrew Balfour who studied at Montpellier. 'Dr. Bendo's' claim

---

[1] F.P. All the details that follow down to the end of the chapter are derived from this source.

that he could cure 'all sorts of distempers, Malladies and Complaints whatsoever' was set forth in a remarkable handbill which was distributed 'by his nimble Emissaries abroad, the sonorous Hawkers', who 'made all the Streets in the Town' ring with 'Dr. Bendo's extraordinary Performances'. By means of this ingenious advertising great crowds of people of all kinds were attracted to the 'doctor's' lodgings. Here they were impressed by his 'free and open way of making his Medicines in the View of all sorts of People, that pleas'd to come to his Laboratory'. The 'medicines', described by Alcock as 'Washes, Paint, Powders, Oyntments, Plaisters, Balsomes, Anodynes, Philters, Salves, Troches, Antidotes, Amuletts, Electuaries, Charms, Apocems, Elixirs, Causticks, Oylo Spirits, Sulphurs, Vitriols, Pills, Potions, Essences, Salts Volatile and fixt, Magisterialls, Pastilles, Lozinges, Opiates, Sudarificks, diureticks, Tinctures, Chemicall Preparations of all sorts with Specificks and Nostrums innumerable', were actually compounded by the 'doctor's' assistants out of 'various mixtures of Ashes, Soote, Lime, Chalk, Clay, old Wall, Soap and indeed anything that came to hand by the Assistances of a little blue Verditer, red Russet, white Lead, Yellow Oaker, Umber, Lamblack, Sheereing Smelt, powdered Brick, Pulverised Slate and Cornish Tyle, with some Gums Artificially to discoulour, tinge and fix Medicaments into the proper view, and Shape'. These 'medicaments', we are told 'cost him nothing but taking up, for where e're he went, he us'd to say it was all Indies; even from the Scullery to the Kitchen & thence to the Hostry or House of Office'.

Alcock gives a lively picture of the activities of the 'operators' in the 'Laboratory': 'some stirring an old boyling Kettle, of Soote and Urine, tinged with a little Asafetida and all the nasty Ingredients that would render the Smell more unsavoury others tending the Fires, some luting the Retorts, others pounding Bricks, and scraping powders from them. Here one busy calcining Mineralls, there another scumming a Crucible; some grinding Oyles with a Stone upon Marble, till they sweat again, whilst the drops from Face and Nose made the Medicine the bigger and consequently more beneficial; others labouring at the pestill & Mortar, and all of them dress't like the old Witches in Mackbeth.' Meanwhile the 'Doctor' sat 'with his Scales and weights, making up Medicines of all sorts and sealing them with his Seal of Office, giving pretended directions to his Operators by his Indicative Gestures in a Language which neither he, nor they understood one word of'. The 'Fraternity' of his assistants similarly 'kept a perpetual Jangling to one another . . . in a Jargon of damn'd unintelligible Gybberish'.

'Dr. Bendo' only accepted payment for his 'medicines', and by this means reaped a rich harvest of 'good Gold and Silver, which was chearfully paid him, by his credulous Patients with thanks to boot'. 'His Affable and communicative Advise' he, '(good man) bestowed Gratis upon all people; and for a world would not Charge his fellow Creatures any thing, for the Tallent he had freely received.' Thus he achieved great popularity among the poor who were 'crying him up for a conscionable good Doctor, and praying for his prosperity'. On the other hand, 'all the Apothicaries and Drugsters in the Neighbourhood' very naturally cursed 'him & his damn'd Operators . . . for spoiling their trade', swearing they were 'all notorious Thieves, and had certainly robbed some Interloper's Cellar'.

The 'Doctor' not only prescribed and dispensed 'medicines' but also indulged in 'predictions, casting Nativities, Interpreting of Dreams, solving of Omens, Responses to Horary Questions, illustrations of Signs and Tokens, Judgments upon Moles, Wenns, Warts and natural Marks, according to their severall kinds, and accidental Positions, in various parts of the naked Body'. Certain modest ladies could not declare the whereabouts of these marks 'without blushing'. In such cases the 'Religious Doctor Bendo' would 'not for all the world, so much as desire to see' the mark in question, but he would arrange for the lady to 'leave a token with the Doctor and appoint an hour when his Wife was to bring it as Credential that she came on that Errand, upon which she was immediately to be admitted into the Bed Chamber, to View and report the matter'. The 'Wife' was no other than the 'Doctor' himself, who 'was divested . . . of his Magisterial Robes, and by the assistance of a Tyre Woman putt into the habit of a grave Matron'. 'So', in Alcock's words, 'away she trudged with the return of the expectant lady's Token, by which Ticket, she soon found the Admittance agreed on between the Lady and the Doctor, and did her business Effectively.' Thus, writes Alcock, the Earl deluded 'his Ignorant and Malicious Enimies; who thought they had exil'd him into France, when he was selling to them, their Wives and Children, Washes, Paint, Powders, Oyntements' and all the other 'medicaments' described above.

Before long, however, we are told that 'the hungry court could no longer sustain her drooping Spirits' without Rochester and the 'Noble Pathologist', as Alcock calls him, was summoned back to Whitehall. He made 'the Quickest Voyage from France that ever Man did, which was the talk and admiration of the whole Town, for those that saw his Ostracism Cancelled this night at Whitehall, did the very next see him there in Splendor dancing in a Ball, in as Great Favour as ever'. Meanwhile 'nobody knew what was become of the Mountebanks'. A rumour went round 'that they were an Inchanted Crew, rais'd and laid by a Necromancie' and the 'credulous Patients' swallowed this story as they had swallowed the 'doctor's' claims and threw away the medicines, which they had purchased 'against all accidents whatsoever', 'for fear of Witchcraft'. The local Apothecaries were convinced that the Devil had run away with the whole band 'for it was not known who or what they were till a long time after'. The poor carpenters who had set up the stage 'were glad to take it for their pains' and all the goldsmith got for his rent was the 'Utensils' left behind in the 'laboratory'.

No copy of the original broadside of Alexander Bendo's Bill has been preserved. Versions of it are printed in some early editions of Rochester's works but the most authentic text is certainly that provided by Alcock for Lady Baynton in the MS already quoted, which he transcribed from a copy of the orginal Bill in his possession. It is Rochester's most sustained and memorable work in prose. After wishing 'all Health and Prosperity to all Gentlemen Ladies & others whether of Citty, Town, or Country' 'Dr. Bendo' begins with a long exordium in which the profession of the Mountebank is defended by means of the ingenious fallacy that the more a man resembles a counterfeit, the more likely he is to be a true man, because the counterfeit necessarily resembles what he is supposed to imitate:

> Whereas this Famous *Metropolis* of *England*, (and were the Endeavours of its worthy Inhabitants equal to their Power, Merit, and Virtue, I should not stick to denounce it, in a short time, the *Metropolis* of the whole *World*:) Whereas I say this City (as most Great ones are) has ever been infested with a numerous Company of such, whose Arrogant Confidence, backing their Ignorance, has enabled them to impose upon the People, either premeditated Cheats, or at best, the palpable, dull, and empty Mistakes of the Self-deluded Imaginations

in Physick, Chymicale, and Gallenick, in Astrology, Physiognomy, Palmestry, Mathematicks, Alchimy, and even in Government itself; the last of which I will not propose to Discourse of, or meddle at all in, since it no ways belongs to my Trade or Vocation, as the rest do; which, thanks to my God, I find much more Safe; I think equally honest, and therefore more profitable. But as to all the former, they have been so erroneously practis'd by many unlearned Wretches, whom Poverty and neediness for the most Part, (if not the restless Itch of Deceiving) has forced to Straggle, and wander in unknown Paths, that even the Professions themselves, though originally the Products of the most learned, and Wise Men's laborious Studies and experiences; and by them left a wealthy and glorious Inheritance for ages to come, seem by this bastard-race of Quacks, and Cheats, to have been run out of all Wisdom, Learning, Perspicuousness, and truth, with which they were so plentifully Stock'd, and now run into a Repute of meer Mists, Imaginations, Errors, and deceits, such as in the Management of these Idle Professors indeed they were.

You will therefore, (I hope) *Gentlemen, Ladies*, and *others*, deem it but Just; that I, who for some years have, with all Faithfulness, and Assiduity, courted these Arts, and receiv'd such signal Favours from them, that they have admitted me to the Happy and full Enjoyment of themselves, and trusted me with their greatest Secrets, should, with an Earnestness and Concern more than ordinary, take their Parts against those impudent Fops, whose saucy, impertinent Addresses and Pretentions have brought such Scandal upon their most immaculate Honours and Reputations.

Besides, I hope you will not think I could be so Imprudent, that if I had intended any such foul play my self, I would have given you so fair warning by my severe Observations upon others. *Qui alterum Incusat probri, ipsum se intueri oportet*, Plaut. However, *Gentlemen*, in a World like this (where Virtue is so frequently counterfeited, and hypocrisie so generally taken notice of, that every one, arm'd with Suspicions, stands upon his Guard against it) 'twill be very hard, for a Stranger especially, to escape a Censure.

All I shall say for my self on this score, is this, If I appear to any one like a Counterfeit, even for the sake of that chiefly, ought I to be constru'd a true Man, who is the Counterfeits example, his Original, and that which he Imploys his Industry and Pains to Imitate and Copy: Is it therefore my Fault, if the Cheat by his Witts and endeavours makes himself so like me, that consequently I cannot avoid resembling him? Consider, pray, the Valiant and the Coward, the wealthy Merchant, and the Bankrupt, the Politician, and the Fool; they are the same in many things and differ but in *one* alone: the Valiant Man holds up his

87

Head, looks confidently round about him, wears a Sword, courts a Lord's Wife, and owns it; So does the Coward; one only Point of Honour, and thats Courage, (which, like false Metal, one only tryal can discover) makes the distinction.

The Bankrupt walks the *Exchange*, buys Bargains, draws Bills, and accepts them with the Richest, whilst Paper and Credit are current Coin: That which makes the difference is reall Cash, a great difference indeed, and yet but one, and that the last found out, and still till then the least perceiv'd.

Now for the Politician, he is a grave, deliberating, close, prying Man: Pray, are there not grave, deliberating, close prying Fools? If then the difference betwixt all these (though infinite in Effect) be so nice in all appearance, will you expect it should be otherwise betwixt the false Physician, Astrologer, &c. and the true? The first calls himself learned Doctor, sends forth his Bills, gives Physick and Council, tells and fore-tells; the other is found to do just as much; 'tis only your Experience must distinguish betwixt them: to which I willingly submit my self: I'll only say something to the honour of the Mountebank, in case you discover me to be one.

Reflect a little what kind of Creature 'tis: He is one then who is fain to supply some higher Ability he pretends to, with Craft: He draws great companies to him, by undertaking Strange things which can never be Effected.

The Politician (by his Example, no doubt) finding how the People are taken with Specious, Miraculous Impossibilities, plays the same Game, protests, declares, promises I know not what things, which he's sure can ne'er be brought about; the people believe, are deluded, and pleas'd. The expectation of a future good, which shall never befall them, draws their Eyes off of a present evil. Thus are *they* kept and establish'd in Subjection, Peace, and Obedience, *He* in Greatness, wealth, and Power: so you see the *Politician* is, and must be a *Mountebank* in State-Affairs, and the *Mountebank* (no doubt if he thrives) is an errant *Politician* in Physick.

This passage is the work of a master of prose style. It has the clarity of the new prose of the Restoration, with an energy, a wit and a subtly varied rhythm that anticipates the best work of Swift. Dr. Bendo (like his predecessor Dr. Themut) proceeds to claim the power of curing a large variety of diseases beginning with 'that Labes Britanica, or grand English Disease, The Scurvy', and pro-ceeding by way of 'Gouts, Ackes, Dropsies and Consumptions' to 'Green-Sickness, Weaknesses, Inflammations or obstructions in the Stomach, Reins, Liver, Spleen, etc.' Then he draws himself up with a superb Puritanical gesture and disclaims the very kind of advertisement in which he has been indulging:

> For I would put no Word in my Bill that bears any unclean sound; it is enough that I make myself understood; I have seen Physician's Bills as Bandy as Aretine's Dialogues; which no Man that walkes warily before God can approve of.

The very accent of the canting religiosity of the day is caught in the last words. The doctor claims not only to be master of the physician's art, but also to practise 'Astrological Predictions, Physiognomy, Divination by dreams and otherwise', but he gives his claim an air of candour by professing disbelief in Palmistry 'because there can be no Reason alledged for it'! The concluding paragraphs of the Bill are addressed to the ladies, and here Alexander Bendo sets up as a beauty specialist, as well as a physician and an astrologer:

> Nor will I be ashamed to set down here, my Willingness to practise rare Secrets, (though somewhat collaterall to my Profession) for the help, conservation and Augmentation of Beauty and Comeliness: a thing created at first by God, chiefly for the Glory of his own Name, and then for the better establishment of mutual Love between Man and Woman: God had bestow'd on Man the Power of Strength and Wisdom, and thereby render'd Woman lyable to the Subjection of his Absolute Will; it seem'd but requisite, that she should be endu'd likewise in recompence, with some Quality, that might beget in him admiration of her, and so inforce his tenderness and Love.
>
> The knowledge of these Secrets I gather'd in my Travels abroad (where I have spent my Time ever since I was fifteen years old, to this my nine and twentieth Year) in *France* and *Italy* : Those that have travell'd in *Italy*, will tell you to what a Miracle there Art does assist nature in the preservation of beauty; how Women of forty bear the same Countenance with those of Fifteen; Ages are there no ways distinguish'd by Faces: whereas here in *England*, look a Horse in the Mouth, and a Woman in the Face, you presently know both their Ages to a Year. I will therefore give you such Remedies, that without destroying your Complexion (as most of your Paints and Daubings do) shall render them purely fair, clearing and preserving them from all Spotts, Freckles, heats, and Pimples, nay Marks of the small-pox, or any other accidental ones, so the Face be not seam'd, nor Scarr'd.
>
> I will also cleanse and preserve your Teeth, white and round as Pearls, fastning them that are loose; your Gums shall be kept Intire, and red as Coral, your Lips of the same Coulour, and Soft as you could wish your lawfull Kisses.

I will likewise Administer that which shall cure the worst breath, provided the Lungs be not totally perished, and Imposthumated; as also certain and infallible Remedies for those whose Breaths are untainted, so that nothing but either a very long Sickness, or old Age it self, shall ever be able to spoil them.

I will besides (if it be desired) take away from their fatness who have over much, and add flesh to those that want it, without the least Detriment to their Constitutions.

Now should *Galen* himself look out of his Grave, and tell me these were Bawbles below the Profession of a Physician, I would boldly answer him, that I take more Glory in preserving God's Image in its unblemished Beauty, upon one good Face, than I should do in patching up all the decay'd Carkasses in the World.

Alexander Bendo's Bill is something more than a joke. It is a little masterpiece of ironical satire written with a sureness of touch and a perfection of poise worthy of the Swift of *An Argument Against Abolishing Christianity* and *A Modest Proposal to the Publick*.

Chapter Five

————⟨⟨⟩⟩⟨⟨⟩⟩————

THIS GAWDY GUILDED STAGE

————⟨⟨⟩⟩⟨⟨⟩⟩————

ROCHESTER had a natural talent for the theatre, and, if he had
been a poor man, might have made a great name for himself as an
actor or a dramatist. As it was, he took a keen interest in theatrical
matters throughout his life, and his patronage was sought by the
chief dramatists of the day. It seems to have been through his
interest in the drama that he made the acquaintance of John Dryden.
The authentic records of the relationship between the two men are
scanty enough, and, unfortunately, they have been overlaid with a
great deal of gossip and legend which has done immense harm to
Rochester's reputation. There is no record of any personal contact
between them before about 1672. Rochester was then twenty-five, at
the height of his powers and one of the most brilliant figures at
Court. Dryden was forty-one. He had been appointed Poet Laureate
in 1670 but he had not yet written any of the works by which he was
to achieve lasting fame. He was the author of the early panegyrical
poems such as *Astraea Redux* and *Annus Mirabilis*, but he was
chiefly known as a popular dramatist, whose rhyming 'heroic'
plays were among the great successes of the contemporary London
theatre. The two figures form a pattern that seems to recur throughout the history of English literature, on the one hand the brilliant,
precocious aristocrat and on the other the slowly maturing, hard-
working professional: Sidney, Rochester, Fielding, Byron and
Swinburne pairing with Spenser, Dryden, Richardson, Wordsworth and Tennyson. At first there was certainly friendship and
even some collaboration between Rochester and the Laureate. In
April 1672 Dryden's gay and delightful tragi-comedy *Marriage à la*

Mode was produced with great success at the theatre in Lincoln's Inn Fields. In 1673 he published the play with a very flattering Epistle Dedicatory addressed to Rochester in which he acknowledges that his work has received 'amendment' from Rochester's 'noble hands ere it was fit to be presented'. He also recalls that Rochester had commended the play to the attention of the King, whose 'approbation of it in writing, made way for its kind reception in the theatre'. Rochester is thanked for being not only careful of Dryden's reputation but of his fortune and this and some other expressions in the epistle may mean that Dryden's appointment to the laureateship was due in some measure to Rochester's influence with the King.[1] That Rochester gave Dryden some help with *Marriage à la Mode* seems very likely. The comic parts of the play have a sparkle and lightness rarely found in Dryden's dramatic work and Rochester's hand may, perhaps, be discerned in the witty, cynical talk of the courtiers Rhodophil and Palamede and the vapourings of the affected, Frenchified lady Melantha. Rochester, apparently, wrote to thank Dryden for this dedication. We know this from the only extant letter from Dryden to Rochester, a copy of which survives in the Harleian Collection in the British Museum.[2] In this letter Dryden describes Rochester's letter to him, which, unfortunately, has not survived, as 'the most handsome compliment couched in the best language I have ever read'. Much of Dryden's letter is in a vein of rather fulsome flattery. 'You are above any incense I can give you', he writes, and there can be detected a note of envy in his description of Rochester as one who has 'all the happiness of an idle life joined with the good nature of an active'. He tries to amuse the Earl who is in the country with some town gossip about Buckingham and Etherege. He is clearly proud of his intimacy with these aristocratic wits and tries to assume the air of ironic gaiety which was characteristic of Rochester's set: 'I dare almost promise', he writes 'to entertain you with a thousand bagatelles every week and not be serious in any part of my letter.' Now Rochester was much too intelligent a man to enjoy large doses of flattery and his keen eye for comedy would see the absurdity of the middle-aged professional writer trying to assume the airs of a gay young courtier. This friendship was clearly a precarious alliance from the outset and it was ominous that Dryden in the epistle

---

[1] Dryden, ed. Scott, IV, 235-40.   [2] H., 293, 294; Malone, I, ii, 6-13.

dedicatory to *Marriage à la Mode* should have written of Rochester, 'Your lordship has but one step to make, and from the patron of wit, you may become its tyrant.' It is true that Dryden seems to mean by this sentence that, if Rochester devoted his energies to authorship, he would outstrip all rivals and be a danger to professional dramatists, but it might be interpreted in a more unpleasant way. Several reasons have been asigned for the interruption of the friendly relations between the two poets and probably there is some truth in all of them. One explanation has been that it was due to the fact that Dryden accepted the patronage of John Sheffield, Earl of Mulgrave, a young nobleman of the same age as Rochester, and, like him, a Gentleman of the Bedchamber. Sheffield was a tall, ungainly youth with a narrow chest and shoulders and a 'sour lofty look'. He was not without literary talent but appears to have been pompous and over-bearing. At first the two young men appear to have been on good terms and Rochester addressed to Mulgrave some amusing and characteristic lines entitled *An Epistolary Essay from M.G. to O.B. Upon their Mutual Poems.*[1] They seem to have quarrelled in November 1669. In his *Memoirs*[2] Mulgrave relates that he had heard that Rochester had spread a malicious report about him 'according to his custom', and he promptly sent him a challenge by Colonel Aston, 'a very mettled friend' of his. By Mulgrave's own admission, Rochester proved that he was quite innocent of what was imputed to him, and Mulgrave declared himself to be satisfied. However, this was a question of 'honour', and 'honour' demanded that there should be a duel. Mulgrave confesses that he 'foolishly thought' that the duel had to be fought. The situation must have appealed to Rochester's sense of humour, and he seems to have resolved to make the affair as absurd as possible. He demanded that the encounter should be on horseback, and it was arranged that it should take place in the fields near Knightsbridge 'to avoid the being secured at *London* upon any suspicion'. Mulgrave and Aston went to spend the night of 2 November at an 'odd Inn', where they 'had all the appearance of Highwaymen'. When they met Rochester in the morning, he was accompanied not by James Porter, whom he had promised to bring as a second, but by 'an errant Life-guardman whom nobody knew'. Rochester and his ally were well mounted and their adversaries had only 'a couple of pads'. Moreover, Aston

---

[1] P., 92-3, 191, 192.   [2] Sheffield, II, 8-10.

'took exception' to the Lifeguard as 'no suitable adversary'. It was therefore agreed that they should fight on foot. Rochester and Mulgrave went off into the next field to fight, and as they were riding there, Rochester declared that he had elected to fight on horseback because he was too 'weak with a certain distemper' to fight on foot, and now he 'found himself unfit to fight at all any way, much less a-foot'. Mulgrave was surprised, 'because at that time no man had a better reputation for courage', and 'took the liberty of representing what a ridiculous story it would make if we returned without fighting'. Rochester, however stuck to his resolution not to fight and 'hoped that' Mulgrave 'would not desire the advantage of having to do with any man in so weak a condition'. . . . Mulgrave solemnly called up the seconds to witness the conditions on which the duel was abandoned, and when they returned to London, Aston wrote an account of the whole affair 'in order to spread everywhere the true reason for our returning without having fought'. According to Mulgrave this 'intirely ruined' Rochester's reputation as to courage '. . . tho' nobody had still a greater as to Wit; which supported him pretty well in the world, not withstanding some more accidents of the same kind, that never fail to succeed one another when once people know a man's weakness'. The truth of the matter may be that Rochester thoroughly enjoyed the fun of dragging Mulgrave and Aston out to Knightsbridge in the raw November weather on a fool's errand, and that his chief object was to ridicule the absurd contemporary conventions of 'honour' and duelling.

This is the story as told by Mulgrave but it does not tally with several entries in *The Journals of the House of Lords*,[1] which deal with the affair. On 23 November the Lord Chamberlain delivered the following message to the house from the King:

'That his Majesty understanding that there was an Intention of a Duel between the Earl of *Mulgrave* and the Earl of *Rochester*; His Majesty hath sent an Officer of His Guards to find them out, but he could not meet with the Earl of *Mulgrave*; and having apprehended the Earl of *Rochester* in his Chamber, his lordship engaged his Honour and Word to him, not to make any Escape; but pretending to have some Occasion to go into a little Back Room, he conveyed himself away at a Back Door and is not yet found: There are several Persons sent abroad to find them out. His Majesty says,

[1] J.H.L., XII, 272–6.

as the Earl of *Rochester* is His Servant, He knows what course to take with him; but, in regard as they are both Peers, and Members of this House, His Majesty held it a Respect to this House, to give their Lordships Notice hereof; and desires their lordships to take some Course with them.' The answer of the Lords to this appeal was an order 'That the gentleman Usher of the Black Rod . . . shall take care speedily to secure the Persons of the Earl of *Mulgrave* and the Earl of *Rochester*, and bring them in safe custody before the Lords in Parliament.' It is interesting to learn from the King's message that Rochester actually seems to have contrived to escape from the officer, no doubt in order to keep his appointment with Mulgrave. On 24 November we hear that the Lord Chamberlain acquainted the House that Mulgrave's person had been secured that he was 'in the safe custody of an Officer of the Guards in Suffolk Street to be disposed of as their Lordships shall think fit'. On the same day Black Rod informed the house that he had Mulgrave in custody, and he was brought in and allowed to sit in his place as a Peer. The Lord Keeper told him about the King's message and informed him that 'their lordships do expect that he should now declare and promise upon his Honour to proceed no further in this Business between him and the Earl of *Rochester*; as neither to give nor receive any Challenge: and if he should receive any Message from the Earl of Rochester concerning any such Matter, this House lays their command upon him, not to do any thing therein, but presently to acquaint their lordships therewith'. Mulgrave 'upon this declared that he would give Obedience to the Commands of this House; and promised, upon his Honour, to observe what was now declared to him as the Pleasure of this House.

On the following day Black Rod informed the House that he had Rochester 'in his safe custody'. On the 26th Rochester was in his place in the House, and was admonished by the Lord Keeper in much the same terms as those which he had used to Mulgrave. Rochester answered as follows:

My Lords
   I shall be ever ready to give Obedience to your Lordships' Commands, and I am sure I shall easily do it in this Particular. I have never been angry with the Earl of *Mulgrave*, and I have no Reason to believe he was so with me; for his Lordship hath always carried himself so gently and civilly towards me, that I am confident that there will be no Occasion of any Difference between us.

95

There was, doubtless, an ironical twinkle in Rochester's eye as he spoke the last words, which seem to imply that Mulgrave was not at all anxious to fight. As far as can be judged from these entries it looks as though Rochester was willing to fight, although he thought the whole affair absurd, and that Mulgrave did his best to avoid the duel. It was probably in order to cover up his own unwillingness to fight that Mulgrave invented the story of Rochester's cowardice. As Mr. Hayward has very well remarked Rochester was 'no more a coward than Falstaff'.[1] When he was really angered, he was quite willing to fight; on 25 March 1673, a duel between him and the notorious hector, Lord Dunbar, was narrowly averted by the Earl Marshal's intervention, and in December 1674, when Mulgrave challenged Henry Savile, Rochester offered to act as second to his friend, though on this occasion also there seems to have been no actual fighting.[2] The intimacy between Dryden and Mulgrave probably appeared to Rochester as an insult to himself and henceforth he was the Laureate's enemy, though he never wavered in his acknowledgment of his genius. It has been frequently stated that he deliberately brought forward the young dramatist Elkanah Settle as a rival to Dryden, but there does not seem to be any evidence to support this report. Settle's tragedy *Cambyses* was produced with great success by the Duke's Company probably in 1670/1 when the poet was only eighteen. He then wrote another heroic drama in the fashionable style called *The Empress of Morocco*, based on hints given to him by the Earl of Norwich who had recently visited Morocco on an embassy.[3] This play was chosen to be performed at Court by a number of distinguished amateurs. Sir Walter Scott in his *Life of Dryden* accuses Rochester of deliberately arranging that this honour should be given to Settle in preference to Dryden,[4] but as a matter of fact it seems unlikely that the production at Court was due to Rochester's influence. Settle himself attributes it to the favour of the Earl of Norwich. Two prologues were written for the play and curiously enough one is by Mulgrave and one by Rochester. Rochester's prologue which was spoken by Lady Elizabeth Howard contains a very graceful and felicitous compliment to the King:

> To you (great Sir) my Message hither tends,
> From Youth, and Beauty, your Allies and Friends
> See my Credentials written in my Face.

[1] Hayward, xxxi.   [2] H.M.C. Le Fleming Papers, 101; E.P., 281; W
[3] S.E.M., Dedication.   [4] Dryden, ed. Scott, I, 183–6.

They challenge your Protection in this Place,
And hither come with such a force of Charms,
As may give check ev'n to your prosp'rous Arms.
Millions of *Cupids* hovering in the Rear,
Like Eagles following fatal Troops appear:
All waiting for the slaughter which draws nigh,
Of those bold Gazers who this Night must dye.
Nor can you 'scape our soft Captivitie,
From which old Age alone must set you free.
Then tremble at the fatal Consequence . . .
Since, 'tis well known, for your own part. (Great Prince)
'Gainst us you still have made a weak Defence.
Be generous, and wise, and take our part:
Remember we have Eyes, and you a Heart;
Else you may find too late that we are things
Born to kill Vassals, and to conquer Kings.
But oh, to what vain Conquest I pretend,
While *Love* is our Commander, and your Friend.
Our Victory your Empire more assures;
For *Love* will ever make the Triumph Yours.[1]

The date of the Court production was probably the spring of
1671/2.[2] This was before the dedication of *Marriage à la Mode* and
the pleasant correspondence between Rochester and Dryden.
Rochester's relations with Settle would, therefore, seem to have
nothing to do with his quarrel with Dryden.

This Court production has sometimes been confused with another
and still more famous one, which took place in the spring of 1675.
The King and the Duke of York wanted a masque to be performed
at Whitehall by the Court ladies, and it would have been natural
for them to have laid their commands on the Poet Laureate. He was
passed over, however, and the choice fell on John Crowne, a young
author, who had already dedicated to Rochester his tragedy, *Charles
VIII of France*. Malone states that this slight to Dryden was due to
Rochester's advice, and this allegation, like that which concerns the
performance of *The Empress of Morocco*, has been repeated regularly
in all the Lives of Rochester. Its origin is to be found in a passage
in John Dennis's *Letters Familiar Moral and Critical* published in
1721.[3] In a letter dated 23 June 1719, he wrotes of Crowne that 'it
was neither to the Favour of the Court, nor of Wilmot, Earl of

---

[1] P., 54.   [2] Boswell, 132, 133.   [3] Dennis, II, 405.

Rochester, one of the shining ornaments of it, that he was indebted for the Nomination, which the King made of him for the writing of the Mask of *Calypso* [*sic*], but to malice of that noble Lord who design'd by that preference to mortify *Mr Dryden*'. Dennis was a youth of eighteen at the time of the production at Court of Crowne's rather poor masque *Callisto*, and this vague piece of gossip retailed forty-four years later, when he could not even remember the correct title of the masque, is entirely worthless as evidence. *Callisto* was performed with great splendour at Whitehall by the Duke of York's two daughters and other great ladies and gentlemen. Dryden composed an epilogue for it, and Malone has conjectured that Rochester prevented it from being spoken.[1] There is not the slightest reason for believing this story. Malone, to do him justice, only mentions it as a possibility, but subsequent writers have frequently stated it as a fact.

Probably the true cause of the rupture between Rochester and Dryden is to be found in the older man's resentment at the young Earl's outspoken criticism of him in his poem called *An Allusion to Horace the 10th Satyr of the 1st Book*. This poem seems to have been written and circulated among Rochester's acquaintance in the spring of 1675. It is a brilliant adaptation of the poem in which Horace defends himself for adversely criticizing Lucilius and passes in review various poets of his day. Rochester, substituting Dryden for Lucilius, gives his frank opinion of the work and personality of the Laureate, and, incidentally, passes judgment on a number of contemporary writers. Taken as a whole, the poem is a powerful protest against affectation, insincerity, playing to the gallery and seeking for cheap applause. The opening lines seem to refer to some previous criticism of Dryden by Rochester, though they may be simply an adaptation of Horace's 'quod sale multo/urbem defricuit, charta laudatur eadem'.

> Well, Sir, tis granted, I said *Dryden's* Rhymes
> Were stoln, unequal, nay dull many times.
> What foolish *Patron* is there found of his,
> So blindly partial to deny me this?
> But that his *Plays* embroidered up and down
> With Wit and *Learning* justly pleas'd the *Town*,
> In the same *Paper*, I as freely own,

---

[1] Malone, I, i, 129.

> Yet having this allow'd, the heavy *Mass*
> That Stuffs up his loose *Volumns* must not pass
> For by that Rule I might as well admit
> *Crown's* tedious *Scenes* for *Poetry* and *Wit*.[1]

The 'foolish Patron' of the third line is probably Mulgrave. It must be remembered that the Dryden to whom Rochester is referring in these lines had not as yet written any of the great satiric and controversial poems or the Pindarique odes or the Fables. He is the author of *Astraea Redux, Annus Mirabilis* and *The Conquest of Granada.* Of this early Dryden Rochester's criticism is fair enough. He goes on to a series of acute comments on poets and dramatists of the day, leading up to a characterization of the poetry of his friends Buckhurst and Sedley, and then returns to Dryden, whose attempts to emulate the manner of the Courts Wit in writing and conversation he finds supremely ridiculous:

> *Dryden*, in vain try'd this nice way of wit,
> For he to be a tearing *Blade*, thought fit,
> But when he wou'd be sharp; he still was blunt . . .

But Rochester saw that this absurd imitator of the 'tearing Blades' was also a poet of genius and he says so emphatically:

> But to be just, 'twill to his praise be found
> His *Excellencies* more than his faults abound,
> Nor dare I from his sacred Temples tear
> That *Lawrel*, which he best deserves to wear.[2]

This is generous praise and in it we can hear the voice of a just and discerning critic. Rochester proceeds to claim the right to treat Dryden's writings with the same freedom as that which Dryden had used in discussing the plays of Shakespeare, Ben Jonson, Beaumont and Fletcher:

> may not I have leave impartially
> To search and censure *Dryden's* Works, and try
> If these gross faults his choice *Pen* does commit
> Proceed from want of Judgment, or of Wit?
> Or if his lumpish fancy does refuse
> Spirit and Grace, to his loose slattern *Muse?*
> Five hundred Verses ev'ry *Morning* writ,
> Proves you no more a *Poet* than a Wit:[3]

[1] P., 95.   [2] Ibid., 97.   [3] Ibid., 98.

Here, surely is the core of Rochester's quarrel with Dryden. He
saw him as a man of genius who prostituted his great gifts by grinding out verses to order, becoming an industrious producer of
popular artefacts instead of a creator of works of art. It may be said
that it was easy enough for a man in Rochester's privileged position
to speak like this about a writer who had to live by his pen. Nevertheless there is much truth in Rochester's criticism. Dryden from
the beginning tried to combine the poet with the journalist and
when the journalist gets the upper hand the poet often suffers.
Like Tennyson and Kipling he was always ready to compromise
with the Philistine, to whom Rochester, like Blake and D. H.
Lawrence, would never yield an inch.

Dryden was deeply offended by Rochester's criticism. In a
letter to his friend Henry Savile written probably in April 1676,
Rochester speaks of the Laureate's reaction to *An Allusion to
Horace*. This is the letter which has done more harm to Rochester's
reputation than anything he ever wrote. The only text which we
have is that printed in the collection called *Familiar Letters* published
in 1697.[1] It is undated and no manuscript survives. It was formerly
supposed that this letter was written in 1679 and that it referred to
the cudgelling of Dryden which took place in Rose Alley, Covent
Garden, in December of that year. It has now been shown by Professor J. H. Wilson from internal evidence that this letter could not
have been written later than 1677 and was almost certainly written
in the spring of 1676.[2] It cannot, therefore, have any connection
with the Rose Alley outrage. Savile had apparently written to
Rochester to tell him that he was out of favour with Dryden, presumably because of the criticism in *An Allusion to Horace*. In his
reply Rochester writes as follows: 'You write me word, That I'm out
of favour with a certain Poet, whom I have ever admir'd for the disproportion of him and his Attributes: He is a Rarity which I cannot
but be fond of, as one would be of a Hog that could fiddle, or a
singing Owl.' These words are not very complimentary to Dryden,
but, again, they go to the root of Rochester's objection to him as a
man and a poet. For Rochester a poet should be a poet through and
through, and a dull dog who wrote fine poetry was something strange

---

[1] W., 88; F.L.I., 4-6.
[2] W., 14; see also J. H. Wilson's article in R.E.S., XV, 59, 294-301 and reply by V. de
S. Pinto in R.E.S., XVI, 62.

and monstrous. It is the sentence that follows this passage which has been taken to mean that Rochester was the instigator:

'If he falls upon me at the Blunt, which is his very good Weapon in Wit, I will forgive him, if you please, and leave the Repartee to Black Will, with a Cudgel.' What Rochester meant by these words (if indeed he wrote them) no one has ever satisfactorily explained. My own belief is that, if the passage be genuine, he only meant that he was not going to take any further action if Dryden lampooned him, but would leave him to the tender mercies of his enemies at Court, who would probably, in the brutal fashion of the day, inflict corporal punishment on him if he developed the habit of satirizing noblemen. Professor Wilson has suggested that 'Black Will' may either be 'a living character, possibly a link-boy, a member of the so-called Black Guard' or that the phrase is either a proverbial expression or a literary allusion to Black Will, the murderer in *Arden of Feversham*.[1] I strongly suspect that 'Black Will' may be a misreading for 'Black Phill' and that it refers to Philip Herbert, seventh Earl of Pembroke, a nobleman notorious for his brutality and almost certainly the real perpetrator of the Rose Alley outrage, of which more hereafter.[2]

Dryden's rejoinder to Rochester's criticism in *An Allusion to Horace* appeared in the Preface to his tragedy *All for Love* published in 1678.[3] He does not mention Rochester by name in this Preface but his remarks are clearly aimed at him and they show all the irritation of the hard-working professional against the rich, idle amateur. *An Allusion to Horace* had been circulated anonymously and Dryden affects to speak of it as though it were the work of some minor aristocratic poetaster. He takes the opportunity of ridiculing the Court Wits whose company he had been cultivating so assiduously a short time before. Now they are described by him as 'Men of pleasant conversation (at least esteemed so) and endued with a trifling kind of fancy, perhaps helped out with some smattering of Latin', who are 'ambitious to distinguish themselves from the herd of gentlemen by their poetry'. 'And is not', he continues, 'this a wretched affectation, not to be contented with what fortune has done for them, . . . but they must call their wits in question, and needlessly expose their nakedness to public view?' Dryden's argument seems a very strange one. It amounts to the contention that writing is

---

[1] W., 88.   [2] See below, p. 182.   [3] Dryden, ed. Scott, V, 311–17.

beneath the dignity of a 'man of quality' who should leave it to the poor professional author: 'We who write, if we want the talent, yet have the excuse that we do it for a poor subsistence; but what can be urged in their defence, who, not having the vocation of poverty to scribble, out of mere wantoness take pains to make themselves ridiculous.' The 'man of quality' is blamed not only for writing but for daring to criticize the professional author: 'Thus the case is hard with writers: If they succeed not, they must starve; and if they do, some malicious satire is prepared to level them, for daring to please without their leave. But while they are so eager to destroy the fame of others, their ambition is manifest in their concernment; some poem of their own is to be produced, and the slaves are to be laid flat with their faces on the ground, that the monarch may appear in the greater majesty.' This is grossly unfair to Rochester. *An Allusion to Horace* is not a 'malicious satire', but a perfectly fair, if severe, piece of criticism, and Rochester never asked anybody to prostrate himself before his poems. Indeed, to judge from the conclusion to *An Allusion to Horace*, he was indifferent to the opinion of anyone outside a small circle of his friends.[1]

The art of patronage in the Restoration period was not an easy one, and Rochester probably lacked the patience and tact which made his friend Charles Sackville, Lord Buckhurst (afterwards Earl of Dorset) the prince of patrons.

Restoration noblemen who had a reputation for literary taste must have suffered a great deal from the importunities of scribblers seeking a patron. A story of the way in which Rochester dealt with one of these pests is preserved in some notes by John Boyle, fifth Earl of Orrery on Roger Boyle, the first Earl. Samuel Pordage had written a tragedy called *Herod and Mariamne*. 'He had taken Infinite Pains to make Herod an errant Jew, & was very unwilling to lose his Labour, after the Work had not only receiv'd the approbation of Himself, but several of his poetical Friends also. A Patron was still wanting; & after consulting some of his Acquaintances, who should have had the honour of patronizing so accomplished a Play, It was resolv'd nemine contradicente, that Wilmot, Earl of Rochester was the most worthy of such a Favour. To This End, the Author, tho not personally, or nominally known to my Lord Rochester, waited upon him & left the Play for his Lordships Perusal, and

---

[1] See below, p. 136.

liv'd for some Days on the Expectation of his approaching Applause. At the Expiration of about a Week, He went a second Time to my Lord's House, where He found the Manuscript in the Hands of the Porter, with this Distick write upon the cover of It.'

> Poet who e'er thou art, God damn Thee
> Go hang thyself, and burn Thy Mariamne',[1]

When he favoured such inferior writers as Settle and Crowne he was probably amusing himself by watching the airs which they gave themselves when they basked in the sunshine of his favour, and maliciously enjoyed their chagrin when he withdrew his patronage from them and allowed them to see how easily their bubble reputations could be pricked. He seems to have behaved in the same capricious way to Thomas Otway, a much greater dramatist than Settle or Crowne. In his dedication of his second play *Don Carlos* to the Duke of York in 1676, Otway boasts of Rochester's patronage and mentions that the Earl had introduced his work to the notice of the King and the Duke.[2] In the following year (1677) he dedicated his *Titus and Berenice* to Rochester himself, and expresses warm gratitude for the support that his patron had given to him.[3] In the autumn of the same year a lampoon attributed to Rochester called *A Session of the Poets* was circulating in the town, and it contained some lines that mock Otway for his boasts, concerning his heroic plays, his 'mange' and 'lice', and his failure as an actor. He is also satirized in *An Allusion to Horace* as 'puzling Otway'.[4] Otway replied to these attacks in his *The Poet's Complaint of his Muse* where he represents Rochester as seeking for the Muse's favour in vain:

> Then next there followed, to make up the Throng,
> *Lord Lampoon* and *Monsieur Song*,
> Who sought her love, and promis'd for't
> To make her famous at the Court.[5]

Against the rather vague and not very reliable reports of Rochester's fickleness as a patron can be placed substantial evidence that he won the unstinted admiration and gratitude of at least two young literary aspirants whom he befriended. One of these was a

---

[1] Orrery, II, 951, 952. The story about Pordage and Rochester is also told in *The History of Herod and Marianne*, London, 1723, where Rochester's couplet is given in a slightly different form.
[2] Otway, I, 174.　　[3] Ibid., I, 253–5.　　[4] P., 106, 96.　　[5] Otway, II, 412.

Lincolnshire knight, Sir Francis Fane, who dedicated to him his lively comedy *Love in the Dark or the Man of Business*, published in 1675, for which Rochester wrote an epilogue. Fane's dedication in the form of a letter to Rochester printed at the head of his play,[1] is a rather absurd piece of highflown compliment, but it shows that the Earl's kindness made a deep impression on the young dramatist. After acknowledging the encouragement he had received from Rochester he describes him as 'an Enthusiast in Wit, a Poet and Philosopher by Revelation', and pays a remarkable tribute to his conversation: 'I must confess, I never return from your Lordship's most Charming and Instructive Conversation, but I am inspir'd to a new Genius, and improv'd in all these Sciences I ever coveted the knowledge of: I find my self, not only a better Poet, a better Philosopher; but more than these, a better Christian: Your Lordship's miraculous Wit and Intellectual pow'rs being the greatest Argument that ever I could meet with for the immateriality of the Soul; they being the highflown exaltation of humane Nature, and, under Divine Authority, much more convincing to suspicious Reason, than all the Pedantick proofs of the most Learnedly peevish Disputants: so that, I hope, I shall be oblig'd to your Lordship, not only for my Reputation in this World, but my future Happiness in the next.' These are strange words to be addressed to the 'atheistical' Wit whose wickedness made the pious shudder, and they show that Rochester's conversation was by no means always frivolous, but that even at this date he was found of discussing philosophical and religious matters.

An even more striking proof of Rochester's capacity for disinterested friendship with a younger writer is to be found in his relationship with the poet John Oldham of which more will be said hereafter.

Rochester's quarrel with Otway has often been connected with his relations with the famous actress Elizabeth Barry. Here again the tendency to represent Rochester as a wicked lord has given rise to a legend which has done much damage to his reputation.

This famous actress claimed to be the daughter of a royalist lawyer called Robert Barry, and she is said to have been the servant of a Lady Shelton in Norfolk. She was not beautiful but her appearance was striking. Antony Aston describes her as 'a fine Creature'

[1] F.L.D., Sigg. A2V., A3.

but 'not handsome, her Mouth op'ning most on the Right Side, which she strove to draw t'other Way, and, at Times, composing her Face, as if sitting to have her Picture drawn'. She was 'middle siz'd, and had darkish Hair, light Eyes, dark Eye-brows, and was indifferently plump'.[1] A certain Lady Davenant, a relative of Sir William Davenant is said to have given her a good education and made her her companion. She wanted to be an actress, but though she had 'a good air and manner and a very strong and pleasing voice',[2] she had a 'a very bad Ear', and the players 'found it so 'difficult to teach her, that they thought it would be impossible to make her fit for the meanest Part'. They tried her three times 'but with so little Success that several Persons of Wit and Quality being at the Play, and observing how she performed, positively gave their opinion she never would be capable of any Part of Acting'. Rochester, however, took a different view and 'entered into a Wager, that by proper Instruction, in less than six months, he would engage she should be the finest Player on the Stage'. He undertook to train her himself, and she became his mistress. It was said that he 'never loved any person so sincerely as he loved Mrs. Barry'.[3] The first parts for which he trained her, according to Curll, were 'the *little Gipsy* in the Comedy of the *Rover* by Mrs. *Behn* and *Isabella*, the Hungarian Queen in the Tragedy of *Mustapha* by the E. of *Orrery*'. She certainly appears in the original cast of Aphra Behn's play *The Rover* as Hellena, described as 'a gay young Woman design'd for a nun',[4] but this play was first produced in the summer of 1677 and Mrs. Barry had played several parts successfully before this. The first part which she is recorded to have played is the small one of Draxilla in Otway's *Alcibiades* produced in September 1675 and this was possibly the performance which made such a bad impression on the 'Persons of Wit and Quality'. If we can believe the story that Rochester played the part of Professor Higgins to Mrs. Barry's Eliza Doolittle, her training, as Professor J. H. Wilson has suggested, probably took place in the autumn and winter of 1675/6. We are told that, in preparing her for a part, Rochester 'made her rehearse near 30 times on the Stage, and about 12 in the Dress she was to Act it in'. He 'took such Extraordinary Pains with her as not omit the least look or Motion, nay, I have been assured', writes Curll, 'from those who were present, that her Page was taught to

---

[1] Cibber, II, 302.   [2] Davies, III, 209.   [3] Curll, 14, 15.   [4] Behn, I, 117.

manager her Train, in such a Manner, so as to give each Movement, a peculiar grace'.

Rochester seems to have belonged to the school of thought that believes that an actor should wholly identify himself with the character he is playing. Mrs. Barry's difficulty had apparently been that, having 'a bad Ear', she could not benefit from the kind of training given by the players, which seems to have consisted of teaching the pupil to imitate parrotwise the instructor's delivery of 'sounding words' without reference to the sense of the passage. When she tried to do this she 'ran into a tone' and they thought her 'dull'. Rochester, on the other hand, perceiving that she was intelligent, appealed to her 'very good Understanding', making her 'enter into the Nature of such Sentiment, perfectly changing herself as it were into the Person, not merely by the proper Stress or Sounding of the Voice, but feeling really, and being in the Humour, the Person she represented, was supposed to be in'.

The experiment had a triumphant success. The first night on which Mrs. Barry acted the part of Isabella in *Mustapha*, she completely captivated the audience. Rochester is said to have brought the King and the Duke and Duchess of York to see her and 'the whole Theatre resounded with Applause'.[1]

Whatever truth there may be in the details of the story, the record of the way in which Rochester trained Mrs. Barry is highly significant. It shows him as a champion of individualism and realism in the theatre as he was in poetry. The players, apparently, were trying to instruct her in an impersonal tradition of dramatic art going back, doubtless, to the Middle Ages. They wanted her to go through the motions of a conventional tragedy queen. Rochester treated her as an individual and made her impersonate a real woman. We can see here the beginnings of a new art of the theatre that was to culminate in the naturalistic drama of Ibsen, Shaw and Chekhov.

Her subsequent career was brilliant, and she became one of the most popular English actresses of the late seventeenth and early eighteenth centuries, acting leading parts in plays by Dryden, Etherege, Otway, Lee, Vanbrugh, Congreve and others.[2] Colley Cibber, who knew her well, praises her in a fine passage in his autobiography: 'in Characters of Greatness', he writes, she 'had a Presence of elevated Dignity, her Mien and Motion superb and

---

[1] Curll, 14–17; Davies, III, 209–12; A.K.L., 50–2.   [2] A.K.L., 110–14.

gracefully majestick, her Voice full, clear and strong, so that no Violence of Passion could be too much for her: And when Distress or Tenderness possess'd her, she subsided into the most affecting Melody and Softness. In the Art of exciting Pity, she had a Power beyond all the Actresses I have yet seen, or what your Imagination can conceive.'[1] Anthony Aston describes her as 'solemn and august' in tragedy and 'in *Free Comedy* alert, easy, and genteel—pleasant in her Face and Action; filling the Stage with Variety of Gesture'. He gives an interesting description of her manner on the stage: 'Her Face somewhat preceded her Action, as the latter did her Words, her Face ever expressing the Passions.'[2] It would seem that Rochester succeeded in imparting something of the fire and energy of his own gestures to this noble and spirited woman. In Elizabeth Malet's company he had been a fine gentleman and a courtier poet; with Elizabeth Barry he was an actor and a bohemian entering into the life of the theatre as if he had been born for it.

The following lovely fragment on Rochester's autograph among the manuscripts formerly at Welbeck Abbey seems to be addressed to an actress, and it is tempting to connect it with Elizabeth Barry:

> Leave this gawdy guilded stage
> From custome more than use frequented
> Where fooles of either sex and age
> Crowd to see themselves presented
> To loves Theatre the Bed
> Youth and Beauty fly together
> And Act soe well it may be said
> The Lawrell there was due to either.
> Twixt strifes of Love & war the difference Lies in this
> When neither overcomes Loves Triumph greater is.[3]

It is curious to notice that Rochester comes close to Shelley twice in this passage. Two of the lines foreshadow the opening of the great epithalamion:

> The golden gates of Sleep unbar,
> Where Strength and Beauty met together. . . .

And the concluding couplet suggests *Epipsychidon*:

> True Love in this differs from gold and clay,
> That to divide is not to take away.

[1] Cibber, I, 160.   [2] Ibid., II, 302, 303.   [3] P., 38, 176.

An old tradition affirms that the quarrel between Otway and Rochester was due to the young dramatist's passion for the Earl's mistress. The origin of this story is a collection of letters published in 1697 by Tom Brown. This collection included, together with a number of Rochester's letters, six which are supposed to have been written by Otway to Mrs. Barry. They are clearly composed by a passionate and disappointed lover, and contain expressions very similar to some of the speeches in Otway's tragedies. Dr. Prinz has pointed out, however, that there is a strong internal evidence against the supposition that the person to whom the letters were addressed was Mrs. Barry.[1] It is true that Oldys in the middle of the eighteenth century reports a vague rumour that Mrs. Barry 'could get bastards with other men, and 'twas a wonderful condescension in her to let Otway kiss her',[2] but such gossip as this has no real value, unless it is supported by contemporary evidence. It is on this slender basis that Sir Edmund Gosse reared the remarkable edifice of fiction that appears in his study of Otway. According to this imaginative critic, Rochester persecuted Otway unmercifully because of his passion for Mrs. Barry, and the poor dramatist never had peace, till the wicked nobleman, that 'plague spot in English literature and English society' 'ceased to be troublesome'.[3] Any stick has been good enough to beat Rochester with in the past, but when a dispassionate search is made for positive evidence of his alleged misdeeds, they are generally found to belong to the world of legend rather than to that of history.

Rochester's own dramatic compositions are very slight. The most famous is his rehandling of Fletcher's famous tragedy *Valentinian*, on which he was working at the end of his life. Although it was left unfinished, it was produced after his death in 1685, and curiously enough both his mistresses, Sarah Cooke and Elizabeth Barry, spoke prologues to it.[4] Of this play more will be said hereafter.

Two fragmentary dramatic pieces by him have survived. One is a scene written to be inserted in a play called *The Conquest of China*, by Sir Robert Howard, Dryden's brother-in-law. Howard seems to have planned this 'heroic' play in 1672, but he laid it aside when Elkanah Settle produced a tragedy with the same title in 1673/4. Many years later, in 1697. Howard thought about this sketch again

---

[1] Prinz, 78–82; F.L.I., 77–92.
[2] W. Oldys, MS. note in B.M. copy of Langbaine (C. 28. g.l.), 397.
[3] G.S.S., 316–22.   [4] V., Sigg. C2–C4.

and asked Dryden to help him to complete it,[1] but the work was never carried out. Howard appears to have asked Rochester to help him with the original plan, and in a letter dated 7 July (? 1672) writes of 'the sceen you are pleas'd to write', and generously declares that he will not 'repine to see how far you can exceed mee'.[2] This scene written by Rochester survives in a manuscript written in a copyist's hand in the British Museum.[3] Its subject is a war between the Chinese and the Tartars. The Chinese Empress Amacoa is a heroic and amazonian figure who believes that women can equal men in war-like deeds. She angers her officer Lycungus by appointing his rival Hyachian commander-in-chief. When the Chinese Army is being beaten and the Empress is in danger, Lycungus plans to kill Hyachian and then seize the Empress and marry her. But Hyachian bravely rallies the defeated troops and Lycungus's treachery is discovered. The fragment ends with the victory of the Chinese Army. The scene is a fine, vigorous piece of work, full of dramatic power and fiery energy. Indeed one modern critic has ascribed it to Dryden himself.[4] But Sir Robert Howard's letter and the attribution at the head of the manuscript furnish decisive proof that it is Rochester's. They are supported by internal evidence. The heroic couplets are in Rochester's best manner and bear a striking resemblance to those of the satires. The Empress's outburst in defence of women is closely akin to the misanthropic passages in the *Satyr against Mankind*:

> Perhaps they think or would perswade ye Foe,
> Warr, led by Women, must bee cold or slow.
> This Day I'le prove ye Injustice of that scorne
> Men treate our Sex withall; Woman is borne
> With equall thirst of Honour and of Fame,
> But treacherous man misguides her in her aime;
> Makes her believe that all her Glories lye
> In dull Obedience, Truth, and Modesty
> That to bee Beautifull is to bee Brave,
> And calls her Conquerer when she's most his Slave,
> Forbidding her those noble Paths to tread
> Which through bold daring deeds to Glory lead,
> With ye poor Hypocriticall pretence
> That Woman's merit is her Innocence
> Who treacherously advis'd, Retaining thus

---

[1] Malone, I, ii, 55, 56.   [2] H., 291.   [3] B.M. Add. MS. 28692; P. 61–9.
[4] Allardyce Nicoll, T.L.S., 13 Jan. 1921.

The sole Ambition to be Vertuous
Thinks' tis enough if she's not Infamous.
On these false grounds is mans stol'n Triumph laid
Through Craft alone ye Nobler Creature made.

In this passage we find exactly the same passionate indignation
against the injustice of irrational conventions that appears in
Rochester's best satire. The concluding speeches in the scene show
what Rochester might have done in romantic narrative or drama if he
had turned his energies to that direction.

HYAC.: The Empresse, by Rash honour, driven on
　　　Into ye thickest of ye Foe was flowne.
　　　I to her Rescue ran midst showers of Darts,
　　　Cutting my Bloudy way through Tartars hearts;
　　　On foot I found her for her horse was kill'd,
　　　Strewing with gasping carcases the field—
　　　Some drops of Blood,
　　　Which from her wounds in her faire neck did flow,
　　　Like Rubies set in Rocks of Silver show—
　　　Alone she fought expos'd to Vulgar Blowes
　　　Like a maim'd Eagle in a flock of Crowes.
　　　While I sought death with her I could not Save,
　　　One more than all the rest generous and Brave,
　　　Presses in through the Assassinating Crowd,
　　　And with a voice of Terrour Cryes alowd:
　　　Desist for shame, [Ye][1] Feeble Murderers,
　　　Stain not with Womans blood your Cymeters!
　　　I'le lead you off to nobler Victories—
　　　The men obey him and away hee flys.
　　　Thus got wee time our Army to regaine
　　　But where's Lycungus? Taken, fled or slaine?
OFF.: Lycungus, sir, has never charg'd at all,
　　　And now stands gazing ore ye City Wall.
HYA.: In him ye stupid Rage of Envy see,
　　　Though Brave, turns Coward to be reveng'd on mee.

Enter an Officer.

OFF.: 　　　　　　　　　　　The scatter'd Troops
　　　At Amacoa's presence stay their flight
　　　And led by her renew a Bloudy fight.

[1] MS., the.

110

HYA.: Noe more shall Nations in distress and thrawll
    On helpless man for Aid in Battails call.
    This Womans Valour is above us all—
    Where ere she fights, Beauty & Ruine joyne.
    Rage on her Arme, While in her Eyes they shine
    With Glory and with Death ye field she fills
    Soe thunder, led by lightning, shines & kills.

In this noble passage, as in Dryden's best riming tragedies, the 'heroic' drama is kindled for a moment into the life of high poetry. The 'Scene' is among Rochester's very finest achievements.

The other dramatic fragment is a passage from the first scene of a prose comedy in Rochester's autograph among Portland manuscripts:

SCENE: 1ST—MR. DAYNTY'S CHAMBER.

Enter Daynty in his Nightgown singing

    D.: *J'ay L'amour dans Le Coeur et La rage dans Les Os,*—I am Confident I shall never sleepe agen, & twere noe great matter if itt did nott make mee Looke thin, for naturally I hate to bee so Long absent from my self, as one is in a manner those seav'n dull how'rs hee snores away, & yett methinks not to sleep till the sun rise, is an odd effect of my disease, and makes the night tædious wth out a Woman, reading would releive mee, but bookes treate of other men's affaires, & to me that's ever tiresome, besides I seldome have Candle, but I am resolv'd to write some Love-passages of my [owne] life, they will make a pritty Novell, & when my boy buy's a linke, itt shall burne by mee when I goe to bedd, while I divert myself wth reading my owne story wch will bee pleasant enough—Boy—!

    Enter Boy—Sr; D; Who knock't att doore just now, was itt some woman; B: Mrs. Mannours maide S^r wth a possett for you; D: And you neaver brought her up, you Rascall, how can you bee soe ill bredd, & belong to mee; see who knocks there, some other Woman; *exit boy* this Mrs. Mannours's [is very] fondness of mee is very usefull, for besides the good things shee allways sends mee, & money I borrow of her somtimes, I have a further prospect, Sr Lyonells Daughters wch are in her charge, both Like mee, but the Youngest I pitch upon, & becaus I can't marry 'em both, my Young Nobility Mr. Squobb shall have the other Sister, butt I'le Bubble him afterwards, thus I'le raise my fortune wch is all I want for I am an agreable Man and ev'ry Body

III

Like's me, *enter boy* B: Tis Mr Squobb S^r, D. Call him up, but comb y^r. perriwigg first, lett mee Comb itt you are the Laziest sloven.[1]

Mr. Daynty is a promising coxcomb, and he might well have become a serious rival to Sir Fopling Flutter. The conception of a man who is so fond of his own company that he does not care to be absent from himself for the 'seav'n dull how'rs' of sleep, and who cannot read books because 'they treat of other men's affaires' is worthy of Etherege or Congreve at their best. It is a pity that Rochester, having launched this pretty cockboat of vanity, never wafted it further on the high seas of comic adventure.

The passage, however, is something more than an amusing fragment of a comedy of manners. It shows a power of psychological analysis that suggests a potential novelist before the novel, as we understand the term, had come into existence. It is also a satiric commentary on the hell of the egotistic individualist in line with that of much of Rochester's poetry:

> In my dear self, I center ev'ry thing,
> My *Servants*, *Friends*, My *Mrs.*, and my *King*[2]

---

[1] Port. f. 12. Words crossed out in MS. are in square brackets.   [2] P., 43.

Chapter Six

───────⟪◆⟫⟪◆⟫───────

THE RIGHT VEINE

───────⟪◆⟫⟪◆⟫───────

O but the World will take offence thereby.
Why then the World shall suffer for't, not I.
Did e're the Sawcy World and I agree
To let it have its beastly will on me?
            Rochester, *An Epistolary Essay from M.G. to*
                    O.B. upon their Mutual Poems.

Every age needs a particular kind of genius, and the genius of
Rochester was exactly what was needed by Restoration England.
His was the representative mind of the English aristocracy under
Charles II as Sir Philip Sidney's had been of the same class under
Elizabeth. In him we can see the spirit of the Renaissance, which
had achieved such a noble civilization in the sixteenth century, still
retaining its pride and its culture, but touched by the cold breath of
the approaching *aufklärung* and turning upon itself in impassioned
and bitter self-criticism. The hardness of the young men of the new
generation shocked Clarendon just as the hardness of the young
people of the post-war period shocked their parents. He was probably thinking of Rochester and his friends when he wrote that 'the
tenderness of the bowels, which is the quintessence of justice and
compassion, the very mention of good nature was laughed at, and
looked upon as the mark and character of a fool; and a roughness
of manners or hard-heartedness and cruelty was affected'.[1] This
apparent hardness was not really lack of sensibility, as Clarendon
thought, but was due to a conviction that such things as honour and

---
[1] C.L., 307.

reverence were empty words which had only led the previous generation into barren warfare. The result was a profound scepticism. If Milton is the great poet of belief in the seventeenth century, Rochester is the great poet of unbelief. *Paradise Lost* is a hymn to the triumph of God over Chaos, of Being over Not-being. One of Rochester's most striking poems is an ironic paean for the victory of Nothing over Existence.

> *Nothing!* thou Elder Brother ev'n to Shade,
> That hadst a Being e're the World was made,
> And (well-fixt) art alone, of ending not afraid.
>
> E'er time and place were, time and place were not,
> When primitive *Nothing* something strait begot,
> Then all proceeded from the great united—What.
>
> Something, the gen'ral Attribute of all,
> Sever'd from thee, its sole Original,
> Into thy boundless self must undistinguish'd fall.
>
> Yet something did thy mighty Pow'r command,
> And from thy fruitful emptiness's Hand,
> Snatch'd Men, Beasts, Birds, Fire, Water, Air and **Land**.
>
> Matter, the wickedst Off-spring of thy Race,
> By Form assisted, flew to thy Embrace,
> And Rebel Light obscur'd thy reverend dusky Face.
>
> With Form, and Matter, Time and Place did joyn;
> Body, thy Foe, with these did Leagues combine,
> To spoil thy peaceful Realm, and ruine all thy Line.
>
> But turn-Coat Time assists the Foe in vain,
> And, brib'd by thee, destroys their short-liv'd Reign,
> And to thy hungry Womb drives back thy Slaves again.
>
> Tho' Mysteries are barr'd from Laick Eyes,
> And the Divine alone, with warrant pryes,
> Into thy Bosom, where the truth in private lies.
>
> Yet this of thee the wise may freely say
> Thou from the virtuous nothing tak'st away,
> And to be part with thee the Wicked wisely pray.

Great Negative, how vainly would the Wise
Enquire, define, distinguish, teach, devise?
Didst thou not stand to point their dull Philosophies.

Is or is not, the two great ends of Fate,
And, true or false, the subject of debate,
That perfect, or destroy, the vast Designs of State.

When they have rack'd the *Politician's* Breast,
Within thy Bosom must securely rest,
And when reduc'd to thee, are least unsafe and best.

But, *Nothing*, why does *Something* still permit,
That sacred Monarchs should at Council sit,
With Persons highly thought at best at best for nothing fit?

Whilst weighty *Something* modestly abstains
From Princes' Coffers, and from States-Men's Brains,
And Nothing there like stately *Nothing* reigns.

Nothing, who dwell'st with Fools in grave disguise,
For whom they Reverend Shapes and Forms devise
Lawn sleeves, and Furs and Gowns, when they like
            thee look wise.

French Truth, *Dutch* Prowess, *Brittish* policy,
Hibernian Learning, *Scotch* Civility,
Spaniards Dispatch, *Danes* Wit, are mainly seen in thee.

The great Man's Gratitude to his best Friend,
King's Promises, Whores Vows, tow'rds thee they bend,
Flow swiftly into thee, and in thee ever end.[1]

Hobbes, in the fourth chapter of *Leviathan*, calls all other names, except those that signify bodies, sense-impressions, parts of speech or relations between words, 'insignificant sounds', or 'names of nothing'. 'Nothing' was what the priests and schoolmen had made the world reverence under such names as 'incorporeity', 'entities', and 'essences'. Rochester, in a flash of vision, sees this 'Nothing', as the oldest of all powers, incarnating itself in all the mummeries of religion and statecraft. Professor R. H. Griffith has truly written

[1] P., 77–79, 185, 6.

that the background of this poem is 'philosophy from Genesis to Plato through Aristotle and St. Augustine to Aquinas'.[1] It is a kind of ironical blasphemy, or to use an expression of Professor Philip Leon 'holy nonsense'. 'The humour of holy nonsense', Professor Leon writes 'is not what appears on the surface. It seems to make fun of the holy, but its deepest effect is to make us aware how comical are our ideas on the holy.' Rochester seems to make fun of the holy by applying its attributes to the Emptiness of a world from which spirit has been banished by the new science and the new philosophy. At a deeper level he is making fun of the Emptiness and so overcoming its horror, and at the same time ridiculing the absurd solemnities of the divines who were worshipping an abstraction (Blake's Nobodaddy) instead of a living God. The true descendant of this poem of Rochester's is Dryden's *Mac Flecknoe*, the first of his great satires. The subject of *Mac Flecknoe* is the majestic and heroic treatment of the kingdom of Dullness. Dryden's kingdom of Dullness is almost certainly derived from Rochester's Empire of Nothing. Indeed the following well-known lines in which Shadwell is described as heir to the kingdom seem to echo the fourteenth stanza of Rochester's poem:

> Besides his goodly fabric fills the eye
> And seems designed for thoughtless Majesty,
> Stately as monarch oaks that shade the plain
> And, spread in solemn state, supremely reign.

Here is Rochester's stanza:

> While weighty *Something* modestly abstains
> From Princes' coffers, and from States-men's Brains
> And Nothing there like stately *Nothing* reigns.

In fact the last line of this stanza may well have been the starting-point of Dryden's poem which is essentially a celebration of the reign of stately Nothing under the name of the kingdom of Dullness.

Rochester was a literary courtier of a new kind, not a writer like Sidney with a love and veneration of the chivalric traditions of his class and nation, but one, who, though he thoroughly relished the pleasures and privileges afforded by his rank, had not the slightest respect for the formalities that surrounded it, and clearly perceived the ugliness, emptiness and brutality of the society of which he was

[1] Ibid., 185, 186.

one of the born leaders. Etherege in his creation of Dorimant divined the paradox of Rochester's character. Like Rochester, Dorimant is both an 'honest man', that is a civilized gentleman, and a Machiavellian 'libertine' satisfying without scruple his insatiable appetite for power and pleasure. The following snatch of dialogue between Bellinda, Lady Townley and Emilia in *The Man of Mode* is an acute summary of this paradox:

L. TOWN.: He's a very well bred man.

BELL.: But strangely ill natur'd.

EMIL.: Then he's a very Witty man.

BELL.: But a man of no principles.[1]

What Etherege missed, or perhaps did not choose to attribute to his comic hero, was a third element in Rochester's character besides the well-bred, witty 'honest man' and the 'ill natur'd' libertine 'man of no principle'. This *tertium quid* saw both the courtly, charming world of 'honest men and women' and the life 'according to nature' of the 'libertines' in the cold light of Hobbes's philosophy as mere combinations of atoms moving according to the immutable laws of mathematics. Regarded in this way, the 'pleasure' and 'power' of the 'libertine' seemed as hollow and ridiculous as the 'honour' and 'courtesy' of the 'man of principle'. The sceptic in Rochester was, in fact, though at this stage he would probably have hated to admit it, already approaching the Christian moralist's condemnation of the 'world'.

Poetry, to survive, had to find a new orientation in the second half of the seventeenth century. The mythological material which had served our own Elizabethans and the poets of the Pléiade in France had become lifeless and frigid. Romantic and sensuous love-poetry was out of place in a mechanical and colourless universe. Symbolic and pictorial thinking was the traditional material of poetry, and now men were so proud of their new way of thinking in concepts that the poets came to despise, or at least only to tolerate, imaginative word pictures as a childish pursuit fit only for elegant triflers. Locke was soon to compare poetry with gaming as pursuits that 'seldom bring any advantage'.[2] The only kinds of subject-matter left for the serious poet, if he were unable to turn to religious themes and if he were not compelled, like

---

[1] Etherege, II, 225–6, cf. Underwood, 36–40, 73–5.   [2] Locke, q. Willey, 293 n.

Dryden, to write dramatic and official poetry, were realism and philosophic argument. There is poetry in these themes, but they are stubborn kinds of material for the imagination to subdue, and the task was doubly hard when the poet had no faith in the dignity of the human mind on the one hand or in the beauty of the world revealed by the senses on the other. Rochester's task was the poetic presentation of naked facts where distance lent no enchantment to the view. A similar task was to present itself to Wordsworth over a century later, but Wordsworth had at his disposal a philosophy of art which had grown up during several generations of discussion and experiment. He recognized the creative imagination as a living force which co-operated with a living universe revealed by the senses and thus created poetic material. Something about Rochester's views on aesthetics may be learnt from the preface written by his friend Robert Wolseley for his *Valentinian*. In this Preface Wolseley defends Rochester from an attack by Mulgrave on the subject-matter of his poem by denying that 'the Wit of a Poet' can be 'measured by the worth of his subject'. 'True Genius,' writes Wolseley in a notable passage which may well be a reminiscence of Rochester's conversation, 'like the *Anima Mundi*, which some of the Ancients believ'd, will enter into the hardest and dryest thing, enrich the most barren Soyl, and inform the meanest and most uncomely matter; nothing within the vast Immensity of Nature is so devoid of Grace, or so remote from Sence, but will obey the Formings of his plastick Heat, and feel the Operations of his vivifying Power, which, when it pleases, can enliven the deadest Lump, beautifie the vilest Dirt, and sweeten the most offensive Filth; this is a Spirit that blows where it lists, and like the Philosopher's Stone, converts into it self whatsoever it touches.'[1] This conception of 'Genius' is very close to the 'Imagination' of Wordsworth and Coleridge. But notice that the material on which it works is regarded as dead ('the deadest Lump'), and is only brought to life by the power of the poet's mind or 'genius'. For the poets of the Restoration the only method of dealing with realistic material was the method of satire. Satire comes naturally to imaginative minds in an age of rationalism and materialism. It arises from their '*sæva indignatio*' because they find themselves amid 'a universe' of death, from the contrast between their instinctive yearning towards beauty and

---

[1] V. sig. A 3v.

118

moral order and the ugly, non-moral world revealed to them by the pitiless vision of the naked reason. Satire, too, was the one kind of realistic poetry for which there was respectable classical precedent and good antique models. For an Englishman there was the famous example of Donne, not only in his formal satires, but in his ironic lyrics and elegies. So it is not surprising that Rochester's most considerable works in verse are realistic satires. The forms that appealed to him particularly are the dramatic monologue or dialogue. His histrionic ability served him here as it served him in his masquerade on Tower Hill. His most notable piece of irony in verse is his *Maim'd Debauchee*, a dramatic monologue which Browning himself never excelled. It must have been inspired by the sight of some worn-out voluptuary at Court like Jermyn or Brouncker, whose appearance and conversation suggested to the poet's mind the martial ardour of one of the battered old naval officers whom he had known in the Dutch Wars. The metre and style obviously parody those of Davenant's *Gondibert* with a side glance at Dryden's *Annus Mirabilis*, and there is also undoubtedly an allusion to two famous Odes of Horace (I, 5 and III, 26).

THE MAIM'D DEBAUCHEE

As some brave *Admiral*, in former War
Depriv'd of Force, but prest with Courage still,
Two Rival Fleets appearing from afar,
Crawls to the Top of an adjacent Hill.

From whence (with thoughts of full Concern) he views
The Wise and daring Conduct of the Fight:
And each bold Action to his mind renews,
His present Glory and his past Delight.

From his fierce Eyes flashes of Rage he throws,
As from black Clouds when Lightning breaks away,
Transported thinks himself amidst his Foes,
And absent, yet enjoys the bloody Day.

So when my Days of Impotence approach
And I'me by Love and Wines unlucky chance
Driv'n from the pleasing Billows of Debauch,
On the dull Shore of lazy Temperance,

My pains at last some respite shall afford,
While I behold the Battels you maintain;
When Fleets of Glasses sail around the Board,
From whose Broad-Sides Volleys of Wit shall rain.

Nor shall the sight of Honourable Scars,
Which my too forward Valour did procure,
Frighten new-listed Souldiers from the Wars,
Past Joys have more than paid what I endure.

Shou'd some brave Youth (worth being drunk) prove
    nice,
And from his fair inviter meanly shrink,
'Twould please the Ghost of my departed Vice,
If, at my Counsel, he repent and drink.

Or should some cold-complexion'd Sot forbid,
With his dull Morals, our Night's brisk Alarms;
I'll fire his Blood, by telling what I did
When I was strong, and able to bear Arms.

I'll tell of Whores attacqu'd their Lords at home,
Bawds Quarters beaten up, and Fortress won;
Windows demolish'd, Watches overcome,
And handsome Ills by my contrivance done.

With Tales like these I will such heat inspire,
As to important mischief shall incline:
I'le make him long some Ancient Church to fire,
And fear no Lewdness they're call'd to by Wine.

Thus Statesman-like I'le saucily impose,
And, safe from Danger, valiantly advise;
Shelter'd in impotence urge you to Blows,
And, being good for nothing else, be wise.[1]

This poem was truly described by Charles Whibley as 'a masterpiece of heroic irony'.[2] 'You can but say of it', writes the same admirable critic, 'that it bears the stamp of Rochester's vigour and

---

[1] P., 75, 76. Whitfield (34–7) has noted the subtle parody of Horace's *Quis te gracilis
puer*, but has missed the equally obvious allusion to *Vixi puellis nuper idoneus*.
[2] C.H.E.L., VIII, 215.

sincerity in every line.' It has the quality of one of the terrible
etchings of Goya, or of such a poem as Baudelaire's *Danse Macabre*.
Rochester's Maim'd Debauchee would have been at home among
the ancient dandies whom Baudelaire apostrophizes:

> Antinöus flétris, dandys à face glabre,
> Cadavres vernissés, lovelaces chenus,
> Le branle universel de la danse macabre
> Vous entraîne en des lieux qui ne sont pas connus!

The object of poetry of this kind is not like that of romantic
poetry to induce in the reader a dream-like condition. It aims at
bringing him close to actuality, and making him see and feel its
ugliness and absurdity and also its grandeur. There is none of what
Hobbes calls 'the frequencies of insignificant Speech'[1] here. Every
word has the weight of a battering-ram, the weight of passion and
feeling behind its conscious, rational meaning.

Rochester's most brilliant and finished social satire is *A Letter
from Artemisa in the Town to Cloe in the Country*.[2] Its setting is like
that of a scene from Etherege or Wycherley, a situation in the life
of the gay, sophisticated *beau-monde* of Restoration London, but
this situation is conceived by a stronger imagination than that of any
contemporary dramatist and the figures in it have the authentic life
of true poetry. The framework is provided by the conception of an
imaginary letter from a witty lady in London to her friend in the
country who has asked for an epistle in verse.

> *Cloe*, by your command in Verse, I write:
> Shortly you'l bid me ride astride, and fight:
> Such Talents better with our Sex agree,
> Than lofty flights of dangerous Poetry.
> Among the men, I mean the men of Wit,
> (At least they pass'd for such before they writ)
> How many bold Advent'rers for the Bays,
> Proudly designing large returns of Praise:
> Who durst that stormy, pathless World explore;
> Were soon dasht back and wreck'd on the dull shore,
> Broke of that little stock they had before.
> How wou'd a Womans tott'ring Barque be tost,
> Where stoutest Ships (the Men of Wit) are lost?

---

[1] Hobbes, III (*Leviathan*, I, i).   [2] P., 78–87.

Artemisa then proceeds to lecture herself on the dangers of writing verse:

> Dear *Artemisa*! Poetry's a Snare:
> *Bedlam* has many Mansions: have a care:
> Your Muse diverts you, makes the Reader sad:
> You think your self inspir'd; He thinks you mad.
> Consider too, 'twill be discreetly done,
> To make yourself the Fiddle of the Town.
> To find th'ill humour'd pleasure at their need:
> Curs'd when you fail, and scorn'd when you succeed.

But the temptation is too great and like an 'arrant woman' she is

> Pleased with the contradiction, and the sin,
> Methinks I stand on Thorns till I begin.

Cloe will naturally want to hear 'what Love has past in this lewd Town', and Rochester makes Artemisa begin her account with a panegyric of love and a lament for the state into which it has fallen that has a curious and pathetic personal ring. They remind us of Burnet's statement that Rochester was 'naturally modest, till the Court corrupted him'.[1] This is one of the most significant passages in Rochester's poetry. It is full of that combination of realism, idealism and disillusion which forms the real basis of his character.

> But how, my dearest *Cloe*, shou'd I set
> My Pen to Write; what I wou'd fain forget
> Or name that lost thing *Love*, without a Tear,
> Since so debauch'd by ill-bred-Customs here?
> *Love*, the most gen'rous Passion of the Mind;
> The softest Refuge Innocence can find;
> The safe Director of unguided Youth:
> Fraught with kind Wishes, and secur'd by Truth:
> That Cordial-drop Heav'n in our Cup hath thrown,
> To make the nauseous draught of life go down:
> On which one only blessing God might raise,
> In Lands of Atheists, Subsidies of Praise:
> For none did e'er so dull and stupid prove,
> But felt a God, and bless'd his Pow'r in Love:
> This only Joy, for which poor we are made,
> Is grown, like Play, to be an arrant Trade:
> The Rocks creep in, and it has got of late
> As many little Cheats, and Tricks, as that.

[1] B.H., I, xii, 264.

But what Artemisa specially deplores is that women are themselves
to blame for the present condition of love:

> Our silly Sex, who, born like Monarchs, free,
> Turn Gipsies for a meaner Liberty;
> And hate Restraint, tho' but from Infamy:

They are blamed because they subdue their natural inclinations and
voluntarily enslave themselves to fashion.

> 'Tis below Wit, they tell you, to admire;
> And ev'n without approving they desire.

After this prelude Artemisa comes to the core of her letter, which
is a brilliant sketch of an affected country lady whom she has met
on the previous night. This person is one of those paradoxical
characters that made a special appeal to the Restoration mind, a
mixture of folly, affectation, good sense and wit. She breaks into
the poem like a whirlwind:

> Where I was visiting the other Night,
> Comes a fine Lady, with her humble Knight,
> Who had prevail'd with her, through her own Skill,
> At his request, though much against his Will,
> To come to *London*—
> As the Coach stopt I heard her Voice, more loud
> Than a great-belly'd Woman's in a Croud;
> Telling the Knight that her Affairs require
> He, for some Hours, obsequiously retire.
> I think she was asham'd he shou'd be seen:
> Hard Fate of Husbands! the Gallant had been,
> Though a diseas'd, ill-favour'd Fool, brought in.
> Dispatch, says she, the business you pretend,
> Your beastly visit to your drunken Friend.
> A Bottle ever makes you look so fine:
> Methinks I long to smell you stink of Wine.
> Your Country-drinking Breath's enough to kill:
> Sour Ale corrected with a Lemmon Pill.
> Prithee farewell: we'll meet again anon.
> The necessary Thing bows, and is gone.
> She flies up stairs, and all the haste does show
> That fifty Antick Postures will allow,
> And then burst out—Dear Madam, am not I
> The strangest, alter'd Creature: Let me dye
> I find my self ridiculously grown,

> Embarrast with my being out of Town:
> Rude and untaught, like any Indian Queen;
> My Country Nakedness is strangely seen.

Like Cloe she wants news about the state of love, but instead of waiting for it launches into a discourse in praise of fools as husbands. Men of wit are to be avoided because they cannot rest content with being deceived, but must pry into their wives' affairs. It is the philosophy of Lady Fidget and her friends in Wycherley's *The Country Wife*:

> They little guess, who at our Arts are griev'd,
> The perfect joy of being well deceiv'd.

Then Rochester suddenly irradiates the prosaic atmosphere of the scene by one of those splendid images that raise him above every poet of his age except Dryden. Woman is conceived as the Irrational, and the Irrational is visualized as a night-bird that flies before the light of reason:

> Women should these, of all Mankind, avoid;
> For wonder, by clear Knowledge, is destroy'd.
> Woman who is an arrant Bird of night,
> Bold in the dusk, before a Fool's dull sight,
> Must flie, when reason brings the glaring light.

Then the lady breaks off her speech to run over to her hostess's pet monkey which is tied up by the window, and while she greets it with 'forty smiles' and as many 'antick bows', and makes it a 'fine tender Speech', Artemisa reflects on the character of this female Sir Fopling Flutter, and makes the wise observation (which was to be repeated by Dryden in his Epilogue to Etherege's famous play[1]) that really excellent fools are produced not by nature but by civilization:

> Nature's as lame in making a true Fop
> As a Philosopher, the very Top
> And Dignity of Folly we attain
> By studious search, and labour of the Brain:
> By Observation, Counsel and deep Thought:
> God never made a Coxcomb worth a Groat.
> We owe that Name to Industry and Arts;
> An eminent Fool must be a Fool of parts.

[1] Etherege, II, 288.

Here the visitor interrupts her reflections, and, leaving the monkey, makes a speech that shows that she is not such a fool after all. She stoutly maintains her thesis that the fool is the best sort of lover, and shows that however low a woman sinks she can always find a fool to deceive. In a mordant couplet, worthy of Byron, Rochester sums up the tragedy of much of the sexual life of his time:

> A Woman's ne're so ruin'd, but she can
> Be still reveng'd on her undoer, Man.

And to support her contention she tells the story of Corinna. The passage is a long one, but it must be quoted as the best example of sustained narrative in Rochester's poems.

> That wretched thing *Corinna*, who has run
> Through all the sev'ral ways of being undone:
> Cozen'd at first by Love, and living then
> By turning the too-dear-bought cheat on Men:
> Gay were the hours, and wing'd with joy they flew,
> When first the Town her early Beauties knew:
> Courted, admir'd, and lov'd, with Presents fed;
> Youth in her Looks, and Pleasure in her Bed:
> 'Till Fate, or her ill Angel, thought it fit
> To make her doat upon a man of Wit:
> Who found 'twas dull to love above a day;
> Made his ill-natur'd jeast, and went away.
> Now scorn'd of all, forsaken and opprest,
> She's a *Memento Mori* to the rest:
> Diseas'd, decay'd, to take up half a Crown
> Must mortgage her Long Scarf, and Manto Gown;
> Poor Creature, who unheard of, as a Flie,
> In some dark hole must all the Winter lye:
> And want, and dirt, endure a whole half year,
> That, for one month, she Tawdry may appear.
> In *Easter* Term she gets her a new Gown;
> When my young Master's Worship comes to Town;
> From Pedagogue, and Mother, just set free;
> The Heir and Hopes of a great Family:
> Who with Strong Beer and Beef, the Country rules;
> And ever since the Conquest, have been Fools:
> And now, with careful Prospect to maintain
> This Character, lest crossing of the Strain
> Should mend the Booby-breed; his Friends provide
> A Cousin of his own to be his Bride;

And thus set out,—
With an Estate, no wit, and a young Wife:
The solid Comforts of a Coxcomb's Life:
Dunghil and Pease forsook, he comes to Town,
Turns Spark, learns to be lewd, and is undone;
Nothing suits worse with Vice than want of sense:
Fools are still wicked at their own expence.
This o're-grown School-Boy lost-*Corinna* wins;
At the first Dash to make an Ass begins:
Pretends to like a Man that has not known
The Vanities or Vices of the Town:
Fresh in his youth, and faithful in his love,
Eager of joys which he does seldom prove:
Healthful and strong, he does no pains endure,
But what the Fair One he adores, can cure.
Grateful for Favour, does the Sex esteem,
And libels none for being kind to him.
Then of the lewdness of the Town complains,
Rails at the Wits, and Atheists, and maintains
'Tis better than good sense, than Pow'r, or Wealth
To have a blood untainted, youth, and health.
The unbred Puppy, who had never seen
A Creature look so gay, or talk so fine,
Believes, then falls in love, and then in debt:
Mortgages all, ev'n to the ancient Seat,
To buy his Mistress a new House for Life:
To give her Plate, and Jewels, robs his Wife.
And when to th' height of fondness he is grown,
'Tis time to poyson him, and all's her own.
Thus, meeting in her common Arms his Fate,
He leaves her Bastard Heir to his Estate:
And, as the Race of such an Owl deserves,
His own dull, lawful Progeny he starves.

Here is poetry made out of ugly and base subject-matter by means
of the vividness with which the poet imagines it and the energy and
vitality with which he expresses it. It is a sketch of contemporary
life and manners worthy of a Hogarth. Artemisa ends her letter by
promising to send Cloe more stories of the kind:

As, joyn'd to these, shall to a Volume swell;
As true as Heav'n, more infamous than Hell.

A draft of a satiric poem in Rochester's autograph among the

Portland manuscripts is in a very similar vein to Artemisa's letter.
Here again a woman is supposed to be the speaker and here again
bitter contempt of men is the main theme.

> What vaine unnecessary things are men
> How well we doe wth out em, tell me then
> Whence comes that meane submissivness wee finde
> This ill bred age has wrought on womankinde
> Fall'n from the rights their sex and beautyes gave
> To make men wish despaire & humbly crave.

There follows a vivid picture of the brutal sensuality of the typical
Restoration rakes:

> To the Pell Mell, Playhous nay the drawing roome
> Their Woemen Fayres, these Woemen Coursers come
> To chaffer, chuse, & ride theire bargaines home,
> Att the appearance of an unknown face
> Up steps the Arrogant pretending ass
> Pulling by th'elbow his companion Huff
> Cryes Looke, de God that wench is well enough
> Faire & well shapt, good lipps & teeth 'twill doe
> She shall be Tawdry for a month or two
> Att my expence, bee rude and take upon her
> Shew her contempt of quallity & honour
> And wth the generall fate of errant women
> Bee very proude awhile, then very Common.[1]

These lines show the obverse side of the Utopia of Gallantry.
Rochester had come to see that it was also the hell of the jaded and
bored sensualist.

None of Rochester's other social satires is as finished as Artemisa's letter, but the poem called *Timon, a Satyr* has very considerable merits. It has been said that this poem was the joint work of
Buckingham and Rochester, but the general conception, as well as
the style and versification show Rochester's hand in it everywhere.
It is suggested by Boileau's third satire, and is one of the pieces
sometimes cited to support the charge of plagiarism against
Rochester. Such a charge is really quite irrelevant. Rochester was
no more a plagiarist than Shakespeare, Milton or Dryden. Like those
great men he freely borrowed from his predecessors, but, when he
borrowed, he transmuted too. 'Sometimes', writes Burnet, 'other

---

[1] P., 116-212.

mens thoughts mixed with his Composures; but that flowed rather
from the Impressions they made on him when he read them, by
which they came to return upon him as his own thoughts, than that
he servilely copied from any. For few men ever had a bolder flight
of fancy, more steddily governed by Judgment, than he had.'[1]

Boileau's own poem is founded on a hint from Horace's eighth
satire of the second book, and, though Rochester knows both his
Horace and his Boileau, he is as original a poet as either of them.
Timon[2] in fact is a sketch of the life of London under Charles II as
Boileau's satire is a sketch of the life of Paris under Louis XIV. In
Boileau's work a poet is carried off by a bore to a supper party where
he has been promised that he shall meet Molière and Lambert. Instead he has to eat a wretched supper every course of which is
eulogized by his host, and listen to the inane conversation of two
country squires who imagine themselves to be great judges of
literature. Rochester's Timon is 'seiz'd i' th' Mall' by 'a dull dining
Sot' who promises him a dinner with some of the famous wits. Unlike Boileau's bore, he carries his victim off in a coach and on the
way reads him a dull satire which he insists on attributing to the
poet. This description is certainly a transcript of Rochester's own
dearly bought experience:

> He takes me to his *Coach*, and as we go;
> *Pulls* out a *Libel*, of a Sheet or two;
> Insipid, as, *The praise of pious queens*,
> Or *Shadwell's* unassisted former *Scenes*;
> Which he admir'd, and prais'd at ev'ry *Line*,
> At last it was so sharp it must be mine.

But there was worse to come. When they reach their destination
they discover that their company is to be as different from what
Timon had expected as that of two 'nobles campagnards' was from
Lambert and Molière:

> He askt, are *Sidley, Buckhurst, Savill* come?
> No, but there were above *Halfwit* and *Huffe*,
> *Kickum* and *Dingboy*, Oh 'tis well enough,
> They're all brave *Fellows* cryes mine *Host*, let's Dine,
> I long to have my *Belly* full of *Wine*,
> They'll write and fight I dare assure you;
> They're Men, *Tam Marte quam Mercurio*.

[1] B.S.P., 8.   [2] P., 99–104, 196.

128

Rochester's dislike of the Jingo element at Court and especially of
the blustering Mulgrave is probably reflected in these lines. But
Timon's oppressor has a horror in store for his guest which Boileau's
sufferer was spared. This is a middle-aged, affected wife:

> In comes my *Lady* strait, she had been *Fair*,
> Fit to give love, and (to) prevent despair,
> But *Age*, *Beauties* incureable Disease,
> Had left her more desire, than pow'r to please.
> As *Cocks* will strike, altho' their *Spurrs* be gone,
> She with her old bleer *Eyes* to smile begun:
> Though, nothing else, she (in despight of time)
> Preserv'd the affectation of her prime.

The lady talks of love and wonders how heaven can bless Louis XIV:

> A *Man* that lov'd two *Women* at one time.

The host professes to despise French wines and French cookery
and to praise an Englishman's hearty fare.

> Our own plain Fare, *and the best* Terse[1] *the* Bull
> *Affords, I'll give you and your* Bellies *full*:
> *As* for your *French* Kickshaws, Cellery, and Champoon,
> Ragous *and* Fricasses, introth w'ave none, . . .

The dinner realizes the worst fears aroused by this preface. It consists of a huge, hard piece of beef and enormous carrots with 'Pig,
Goose and Capon'.

> Served up with Sauces all of *Eighty Eight*
> When our tough *Youth* wrestled and threw the Weight.

The wine is wrapped in a wet clout instead of ice, and the host begins the conversation by boasting of his services as a colonel in the
Civil War. Rochester and the men of his generation must have had
to endure a lot of this kind of thing:

> And now the *Wine* began to work, mine *Host*
> Had been a *Collonel*, we must hear him boast
> Not of *Towns* won, but an *Estate* he lost
> For the *King's* Service, which indeed he spent
> Whoring, and Drinking, but with good intent.
> He talkt much of a Plot and *Money* lent
> In *Cromwel's* time . . .

[1] Claret.

His lady praises the manners and the poetry of her youth in the days
of Charles I. The poetry of today, she declares, is 'unfit for modest
ears', and contemporary youth only cares for 'small *Whores* and
Play'rs'. Like Clarendon she admires Falkland as the model of a
fine gentleman and her poet is 'easie' Suckling. When she quits the
room the gentlemen discuss literature. This is the best passage in
the poem. It is certainly Rochester's and a magnificent example of his
genius for satiric drama:

> *Halfwit* cries up my Lord of *Orrery*;
> Ah how well *Mustapha*, and *Zanger* dye!
> His sense so little forc'd, that by one *Line*,
> You may the other easily divine.
> > *And which is worse, if any worse can be,*
> > *He never said one word of it to me.*
> There's fine *Poetry*! you'd swear 'twere *Prose*,
> So little on the Sense, the Rhymes impose.
> Damn me (says *Dingboy*) in my mind *Gods swounds*,
> *Etherege* writes *Airy Songs*, and soft *Lampoons*,
> The best of any *Man*; as for your *Nowns*,
> *Grammar*, and Rules of Art, he knows 'em not,
> Yet writ two talking *Plays* without one *Plot*.
> *Huffe* was for *Settle*, and *Morocco* prais'd,
> Said rumbling words, like Drums, his courage rais'd.
> > *Whose broad built-bulks, the boystrous Billows bear,*
> > *Zaphee and Sally, Mugadore, Oran,*
> > *The fam'd Arzile, Alcazer, Tituan.*
> Was ever braver language writ by *Man*?
> > *Kickum* for *Crown* declar'd, said in *Romance*,
> He had outdone the very Wits of *France*.
> Witness *Pandion*, and his *Charles the Eight*,
> Where a young *Monarch*, careless of his Fate,
> Though Forreign Troops and *Rebels*, shock his State,
> Complains another sight afflicts him more
> (*Videl.*) The *Queen's Galleys* rowing from the *Shore*:
> > *Fitting their Oars and Tacklings to be gon;*
> > *Whilst sporting Waves smil'd on the rising Sun.*
> Waves smiling on the *Sun*! I am sure that's new,
> And 'twas well thought on, give the *Devil* his due.
> Mine *Host*, who had said nothing in an hour,
> Rose up and prais'd the *Indian Emperor*.
> > *As if our Old* World *modestly withdrew,*
> > *And here in private had brought forth a New.*

> There are two *Lines*! who but he durst presume
> To make the old *World* a withdrawing Room,
> Where of another *World* she's brought to *Bed*!
> What a brave *Midwife* is a *Laureat's* Head!

This is an astonishing feat. It is poetry made out of inane conversation. Rochester has discovered the beauty of pure silliness and enjoys it as much as a romantic poet would have enjoyed a flower or a sunset. Notice the ingenuity with which the quotations from the fashionable 'heroic' plays of Orrery, Settle, Crowne and Dryden are woven into the text and form an integral part of the satiric pattern.

From literature the conversation turns to international politics and war. Huffe champions the French, and Dingboy the Imperialists. Soon they come to blows. A greasy plate is thrown but 'Their Swords were safe', and they are left to 'cuff' till peace is restored and six fresh bottles are sent for. But by now Timon has had enough and makes his escape.

The satire called *Tunbridge Wells* has less unity of design than Artemisa's Letter or *Timon*, but it bears the authentic stamp of Rochester's keen observation and energetic expression. Hamilton's delightful description of the little watering-place as it was in the days of Charles II may serve as an introduction to the poem:

> Tunbridge is at the same distance from London as Fontainebleau is from Paris, and is, in the season, the general meeting-place of all the fair and the gallant of both sexes. The company, though always large, is always select: since those who go there in search of amusement are always more numerous than those who go there in search of health; every thing there breathes mirth and pleasure; constraint is banished, familiarity is established upon the first acquaintance, and the life that one leads is delicious. The visitors are accommodated with lodgings, in little, clean, and convenient houses, that lie straggling and apart from each other for a half a mile all round the Wells, where the company meet in the morning; this place consists of a long avenue of spreading trees, under which they walk when they drink the waters. On one side of this walk there is a long row of shops, supplied with all kinds of toys, lace, stockings and gloves, and where there is raffling, as in the Foire St. Germain; on the other side of the walk is the market: and, as it is the custom here for every person to choose and bargain for his own food, care is taken that nothing offensive appears on the stalls. Here young, fair, fresh-faced village girls, with clean, white linen, small straw hats, and neat shoes and stockings, sell game, vegetables, flowers

and fruit. Here one may live as well as one likes: here likewise, there is deep play and plenty of amorous intrigue. As soon as evening comes everyone quits his little palace to assemble on the bowling-green, where, in the open air, everyone who cares to, may dance on a turf that is softer and smoother than the finest carpet in the world.[1]

Rochester's *Tunbridge Wells* is dated 30 June 1675, in the old editions. It gives us a spirited panorama not of the rural beauty of the place but of the 'Fools, Buffons and Praters, Cuckolds, Whores, Citizens, their Wives and Daughters'.[2] Rising at five, Rochester, who has been ordered to drink the waters, rides over from London. At the Wells he finds a series of grotesque figures. Here is an apparition that greets him on the Lower Walk:

> A tall stiff Fool, that walk'd in Spanish guise;
> The Buckram Puppet never stir'd his Eyes,
> But grave as Owlct look'd, as Woodcock wise.
> He scorns the empty talk of this mad Age
> And speaks all Proverb, Sentences, Adage.
> Can with as great solemnity buy Eggs,
> As a Cabal can talk of their Intrigues . . .

Then there is a tribe of 'Curates, Priests, Canonical Elves,' and among them 'pert *Bayes*', or Samuel Parker, the High Church divine:

> He being rais'd to an Archdeaconry,
> By trampling on Religious Liberty,
> Was grown so fat, and look'd so big and jolly,
> Not being disturbed with care and melancholly,
> Tho' *Marvel* has enough expos'd his folly.

This allusion to Andrew Marvell's brilliant attack on Parker in the pamphlet called *The Rehearsall Transpros'd* is the only reference to Marvell in Rochester's works. It is interesting to set it beside Marvell's own high praise of Rochester as a satirist.[3] The best passage in *Tunbridge Wells* is, perhaps, the following admirable conversation piece:

> Here waiting for Gallant, young Damsel stood,
> Leaning on Cane, and Muffled up in Hood:
> That would be wit—whose business 'twas to woo,
> With Hat remov'd and solemn scrape of Shooe
> Bowing advanc'd, (and) then he gently shrugs,

---

[1] Hamilton, 294, 295.   [2] P., 87.   [3] See above, p. 75, and note 1.

And ruffled Foretop, he in order tugs;
And thus accosts her, 'Madam, methinks the Weather
Is grown much more serene since you came hither;
You influence the Heavens; and should the Sun,
Withdraw himself to see his Rays out-done,
Your Luminaries would supply the Morn,
And make a Day, before the Day be born.'
With Mouth screw'd up, and awkward winking Eyes,
And breast thrust forward; Lord, Sir, she replies:
It is your goodness, and not my deserts,
Which makes you shew your Learning, Wit and Parts.
He, puzzled, bites his Nails, both to display
The Sparkling Ring, and think what next to say:
And thus breaks out afresh. Madam I'gad
Your Luck, last Night, at Cards was mighty bad . . .

Equally vivid and amusing is the picture of the younger brothers.

Some warlike Men were now got to the Throng,
With Hair ty'd back, singing a bawdy Song:
Not much afraid, I got a nearer View,
And 'twas my Chance to know the dreadful Crew:
They were Cadets, that seldom did appear,
Damn'd to the stint of Thirty Pounds a Year.
With Hawk on Fist, or Greyhound led in Hand,
They Dog and Foot-boy sometimes do command;
But now having trim'd a Leash of spavin'd Horse,
With three hard-pincht-for Guineas in their Purse
Two rusty Pistols, scarf about the Arse—
Coat lin'd with Red, they here presum'd to swell;
This goes for Captain, that for Collonel.

Rochester alone among the satirists of his age seems to have eyes and ears. Dryden's satires live by their ironic arguments and their intellectual portraits. He never shows us what a group of his contemporaries looked like or how they talked. In Rochester's satires we see them and hear them as clearly as in Pepys's diary or in the plays of Etherege or Shadwell, but irradiated by the powerful light of a poet's imagination.

Closely akin to those social satires are the poems that may be called literary criticism in verse. This kind of writing was naturally fashionable in a society that delighted in the discussion of critical questions. We may notice that Rochester does not attempt the formal versified 'Essay in Criticism' like Boileau, Roscommon and

133

Pope. He does not discuss the abstract principles of criticism, but gives a series of penetrating and witty judgments on contemporary writers. He is always more at home with the particular and the concrete than with the general and the abstract. Like Swift's, his mind successfully resisted the Augustan tendency towards high-sounding generalizations. Twice he passes in review the chief authors of the day. In *A Session of the Poets*[1] he uses the style and metre of the popular lampoon or street ballad. The poem is not, as some old editions say, an 'Imitation of a Satyr of Boileau', but is modelled on Sir John Suckling's *A Session of the Poets*, written in the reign of Charles I, an amusing skit, the form of which seems to be derived from Boccalini's *De Ragguagli di Parnaso* published at Venice in 1612. *A Session of the Poets* is perhaps the best example of Rochester's use of the rough four-accent 'tumbling metre' which is the classic English form for this kind of poem. The poets appear before Apollo in turn, headed by that 'ancient grave wit', John Dryden. Each is hit off in a few witty lines that sum up their merits and defects with pitiless accuracy. Etherege is too idle, Wycherley too much of a gentleman, Shadwell too boastful, Lee strains too hard, Settle is too silly, Otway brags of the success of *Don Carlos* and Crowne is 'past sense of shame'. When others like the poetess Afra Behn and Tom d'Urfey have been dismissed, Apollo awards the laurel to Betterton, and the conclusion is a charming compliment to the great actor, which shows that Rochester fully appreciated both his artistic genius and his genuine, unassuming character.

An Allusion to Horace the 10th Satyr of the 1st Book,[2] already mentioned in connection with Rochester's quarrel with Dryden, is a much more important work. This was one of the poems which, in Dr. Johnson's words, 'began that adaptation, which has since been very frequent, of ancient poetry to present times'. It is not a translation of Horace's poem but an 'imitation' in which the Horatian theme is most happily adapted to contemporary English life. It was a method that was to produce such masterpieces as Pope's *Imitations of Horace* and Johnson's *Vanity of Human Wishes*. Horace's poem is, in the main, a protest against the slavish admirers of Lucilius who would not admit that their idol had any faults. It is a plea for the liberty of the critic to censure the shortcoming of writers with

---

[1] P., 104–7. See also *A Journal from Parnassus*, ed. Hugh Macdonald (P. S. Dobell), 1937.
[2] P. 95–98.

established reputations. Such a plea suited Rochester's independent spirit excellently. *An Allusion to Horace* is a rejection of the cant of the uncritical admirers of Dryden, but it is far more than this. It may be described as the manifesto of Rochester's literary creed, a plea for artistic integrity and a protest against playing to the gallery and the debasement of the poetic currency. One of the most interesting passages in the poem, and perhaps Rochester's most notable performance as a critic, is that in which he describes his ideal poetic style:

> But within due proportions circumscribe
> What e're you write; that with a flowing Tide,
> The *Style* may rise, yet in its rise forbear,
> With useless words, t'oppress the weary'd Ear.
> Here be your Language lofty, there more light,
> Your *Rethorick* with your *Poetry* unite:
> For *Elegance* sake, sometime allay the force
> Of *Epithets*, 'twill soften the discourse;
> A jeast in scorn, points out, and hits the thing,
> More home, than the *Morosest Satyrs* sting.

The style recommended here is one that can express passion without superfluous verbiage. It is to have the grace of easy unaffected speech. Shakespeare and Jonson are praised as models of this kind of writing, and in one of those sudden turns of thought in which Rochester delights, Etherege is declared to be excellent, although he does *not* imitate them:

> Whom refin'd *Etherege* coppy's not at all
> But is himself, a sheer *Original*.

One is reminded of Gerard Manley Hopkins's advice: 'Go thou and do otherwise.' Flatman is censured as a poor imitator of Cowley and Lee as a 'hot-brained *Fustian* Fool', and then in a memorable passage, Rochester draws a comparison between Shadwell and Wycherley, whom he considers to be the two best comic dramatists of the day:

> Of all our *Modern Wits* none seems to me,
> Once to have toucht upon true *Comedy*,
> But hasty *Shadwel*, and slow *Wicherley*,
> *Shadwells* unfinish'd works, do yet impart,
> Great proofs of force of *Nature*, none of Art;
> With just bold strokes he dashes here, and there,
> Shewing great *Mastery* with little Care,

And scorns to varnish his good Touches o're,
To make the *Fools* and *Women* praise 'em more.
But *Wicherley*, earnes hard what e're he gains,
He wants no judgement, nor he spares no pains;
He frequently excells, and at the least,
Makes fewer faults than any of the best.

This is poetic criticism like Drayton's of Marlowe and Shelley's of Coleridge; it seizes the essential qualities of its subject and expresses them in the living language of genius.

For Rochester, poetry and life were one, and Dryden seemed to him to be prostituting his genius by turning out verses to order without any real inspiration. He bids him bestow more care on his work and write to please not 'the vile *Rout*', but the 'few who know'.

Canst thou be such a vain mistaken Thing,
To wish thy *Works* might make a *Play-house* ring
With the unthinking Laughter, and poor praise,
Of *Fops* and *Ladies*, factious for thy *Plays*;
Then send a cunning *Friend* to learn thy doom,
From the shrewd Judges of the *Drawing Room*.

This itch for popularity in Dryden is compared by Rochester with his own scorn for it, and the poem ends with a superb affirmation of literary independence:

I loath the *Rabble*, 'tis enough for me,
If *Sedley, Shadwell, Sheppard, Wicherley,*
Godolphin, Butler, Buckhurst, Buckingham
And some few more whom I omit to name,
Approve my sense, I count their censure *Fame*.

It is worthy of notice that this passage has nothing whatever to do with the snobbery of an exclusive aristocracy. The Rabble to which Rochester refers is not the common folk. The preceding verses show that it refers to the senseless courtiers and fine ladies, the 'shrewd judges' of the drawing-room. The aristocracy for which Rochester wanted to write is an aristocracy of brains and taste. It includes the plebeian professional authors, Shadwell and Butler as well as the Duke of Buckingham, Lord Buckhurst and Sir Charles Sedley.

In this poem Rochester shows that he is one of the first of the great Augustans as well as one of the last of the great Metaphysicals.

Pope censured its versification,[1] but Rochester's aim in versification was not the same as Pope's. He is not trying to give an impression of high finish. His verses are meant to be read or recited rapidly. The sense carries the reader forward on 'a flowing tide', and the occasional imperfect rimes and assonances and the frequent triplets add to the impression of variety and copious energy. There can be no doubt that the *Allusion to Horace* was an important influence on the development of Pope's genius. This was the kind of poetry which the Augustans were always trying to write, poetry that has the grace, the coolness, the ease and the equable flow of good conversation. We seem to hear Rochester talking to his friends as he must have talked often at Will's or the Rose, but the talk has somehow glided into the mould of easily flowing and harmonious verse.

[1] Spence, 213.

Chapter Seven

———⟨⟨◆⟩⟩⟨⟨◆⟩⟩———

DOUBT'S BOUNDLESS SEA

———⟨⟨◆⟩⟩⟨⟨◆⟩⟩———

He used to say that 'when he came to Brentford, the devill entred into him and never left him till he came into the country again to Alderbury or Woodstock'. Once a year in the summer he would go back to his own country, and there, according to Aubrey, he was 'generally civill enough'.[1] Indeed one has the curious impression sometimes that there were two different Earls of Rochester, the wild poet and rake of Whitehall and Covent Garden, and the respectable country gentleman who had married a lady of his own class and lived the life of his ancestors, hunting, hawking and dancing among his neighbours, becoming 'Gamekeeper of the County of Oxford' and obtaining 'the Grant of four bailiwicks in Whittlewood Forest'.[2]

Sometimes, indeed, he was bored by country life and angered by its stupidities. Some lines that he is supposed to have 'spoken extempore to a country clerk after hearing him sing psalms' at Bodicot near Adderbury express his disgust at the quality of the music in country churches and of the poetry of the old metrical version of the psalms that was still in use.

> *Sternhold* and *Hopkins* had great Qualms,
> When they Translated *David's Psalms*,
>   To make the Heart full glad:
> But had it been poor *David's* Fate,
>   To hear thee Sing and them Translate,
> By G— 'twould have made him Mad.[3]

---

[1] Aubrey, II, 304.   [2] C.S.P.D., 1667–8, 253, 343; C.T.B., 1667–8, 320, 566.
[3] P., 148, 229; Longueville, 273.

A story is told that he was once bitten by a dog, and that the worst he said to the animal was, 'I wish you were married and living in the country'. Local tradition preserved some anecdotes of the ways in which the 'mad Earl' amused himself in the country. These stories recall Robert Wolseley's description of the 'strange facility' Rochester 'had to talk to all capacities in their own Dialect, and make himself good Company to all kind of people at all times'.[1] Once he is said to have disguised himself as a tinker and walked from Adderbury to Burford where he once went to school. Here he collected from the villagers a number of pots and pans which he promised to mend. Instead he knocked the bottoms out and the irate villagers seized him and put him in the stocks. He then succeeded in sending a man to Adderbury with a note to Lord Rochester. Soon after, his coach and four arrived, his servants dug up the stocks and released him, and he drove home. The good people of Burford, however, suffered no loss, as new pots and pans soon arrived from the Earl to replace those which he had spoilt. On another occasion he disguised himself as a beggar, and, meeting another member of the fraternity on a country road, he asked him where he was going. The real beggar said he was going to Lord Rochester's, but it was not much use as he never gave anything to beggars. Rochester offered to accompany him. When the pair reached Adderbury, the beggar modestly went in by the back door. Rochester quickly went round to the front and told the servants to seize the visitor and put him in a great barrel of beer. Every time the unfortunate man put his head up, the Earl threatened to knock it down again. Finally he relented. The beggar was taken out of the barrel, given a good meal and a new suit of clothes, and told never to say again that Lord Rochester was ungenerous.

In the first years of his married life his country seat was the old house on the green at Adderbury, near Banbury, which his father had left him. Thither Elizabeth Malet after her brief springtime of gaiety at Court went to live the humdrum life of a country squire's wife, and there she gave birth to four children, a girl, called Anne, in the summer of 1669, an only son, Charles, who was baptized on 2 January 1671, a second daughter, Elizabeth, in 1674, and a third, Mallet, in 1675.[2]

---

[1] The first story comes from Longueville, 267, and the other two from Gepp, 59. The quotation by Wolseley is from V., sig. A 4.

[2] D.N.B., s.a. John Wilmot, Earl of Rochester; Prinz, 239, 240.

The old Countess, Rochester's mother, seems to have lived sometimes at Ditchley and sometimes at Adderbury. It would appear
from some of the Earl's letters to his wife, that at first she did
not get on very well with her daughter-in-law. The old lady must
have been somewhat of a trial to the young people. Once Rochester tells his wife not 'to bee too much amazd at the thoughts my
mother has of you, since being meere immaginations they will as
easily vanish as they were groundlessly created'.[1] From another
letter we learn that once he fled, presumably to avoid a family
'scene':

> Runn away like a rascall without taking leave, deare wife, it is an
> unpollish'd way of proceeding wch a modest man ought to bee asham'd
> of, I have left you a prey to your owne immaginations, amongst my
> Relations, the worst of damnations; but there will come an hower of
> deliverance, till when, may my mother bee mercifull upon you, soe I
> committ you to what shall ensue, woman to woman, wife to mother, in
> hopes of a future appearance in glory; . . .[2]

The gentle humour of this letter is characteristic of much of
Rochester's correspondence with his wife. His letters (which unfortunately are undated) are full of domestic details, presents sent
from London to the Countess, commissions given by her to her
husband, affectionate messages to the children and money matters.
One of the most charming, a little masterpiece of tender *badinage*,
is an acknowledgment of some pictures:

> Dear Wife, I receiv'd y^r three pictures & am in a greate fright least they
> should bee like you, by the biggnes of ye heade I should apprehend
> you farr gone in ye Ricketts, by the severity of the Count'nance, som-
> what inclin'd to prayer & prophesy, yett there is an alacrity in the plump
> cheeke, that seemes to signify sack & sugar, & the sharp sighted nose
> has borrowed quickness from the sweete & melting eye, I never saw a
> chin smile before, a mouth frowne, & a forhead mump, truly ye Artist
> has done his part, (god keep him humble) & a fine man hee is if his
> excellencyes doe not puff him up like his pictures; the next impertin-
> ence I have to tell you is that I am coming down to you I have gott
> horses but want a coach when that defect is supply'd you shall quickly
> have the trouble of
> Y^r humble servant.
> Present my duty to my Lady & my humble service to my Sister,
> my brother, & all the Babyes, not forgetting Madam Jane.[3]

[1] H., 260.   [2] Ibid., 192.   [3] Ibid., 228.

It is curious to find that Rochester, who is usually considered to be the most profligate of English poets, is also one of the most domestic. His little notes to his wife reveal a side of his character that would be hardly suspected if we knew of him only from the descriptions of Hamilton and Pepys. To her he opened his heart as he opened it to no one, except, perhaps, to his friend Henry Savile. A fragment of a letter addressed to her is perhaps the most self-revealing statement in the whole of his correspondence:

> . . . so greate a disproportion 'twixt our desires & what is ordained to content them; but you will say this is pride & madness, for theire are those soe intirely satisfyed with theire shares in this world, that theire wishes nor theire thoughts have not a farther prospect of felicity & glory, I'le tell you were that mans soule plac't in a body fitt for it, hee were a dogg, that could count anything a benifitt obtain'd wth flattery feare, & service,
>
> > Is there a man yee gods whome I doe hate
> > Dependance & Attendance bee his fate
> > Lett him bee busy still & in a crowde
> > And very much a slave & very proude.[1]

Here is indeed the true Rochester, a spirit full of boundless aspiration after 'felicity and glory' and of boundless contempt for meanness and servility. At the end of this fragment he writes: 'I would not have you lose my letter; it is not fitt for every body to finde.' Lady Rochester appears to have destroyed the first sheet of it. Probably that sheet contained daring reproaches against the power that made 'so great a disproportion' between our desires and 'what is ordained to content them'. The fact that Rochester wrote thus to his wife shows that he believed her to be capable of understanding him and that he had complete faith in her. That these pleasant domestic relations should suffer some interruptions was inevitable. According to Rochester, Lady Warre, his mother-in-law, was the cause of the trouble, and he accuses her of visiting Lady Rochester once a year and bewitching her for eleven months after.[2] No doubt such visitors told tales about the wild life that the Earl lived in London,

---

[1] Ibid., 191. The four lines of verse in this letter are slightly misquoted from a translation by Cowley of a poem by Martial appended to his essay 'Of Liberty' (*Essays, Plays and Poems* by A. Cowley, ed. Waller, Cambridge University Press, 386, 387). The abbreviation 'Cow' is written in the margin against the passage in the MS. See D. Vieth, letter in T.L.S., 12 Oct. 1951.

[2] Ibid., 245.

and then he would be in disgrace at Adderbury. What annoyed him especially was the cant concerning 'heroic' virtue which these friends of Lady Rochester endeavoured to instil into her mind. He writes a long letter expressing his contempt of this kind of sentimentality and asking his wife to consider

> how men & woemen are compounded, that as heate and cold, soe greatness and meanness are necessary ingredients that enter into the making up of everyone that is borne, now when heat is predominant we are term'd hott, when cold is, wee are call'd cold; though in the mixture both take theire places, els our warmeth would bee a burning, & our cold an excessive freezing, soe greatness or virtue that sparke of primitive grace is in every one alive, & likewise meaness or vice that seede of originall sin is (in a measure) alsoe; for if either of them were totally absent, men & woemen must bee perfect angels, or absolute divills. . . .[1]

On the other hand it is certain that Lady Rochester must have suffered a great deal from her husband's uncertain and capricious temper as well as from his numerous infidelities, and the few of her letters that survive are in a somewhat pathetic strain. She seems to have been a brave and patient woman, who was always endeavouring to please a husband, who, in some moods, could not be pleased. The following undated letter from her to the Earl deserves to be quoted:

> If I could have been troubled att any thing when I had the happyness of resceiving a letter from you I should be soe because you did not name a time when I might hope to see you: The uncertainty of which very much aflicts me whether this ode kind of proceeding be to try my patience or obedyence I cannot but guesse, but I will never faile of ether where my duty to you requier them, I doe not think you design staying att bath now that it is like to be soe full and God knows when you will find in your hart to leave the place you are in: pray consider with your selfe wheather this be a reasonable way of proceeding and be pleased to lett me know what I am to expect for thear being soe short a time between this and the next sitting of the Parlemant. I am confident you will find soe much bussines as will not allow you to come into the country thearfore pray lay your commands upon me what I am to doe and though it be to forgett my children and the long hopes I have lived in of seeing you, yet I will endeavour to obey you Or in the memory only torment myselfe without giving you the trouble of puting you in mind that thear lives such a creature as your faithful
>
> humble,[2]

[1] Ibid., 247. [2] Ibid., 261.

There are several passages in his letters that show that he often felt remorse for his treatment of his wife. In one of these he writes the following significant words:

> My most neglected Wife, till you are a much respected Widdow, I find you will scarce bee a contented Woman, and to say noe more than the plaine truth, I doe endeavour soe fairly to do you that last good service, that non but the most impatient would refuse to rest satisfy'd.[1]

He had a habit of extemporizing in verse and a number of little comic impromptus have been ascribed to him. One of them is the following reply which he is said to have dispatched 'to his Lady, who sent a servant on purpose desiring to hear from him, being very uneasy at his long silence'.

> To his more than meritorious Wife
> I am by fate, slave to your will,
> And I will be obedient still.
> To shew my love, I will compose ye,
> For your fair fingers ring a posey.
> In which shall be express'd my duty,
> And how I'll be for ever true t'ye;
> With low made legs and sugar's speeches,
> Yielding to your fair bum the breeches,
> To prove myself in all I can
> Your faithful humble servant,
> John.[2]

When he is lying ill and unhappy in London it is of his wife at Adderbury that he thinks, and the following letter, one of the most touching that he wrote, is a testimony to the real strength of his attachment:

> Deare Wife
> I recover soe slowly, and relaps so continually that I am allmost weary of my self, if I had the least strength I would come to Adderbury, but in the condition I am, Kensington and back is a voyage I can hardly support; I hope you excuse my sending you noe money, for till I am well enough to fetch itt myself they will not give mee a farthing, & if I had not pawn'd my Plate, I beleive I must have starv'd in my sickness, well god Bless you & the Children whate'r becomes of
> y^r humble
> servant
> Rochester.[3]

[1] Ibid., 245.   [2] P., 148.   [3] H., 214, 215.

From another note it is pleasant to learn that Rochester, in spite of financial difficulties, kept his wife's estate entirely for her own use and that of her children:

'I know nott', he writes, 'who has perswaded you that you want five pounds to pay a Servants wages, but next weeke Blancourt is going into the West, att whose returne you may expect an Account of y^r intire revenue, wch I will be bound to say has hitherto, & shall (as Long as I can gett bread without itt) bee wholly imployed for the use of y^{r}self & those who depend on you, if I prouve an ill steward att least you never had a better, wch is some kind of satisfaction to
Your humble servant.[1]

In days when a wife's estate was considered to be legally and morally her husband's property, Rochester's attitude reveals a sense of justice far in advance of the accepted ethics of the age, and shows that in some respects he had a good deal more practical morality than many of the severe critics of his ways of living.

His affection for his children appears in many passages in his letters to his wife. There were great rejoicings at Adderbury when his son Charles was born. The child was baptized on 2 January 1670/1 and Buckhurst and Sedley were his godfathers.[2] He grew up to be a pretty, delicate, intelligent boy who must have been very like Rochester himself when he was a child. We hear of the Duke of Monmouth, giving him 'a fine little horse' and walking with him and his father in the Park at Woodstock.[3] Two letters from Rochester to his son have been preserved. They are among the most delightful that he ever wrote. The first seems to have been sent with a tutor whom Rochester had engaged:

I hope Charles when you receive this, and know that I have sent this gentleman to bee y^r tutour, you will be very glad to see I take such care of you, and bee very gratefull, wch is best showne in beeing obedient & dilligent, you are now grown bigg enough to bee a man, if you can bee wise enough; & the way to bee truly wise is to serve god, Learne y^r booke and observe the instructions of y^r Parents first and next y^r Tutour, to whom I have intirely resign'd you for this seven yeare, and according as you imploy that time, you are to bee happy or unhappy for ever; but I have soe good an opinion of you y^t I am glad to thinke you will never deceive me, dear Child Learne y^r Booke, & bee obedient,

& you shall see what a father I will bee to you. you shall want noe pleasure while you are good, & that you may be soe are my Constant Prayers.

Rochester.

The other letter seems to have been written when the little Lord Wilmot was staying with his grandmother, the old Countess:

> Charles, I take itt very kindly that you write to mee (though seldome) & wish heartily you would behave y^r selfe soe as that I myght show how much I love you wth out being asham'd; Obedience to y^r grandmother & those who instruct you in good things, is the way to make you happy here & for ever, avoyde Idleness, scorn Lying, & God will Bless you, for wch I pray.

Rochester.[1]

It is hard to believe that these letters were written by the wild libertine whose defiance of traditional morality was a byword at Court, the man whom Henry Savile tells us was elected the 'Generall' of the Ballers, the fastest set in Restoration London.[2] But they are not the letters of a hypocrite. Rochester, like Milton's Satan,

Saw

> Vertue in her shape how lovly, saw and pin'd
> His loss . . .

One of the most curious stories told about Rochester is the fairly well-authenticated report that he persuaded his wife to join the Roman Catholic Church. There is no doubt whatever that Lady Rochester became a Roman Catholic and reverted to Protestantism at the time of her husband's last illness. Burnet states that 'he himself (i.e. Rochester) had been not a little instrumental in procuring it[3] (i.e. Lady Rochester's 'perversion'). The strangest part of the story is the allegation that Stephen College, afterwards notorious at the time of the Popish Plot agitation as 'the Protestant Joiner', was somehow concerned in bringing about Lady Rochester's change of religion. College stated in 1681 to William Clarke of Sandford, who was one of the trustees of Rochester's estate, that 'being 14 years since a trooper under the Earl of Rochester, my lord employed him to bring Tomson, a priest, to his lady to pervert her, and that he did so several times and by means of that priest she was perverted'.[4]

---

[1] H., 249–51. [2] W., 31. [3] B.S.P., 143.
[4] C.S.P.D., 1680–1, 415, 416, cf. also 406, 409, 420. Williams in his *Rochester* gives a more circumstantial account of the affair, but quotes no authority.

If we can believe College, this event took place in 1667, shortly after Rochester's marriage, when he was commanding a troop of horse in Prince Rupert's regiment, in which apparently College was serving as a trooper. Rochester's action seems inconsistent with the strongly anti-Catholic tone of some of the poems ascribed to him. One possible motive may have been that he was convinced that Catholicism would triumph in England on the accession to the throne of the Catholic Duke of York, or, perhaps, even earlier, and that, if the Countess survived him, she would have a better chance of obtaining royal protection and favour than if she remained a Protestant. Another possibility is that, as a freethinker, he regarded all religions as different forms of 'opium for the people', but, like Byron, favoured Catholicism as a good religion for women because it 'is by far the most elegant worship, hardly excepting the Greek mythology. What with incense, pictures, statues, altars, shrines, relics, and the real presence, confession, absolution,—there is something sensible to grasp at'.[1]

Rochester often visited his wife's estates in Somerset. Both the Earl and the Countess were at Enmore, their Somersetshire house, in the summer of 1672, and we have a delightful glimpse of festivities in June of that year, when in honour of a friend's birthday they caused 'the bell to be rung' and gave a great dinner after which there were sixteen dances and 'because the weather was hot', the dancing took place in the forecourt and the garden as well as the hall.[2] But Rochester did not go into the West only for merry-making. He took his duties as a Somersetshire landlord seriously. As early as August 1670, we find him at the head of a number of gentlemen whose manors adjoined the 'Chase of Kingswood, Co. Gloucester', petitioning the King because a certain Sir Baynham Throckmorton instead of getting a patent for the rangership, had obtained a lease of sixty years (contrary to all former example) of all the King's rights and oppressed the commoners and cottagers.[3] This action shows that Rochester had a sense of the responsibilities attached to his rank with which he has been rarely credited, and it accords ill with the picture of the heartless Court fribble perpetuated by eighteenth- and nineteenth-century biographies. At any rate his neighbours in the West seem to have trusted him. On 30 October

---

[1] *Byron, a Biography* by L. A. Marchand (1957), 977, 978.
[2] H.M.C., Rutland MSS. at Belvoir Castle, II, 25, 26.
[3] H.M.C., 5th Rep. App., 324.

1672, he was appointed Deputy Lieutenant of Somerset and in November 1677, he was elected an Alderman of Taunton.[1] He held various offices also in his own county of Oxford. On 28 February 1668, he was appointed Gamekeeper for the county of Oxford.[2] The posts that he coveted, however, were those of Keeper and Ranger of the ancient and royal hunting-forest of Woodstock near his ancestral estate. These two offices were granted on 2 November 1674, to Lord Lovelace, but on 27th of the following February the grant was revoked in so far as it concerned the rangership, which was now given to Rochester. On 2 May his triumph was complete and he received the keepership as well.[3] Rochester's principal object in seeking these offices was, no doubt, to obtain possession of the pretty old High Lodge at the west end of Woodstock Forest, which was the Ranger's official residence. The lodge commands one of the finest views in Oxfordshire over the great forest 'Walk' that runs between magnificent expanses of oaks stretching towards Witney and the distant blue Cotswolds.[4] Here Rochester could retreat, when he was in the country, from the house at Adderbury, which was now full of children, and often, doubtless, of relations. Here he could be at peace among his books and often spend, as Burnet writes 'some months wholly imployed in Study, or the Sallies of his Wit'.[5] He decorated the old lodge according to his taste, and Aubrey writes

---

[1] C.S.P.D., 1672, 101; Marvell, II, 331.   [2] See above, p. 138.
[3] C.S.P.D., 1673–5, 182, 238.
[4] It is still in existence, though structurally somewhat altered. An engraving made in 1732 probably gives a fair idea of the appearance of the house in Rochester's time. When I visited it in 1934 by kind permission of the Duke of Marlborough I found there an old fourposter bed and a sword which were supposed to have belonged to Rochester.
[5] B.S.P., 25. If we can believe Thomas Hearne, the Earl sometimes amused himself with the village girls at Woodstock. Under the date 8 Jan. 1725/6, he records that Rochester 'among the girls us'd the body of Nell Browne of Woodstock, who, tho' she look'd pretty well when clean, yet was a very nasty, ordinary, silly Creature, wch made people much admire'. (H.R.C., IX, 78, 79.) The tone of this piece of gossip suggests that it may have come to Hearne from some old woman at Woodstock, who, after nearly half a century, still resented the favour shown by Rochester to pretty Nell Browne. In the same place (H.R.C., IX, 78) Hearne also tells a story of a rather disgusting prank alleged to have been played by Rochester and his friends at Woodstock. As this story is mere gossip retailed about forty-five years after Rochester's death, I relegate it to a note: 'Once the wild Earl of Rochester, and some of his Companions, a little way from Wood-stock, meeting in a morning with a fine young Maid going with butter to Market, they bought all the butter of her, and paid her for it, & afterwards stuck it against a tree, wch the Maid perceiving, after they had gone, she went & took it off, thinking it a pity that it should be quite spoil'd. They observ'd her, & riding after her, soon overtook her, &, as a punishment, set her upon her head & clapt the Butter upon her Breech.'

that 'his lordship had severall lascivious pictures drawen' there.[1]
Buckingham, Buckhurst, Savile and Fleetwood Shepherd were frequent vistors. Rochester was no mere bookworm; he delighted in outdoor sports. His addiction to the ancient pastime of falconry received
official recognition when he was appointed on 24 January 1674/5
'Master, Surveyor and Keeper' of the King's Hawks. On 8 October
1677 Buckingham in a letter from Cliveden wrote that he would
'imediatly wayte upon' him 'with the best pack of Hownds that ever
ran upon English grownd'.[2]

Rochester's health, which had never been robust, declined steadily
from about 1671 onward. The venereal disease which he had contracted early in life was probably aggravated rather than mitigated
by the prescriptions of contemporary physicians, and he appears to
have been consumptive as well. A constitution of this kind could not
stand up for long against the strain of the life of pleasure at Whitehall and Covent Garden.

One day in September, 1671, he had suddenly walked out of
Garraway's coffee-house where he had been sitting with John Mud-
diman, Killigrew, and other merry friends,[3] and posted down to the
country, where he suffered much from trouble in his eyes. This
physical change was accompanied by a mental development. The life
of pleasure became more and more distasteful to him. He had
accepted the materialism of Hobbes and had applied it to the art of
living. It led logically to complete egoism, and in one of his poems
this egoism is stated frankly and with a boldness that must have
shocked many who practised it in their lives, but who never had the
courage to admit such principles openly. The poem is entitled *A
Very Heroical Epistle in Answer to Ephelia*:

> Madam,
>> If you're deceiv'd it is not by my Cheat,
>> For all disguises are below the Great.
>> What *Man* or *Woman* upon *Earth* can say
>> I ever us'd 'em well above a Day?
>> How is it then, that I unconstant am?

---

[1] Aubrey, II, 304. Grants were made to Rochester for the repairs to 'the King's Lodge
at Woodstock' on 23 June 1675 and 20 Feb., 1679/80. See C.T.B. 1672–5, 761 and 1679–
1680, 438.
[2] For Rochester's appointment as Master of the Hawks see C.T.B. 1672–5, 655, 688;
for Buckingham's letter H., 274, Prinz, 278.
[3] H.M.C., Bath Papers at Longleat, 152, 153.

He changes not, who always is the same.
In my dear self I center ev'ry thing,
My *Servants*, *Friends*, My *M^rs* and my *King*,
Nay Heav'n, and *Earth* to that one poynt I bring.
Well manner'd, honest, generous, and stout,
Names by dull *Fools*, to plague Mankind found out;
Shou'd I regard, I must myself constrain.
And 'tis my *Maxim* to avoid all pain.
You fondly look for what none e're cou'd find,
Deceive your self, and then call me unkind;
And by false Reasons, wou'd my falshood prove,
For 'tis as natural to change, as love:
You may as justly as the *Sun* repine,
Because alike it does not often shine:
No glorious thing, was ever made to stay,
My Blazing *Star* but visits, and away.
As fatal to(o) it shines, as those i' th' Skyes,
'Tis never seen, but some great *Lady* dyes,
The boasted favour you so precious hold,
To me's no more than changing of my Gold;
What e're you gave, I paid you back in Bliss,
Then where's the Obligation pray of this?
If heretofore you found grace in my *Eyes*,
Be thankful for it, and let that suffice
But *Woman*, *Beggar like*, still haunt[s] the Door,
Where they've received a *Charity* before.
Oh happy Sultan! whom we barb'rous call,
How much refin'd art thou above us all!
Who envies not the Joys of thy *Serail?*
Thee like some God! the trembling Crowd adore,
Each Man's thy *Slave* and *Woman kind* thy *Whore* . . .[1]

If only he could have been an Oriental monarch, enjoying the life of the senses under perfect conditions. Instead, he was lying at Woodstock, with a shattered body and a tortured, restless mind. His dream of Oriental luxury was the will-o'-the-wisp of the defeated sensualist. Wherever he had been, he would have been bored and unhappy. The life of the senses, as Rochester's contemporary, Pascal, showed in his *Pensées* (published in 1670) is only endurable while the mind is distracted. When the sensualist comes to be alone with himself, he finds no spring of happiness within, but only desolation.

[1] P., 44, 45.

Mais quand j'y ai regardé de plus près, j'ai trouvé que cet éloignement que les hommes ont du repos, et de demeurer avec eux-mêmes, vient d'une cause bien effective; c'est-à-dire du malheur naturel de notre condition faible et mortelle, et si miserable que rien ne peut nous consoler, lorsque rien ne nous empêche d'y penser, et que nous ne voyons que nous. . . .

Mais pour ceux qui n'agissent que par les mouvemens qu'ils trouvent en eux et dans leur nature, il est impossible qu'ils subsistent dans ce repos, qui leur donne lieu de se considérer et de se voir, sans être incontinent attaqués de chagrin et de tristesse. *L'homme qui n'aime que soi ne hait rien tant que d'être seul avec soi. Il ne recherche rien que pour soi, et ne fuit rien tant que soi; parce que, quand il se voit, il ne se voit tel qu'il se désire, et qu'il trouve en soi-même un amas de misères inévitables, et un vide de biens réels et solides, qu'il est incapable de remplir.*[1]

The words which I have italicized describe exactly the state of mind in which Rochester found himself in the latter years of his life. He was alone with himself, and he was miserable. For the ordinary mind, which hardens and becomes static, when it reaches a certain stage of development, materialism and egoism, politely masked by the disguises of conventional religion and good manners, might suffice. But Rochester's mind was not an ordinary one. It had in it what Chapman called that 'strangely-intellectuall fire' which must be fed with living experience, by significant emotion. He had found that emotion once, in love-making and the aesthetic satisfactions of the life of pleasure. But those satisfactions could no longer content his restless and aspiring spirit. Already, as we have seen in his satires, he had come to see through the world of pleasure and to recognize and despise the ugliness and folly that lay behind it. In that recognition too he found significant emotion for a while. Now, when he was alone with himself, it developed into misanthropy, the end of the cul-de-sac of which materialism had been the beginning. It was in this mood of misanthropy—hatred of the world, hatred of himself and complete scepticism—that his greatest poem was written. The first sketch for it may, perhaps, be found in the following lines published anonymously as a broadside under the title, 'On Man: A Satyr By a Person of Honour':

> To what Intent and Purpose was Man made,
> Who is by Birth to Misery betray'd!
> That in the slender Course of life runs thrô

---

[1] Pascal, I, vii.

More Plagues than all the Land of *Egypt* knew.
Doctors, Divines, great Dispensations, Punns,
Ill-lookt Citizens, and scurvy Dunns;
Conceited Laureats, dull, long Opera's,
And those that ne'er were Poets, yet write Plays.
Insipid Squires, fat Bishops, Deans and Chapters,
Enthusiasts, Prophecies, new Rants and Raptures;
Pox, Gout, Catarrhs, old Sores, Cramps, Rheums
        and Aches,
Half-witted Lords, double-chinn'd Bawds, and Patches;
Illiterate Courtiers, Chancery-suits for Life,
A tracing Whore, and a most tedious Wife.
Raw Innes-of-Court Men, empty Fops, Buffoons,
Bullies Robust, raw Aldermen, and Clowns.
Gownmen that argue about, discuss, and prate
And vent dull Notions of a future State;
Sure of another World and do not know
Whether they shall be sav'd, or damn'd, or how.
'Twere better therefore that Men ne'er had been,
Than thus Unfortunate. *God save the Queen.*[1]

If this poem be Rochester's—and the energy of the language and
versification suggest that it is—we have in it a powerful expression
of his own misery in the midst of what had now come to appear to
him to be an ugly and meaningless world. His greatest poem, *A
Satyr against Mankind,* is something far more significant. It is a
reasoned statement of the causes of that misery and an announce-
ment of the discovery that reason divorced from morality was the
chief cause. This poem was first printed as a broadside in June 1679,[2]
but it was composed before 23 March 1675/6.[3] Like *Timon,* it is suggested by a satire of Boileau, but like *Timon,* too, it is a thoroughly
original poem. Boileau's eighth satire is a somewhat long-winded
discussion with an imaginary divine concerning the alleged inferiority
of man to the beasts. Rochester's poem is much shorter, much more
concentrated and informed throughout by a passionate vehemence
which makes the elegant and carefully meditated art of Boileau's
satire seem frigid. Boileau discusses the matter as a pure affair of

[1] This poem was printed as Rochester's in *Poems Upon Several Occasions by the R.H.,
the E. of R.,* London, 1712; see P., 131, 219.
[2] W.A.O., II, 1229.
[3] H.M.C. 7th Rep. App. 467, Letter from J. Verney to Sir R. Verney, 23 Mar.,
1675/6.

speculation. Rochester discusses it as though his life depends upon it. As Thomas Rymer writes, 'My Lord Rochester gives us another Cast of Thought, another Turn of Expression, a strength, a Spirit, and Manly Vigour. . . .'[1] It is indeed one of the most notable examples of what Roscommon called the 'comprehensive English Energy', which was the ideal of our early Augustan poets. The meaning of this kind of poetry is indeed explicit. It is on the surface, but below the surface there is the irresistible force of passion which, instead of distracting the mind from it as in romantic poetry, reinforces it and kindles it into the life of great art.

The *Satyr against Mankind* opens with the most memorable lines that Rochester ever wrote. They are an attack on Man, but still more an attack on Reason, the idol of Hobbes and the freethinkers of the age. Hence they are in some measure a recantation, a turning-back of Rochester on himself. 'Reason', naked rationality, has led Man only to misery, and Rochester sees the process in a moment of vision as the picture of a wanderer misled by a will-o'-the-wisp, through all kinds of difficulties to a miserable death. He is seeing an image of his own fate:

> Were I (who to my cost already am
> One of those strange prodigious Creatures *Man*)
> A Spirit free to choose for my own share,
> What Case of Flesh, and Blood I pleased to weare,
> I'd be a *Dog*, a *Monkey*, or a *Bear*,
> Or any thing but that vain *Animal*,
> Who is so proud of being rational.
> The senses are too gross, and he'll contrive
> A Sixth to contradict the other Five;
> And, before certain Instinct, will preferr
> *Reason*, which Fifty times for one does err.
> *Reason*, an *Ignis fatuus* in the *Mind*,
> Which, leaving light of Nature, sense behind,
> Pathless and dang'rous wand'ring ways it takes,
> Through errors, Fenny-*Boggs*, and Thorny *Brakes*;
> While the misguided follower climbs with pain
> *Mountains* of Whimseys, heap'd in his own *Brain*,
> Stumbling from thought to thought, falls head-long down
> Into doubts boundless Sea, where, like to drown,
> Books bear him up awhile, and make him try,

[1] Preface to the Reader [by Thomas Rymer], 1691, Sigg.

To swim with Bladders of *Philosophy*,
In hopes still t'oretake th' escaping light;
The *Vapour* dances in his dazled sight,
Till spent, it leaves him to Eternal Night.
Then Old Age, and experience, hand in hand,
Lead him to death, and make him understand,
After a search so painful, and so long,
That all his Life he has been in the wrong;
Hudled in dirt, the reas'ning *Engine* lyes,
Who was so proud, so witty, and so wise.
Pride drew him in, as *Cheats* their *Bubbles* catch,
And makes him venture to be made a *Wretch*.
His wisdom did his happiness destroy,
Aiming to know that *World* he shou'd enjoy.[1]

This passage was a favourite of Tennyson, and W. E. H. Lecky writes of the 'almost terrible force' which the Victorian laureate threw into the reading of it.[2]

Rochester, not content with this assault on Reason, couples with it a denunciation of Wit, the other idol of the set to which he had belonged. Wit is declared to be only Man's

>   vain frivolous pretence
> Of pleasing others, at his own expence.

Then the poet imagines himself to be taken to task by a clerical opponent, 'a formal Band and Beard', who is delighted with the attack on Wit

> '*that gibeing, jingling knack*,'

which he too longs 'to lash' '*in some sharp Essay*', but he is surprised and indignant at the outbursts against Mankind and Reason, which he defends in some fine lines partly suggested by Lucretius, who was one of Rochester's favourite poets:

> *What rage ferments in your degen'rate mind*
> *To make you rail at Reason, and Mankind?*
> *Blest glorious* Man! *to whom alone kind* Heav'n,
> *An everlasting* Soul *has freely giv'n*;
> *Whom his great* Maker *took such care to make,*
> *That from himself he did the* Image *take,*

---

[1] P., 118, 119. The punctuation of this and the succeeding quotations from *A Satyr Against Mankind* has been normalized.
[2] See *Tennyson, A Memoir* by Hallam Tennyson, 1898, II, 301.

And this fair frame in shining Reason drest,
To dignifie his Nature, *above* Beast,
Reason, *by whose aspiring influence,*
We take a flight beyond material sense
Dive into Mysteries, then soaring pierce,
The flaming limits of the Universe,
Search Heav'n and Hell, find out what's acted there,
And give the World true grounds of hope and fear?

In these noble lines we can find Rochester's own baffled idealism.
This is what he would have liked to believe, what he might have
believed, if he had lived in another and happier 'climate of opinion'.
But now he affects to brush these arguments aside. They are only the
kind of thing that was to be found in all the musty conventional
books of the orthodox. He could have learnt such stuff

From the Pathetique Pen of *Ingello,*
From Patrick's *Pilgrim, Sibbs'* Soliloquies, . . .[1]

These were books that may well have been favourites in the house
of old Lady Rochester. Nathaniel Ingelo was the author of a dreary
allegorical romance called *Bentivolio and Urania.* Simon Patrick's
The Parable of the Pilgrim was another allegorical work by a famous
contemporary divine. Richard Sibbes is the popular Puritan preacher
from whose writings a passage has already been quoted.[2] Taken together the three names sum up very well the pedantic dullness with
which religion must have been presented to Rochester in his youth.
The reply to the 'formal Band and Beard' is that 'Reason' is useless
because it has contributed nothing to man's happiness. Rochester
is a true child of the England of his age in his appeal to the practical,
the empirical test:

'tis this very reason I despise,
This supernaturall gift that makes a *Myte*
Think he is the Image of the Infinite:
Comparing his short life, void of all rest,
To the *Eternal,* and the ever blest.
This busie, puzling, stirrer up of doubt,
That frames deep *Mysteries,* then finds 'em out;
Filling with Frantick Crowds of thinking *Fools,*
Those Reverend *Bedlams, Colledges* and *Schools,*
Borne on whose Wings, each heavy *Sot* can pierce

---

[1] P., 120.   [2] See above, Chapter II, p. 25, note 2.

The limits of the boundless Universe,
So charming Oyntments, make an Old *Witch* flie,
And bear a Crippled Carcass through the Skie.
'Tis this exalted Pow'r whose bus'ness lies
In *Nonsense* and impossibilities.
This made a Whimsicall *Philosopher*,
Before the spacious World, his *Tub* preferr
And we have modern *Cloysterd Coxcombs*, who
Retire to think, cause they have naught to do.
But thoughts are giv'n for Actions government,
Where Action ceases, thoughts impertinent:
Our *Sphere* of Action is lifes happiness,
And he who thinks Beyond, thinks like an *Ass*.

Nowhere is the peculiar quality of Rochester's genius better illustrated than in the lines that compare the 'thinking *Fools*' borne upon the wings of reason to the old Witch's 'Crippled Carkass' flying by means of the 'charming Oyntments'. It is an image that combines humour with grotesque pictorial effect in a way that has rarely been paralleled in English poetry.

Rochester is too much of a child of the Enlightenment to deny Reason altogether. He claims that true Reason co-operates with the senses instead of working against them.

Thus, whilst 'gainst false reas'ning I inveigh,
I own right *Reason*, which I wou'd obey:
That *Reason* that distinguishes by sense,
And gives us *Rules* of good and ill from thence:
That bounds desires with a reforming Will,
To keep 'em more in vigour, not to kill.
Your *Reason* hinders, mine helps t'enjoy,
Renewing Appetites, yours wou'd destroy.
My Reason is my *Friend*, yours is a *Cheat*,
Hunger calls out, my Reason bids me eat;
Perversely yours, your Appetite does mock,
This asks for Food, that answers what's a Clock?

This is the epicurean philosophy of the 'merry gang' at Whitehall. It was still Rochester's practical creed. Thus, he says, he has 'righted' Reason, but he proceeds now to launch a new onslaught on Man, and this time, it is important to notice, he attacks Man not for being absurd but for being 'base', much baser than the beasts whom he affects to despise. Rochester here implicitly abandons the egoistic immoralism which he had hitherto flaunted:

M   155

But for *Man*,
I'le ne'er recant, defend him if you can.
For all his Pride, and his Philosophy,
'Tis evident *Beasts* are in their degree,
As wise at least, and better far than he.
Those *Creatures* are the wisest who attain
By surest means the ends at which they aim.
If therefore *Jowler* finds, and Kills his *Hares*
Better than *Meres* supplyes Committee Chairs,
Though one's a *States-man*, th'other but a *Hound*,
Jowler, in Justice, wou'd be wiser found.
You see how far *Mans* wisedom here extends,
Look next if humane Nature makes amends;
Whose Principles most generous are and just,
And to those *Moralls*, you wou'd sooner trust.
Be Judge your self, I'le bring it to the test,
Which is the basest *Creature*, *Man*, or *Beast?*
Birds feed on *Birds*, *Beasts* on each prey,
But Savage *Man* alone does *Man* betray:
Prest by necessity, they Kill for Food,
Man undoes *Man* to do himself no good.
With Teeth and Claws by Nature arm'd they hunt,
Natures allowances to supply their want.
But *Man*, with smiles, embraces, Friendships, praise,
Unhumanely his Fellows life betrays;
With voluntary pains works his distress,
Not through necessity, but wantonness.
For hunger, or for Love, they fight or tear,
Whilst wretched *Man* is still in Arms for fear;
For fear he armes, and is of Armes afraid,
By fear to fear successively betray'd,
Base fear, the source whence his best passions came,
His boasted Honor, and his dear bought Fame,
That lust of Pow'r, to which he's such a *Slave*.
And for the which alone he dares be brave:
To which his various Projects are design'd
Which makes him gen'rous, affable and kind,
For which he takes such pains to be thought wise,
And screws his actions in a forc'd disguise:
Leading a tedious life in Misery,
Under laborious, mean *Hypocrisie*.
Look to the bottom of his vast design,
Wherein *Mans* Wisdom, Pow'r and Glory joyn;

> The good he acts, the ill he does endure,
> 'Tis all for fear to make himself secure.
> Meerly for safety, after Fame we thirst,
> For all Men wou'd be *Cowards* if they durst.[1]

This passage is the result of profound moral agitation. It is the poetry of argument indeed, but its passionate vehemence is very different from the cool reasoning of the *Religio Laici* or the *Essay on Man*. Its place is rather beside the great things in Swift, and it recalls the King of Brobdingnag's denunciation of the human race.

A curious epilogue to *The Satyr against Mankind* is printed in some of the old editions.[2] It is undoubtedly the work of Rochester. These lines contain a sort of conditional recantation. Rochester is an idealist at heart, and he wants to find a man whom he can admire. It is above all a just man that he wants:

> Who does his needful flattery direct
> Not to oppress and ruine, but protect . . .

He must be a true patriot

> Who does his Arts, and *Policies* apply,
> To raise his *Country*, not his *Family*.

Then we learn, with surprise, perhaps, that Rochester is thinking of a priest:

> Is there a *Church-Man* who on *God* relyes,
> Whose Life, his Faith, and Doctrine Justifies?

Such a man is compared in bitterly satiric lines to the typical parson of the day:

> Who from his Pulpit vents more peevish Lyes,
> More bitter railings, scandals, Calumnies,
> Than at a Gossipping are thrown about,
> When the good *Wives* get drunk, and then fall out.
> None of that sensual *Tribe* whose Tallents lye
> In Avarice, *Price, Sloth*, and *Gluttony*,
> Who hunt good Livings, but abhor good Lives,
> Whose Lust exalted to that height arrives
> They act *Adultery* with their own *Wives*.
> And e're a score of Years compleated be,
> Can from the lofty *Pulpit* proudly see
> Half a large *Parish*, their own *Progeny*.

---

[1] P., 121-3.   [2] Ibid., 123, 124, 214, 215.

The man for whom Rochester was seeking was

> a meek humble Man of modest sense,
> Who Preaching peace, does practice continence;
> Whose pious life's a proof he does believe,
> Misterious truths, which no *Man* can conceive

He ends the epilogue with an offer to 'recant' his '*Paradox*' if 'such *Godlike Men*' can be found. He will do more. He will

> Adore these *Shrines* of *Virtue*, *Homage* pay,
> And with the *Rabble World*, their *Laws* obey.

But, even if he is convinced of the existence of truly good men, he will still retain his former opinion of the rest, and his conclusion will be that of Montaigne:

> *Man* differs more from *Man*, than *Man* from *Beast*.[1]

The epilogue to *A Satyr against Mankind* is of great biographical significance. Rochester had reached the end of the cul-de-sac into which he had been led by materialism. In the epilogue we see the truth beginning to dawn upon him that he must retreat from it, and find a new direction in which his starved moral and spiritual life can develop freely.

---

[1] Ibid., 124, cf. Montaigne, *Essais*, I, xlii.

Chapter Eight

———«◆»«◆»———

THE DANCE OF DEATH

———«◆»«◆»———

It was still possible to escape from the nightmare of boredom and despair by plunging into dissipation. He would call for louder music and for stronger wine. It was possible, but it was becoming more and more difficult. The lights were blinding his tired eyes and the music was stunning his dizzy brain. The Utopia of Gallantry was turning into a kind of weird *danse macabre*, a ballet of figures that were becoming ghostly and incredible:

> Mishapen Monsters round in Measures went
> Horrid in Form with Gestures insolent;
> Grinning throu Goatish Beards with half clos'd Eyes.[1]

These lines come from the adaptation of Fletcher's *Valentinian* (called in a manuscript copy *Lucina's Rape*[2]), on which Rochester was working in the last years of his life. They are spoken by Lucina, the chaste wife of the Roman general Maximus, whom the emperor Valentinian is trying to seduce. *Lucina's Rape* was left unfinished at Rochester's death, but the text as we have it is certainly one of his most interesting and revealing works. Fletcher's play is a vigorous, loosely constructed melodrama in flowing rhetorical verse. In Rochester's adaptation we can see it in process of being transformed into a symbolic poem full of profound meaning. The three main characters Lucina, the chaste wife ravished by force, Maximus, the upright Roman general and Valentinian the lustful Tyrant all represent different aspects of Rochester's own character. Valentinian is Rochester the selfish libertine ('In my dear self, I center ev'ry thing'),

---

[1] P., 70; V., 21, 32. [2] B.M. Add. MS. 28692.

159

with perhaps a suggestion of Charles II, a man who is totally devoid
of moral sense and who, unlike Fletcher's rather sentimental tyrant,
dies unrepentant. Lucina is the *anima* or soul of Rochester, remain-
ing pure in spirit in spite of her rape, bewildered by the phantas-
magoria or witches' rout of contemporary life and longing for
'felicity and glory'. Maximus is Rochester the deeply troubled and
clearsighted satirist of Restoration morals and manners. In a sombre
and powerful lyrical passage in Act IV, Scene 3 of *Lucina's Rape* we
can hear the voice of the unhappy Rochester speaking through the
mouth of Maximus. It is the voice of a man whose moral sense is re-
volted by the world's evil and who can find no comfort in the answers
of conventional piety:

> Bear me, cold Earth, who am too weak to move
> Beneath my load of Shame and Misery,
> Wrong'd by my lawful Prince, robb'd of my Love,
> Branded with everlasting infamy.
> Take pity, Fate, and give me leave to die.
>
> Gods! would you be ador'd for being good,
> Or only fear'd for proving mischievous?
> How would you have your Mercy understood?
> Who would create a Wretch like *Maximus*,
> Ordain'd tho' guiltless to be infamous?
>
> Supream first Causes? you, whence all things flow,
> Whose infiniteness does each little fill,
> You who decree each seeming Chance below,
> (So great in Power) were you as good in Will,
> How could you ever have produc't such ill?
>
> Had your eternal minds been bent to good?
> Could humane happiness have prov'd so lame
> Rapine, Revenge, Injustice, thirst of Blood,
> Grief, Anguish, Horror, Want, Despair and Shame,
> Had never found a Being nor a Name.
>
> 'Tis therefore less impiety to say,
> Evil with you has Coeternity,
> Than blindly taking it the other way,
> That, merciful, and of election free,
> You did create the mischiefs you foresee.[1]

[1] P., 71, 72.

These lines are not the work of a shallow rebel or scoffer; they represent the feelings of a poet who is profoundly troubled, like Thomas Hardy two centuries later, by the spectacle of a non-moral universe.

Rochester's 'time of troubles' seems to have really begun in the summer of 1675. From a letter written by him to his friend Henry Savile in late August of that year[1] we learn that he was not only severely injured by a fall from his horse but also 'us'd barbarously' by certain enemies of his at Court who had slandered him to the King's powerful French mistress, the haughty Louise de Kéroualle, Duchess of Portsmouth and her sister, the Countess of Pembroke. On account of this 'false idle story' he was in disgrace at Court. The Duchess, he was told, had made 'a generous Resolution of not hurting' him to the King. But he places little reliance on this promise: 'I do not know how to assure myself the D. will spare me to the King who would not to you.' It is pathetic to read his plea to Savile 'to desire her [the Duchess] to give me the fair hearing she would afford to any Footman of hers, who had been comlain'd of to her by a less-worthy Creature'. A letter to Savile written in September of the same year seems to show that his fears have been justified and he writes, 'I shall scarce think of coming [to London], till you call me, as not having many Prevalent Motives to draw me to Court, if it be so that my Master has no need of my Service, nor my Friends of my Company'. In a letter written in a very bitter tone in the following February he speaks sarcastically on arrangements that were apparently being made at Court for the reversion of his offices when he should die. On 9 October 1675 the King had signed 'a warrant for a grant to Sir Walter St. John and three others for the office of Ranger of Woodstock Park, after the determination of the Earl of Rochester's estate during the lives of the Earl and Countess of Lichfield'.[2] The same people also sought the reversion of Lord Lovelace's rights as Lieutenant of Woodstock. Both Lovelace and Rochester filed caveats, and on Friday, 29 October, Secretary Williamson wrote to Rochester advising him that 'to-morrow being appointed for hearing the matter in difference . . . concerning Woodstock . . . the King commands me to signify to you that you take order that some person, whomever you shall choose, be there to hear it jointly with the Lord Keeper'.[3] The affair probably dragged on through the autumn and winter and it seems likely that Rochester

[1] W., 35, 36. [2] C.S.P.D., 1675–6, 341, 342; C.T.B., 1672–3, 818; W., 38, 39.
[3] Ibid., 367; W., 14.

and Lovelace lost. Rochester's ironical comment on these intrigues must be given in his own words. 'This day I have receiv'd the un-happy News of my own Death and Burial. But hearing what Heirs and Successors were decreed me in my Place, and chiefly in my Lodgings, it was no small Joy to me that these Tidings prove untrue; my Passion for living is so encreased, that I omit no Care of myself, which before I never thought Life worth the trouble of taking. The King, who knows me to be a very ill-natur'd Man, will not think it an easie matter for me to dye, now I live chiefly out of spight.'[1] The 'Lodgings' are undoubtedly his beloved Ranger's lodge at Wood-stock. Another letter written to Savile at Lent in 1676 ('a season of tribulation') shows that he was bored by 'the tediousness of doing nothing' in the country, and, although he realized that the World was 'still unsupportably the same' and he had 'no curiosity for News', he is anxious to hear if Parliament is likely to sit. He notes that 'the Peers of England' have 'grown of late Years very consider-able in the Government' and would like to attend a session of the House of Lords. He has been reading Livy and thinking of state affairs: 'Livy and Sickness' he writes 'has a little inclin'd me to Policy.' Nevertheless he has no political ambitions and he prefers the 'generous Philosophy' of Philip Sidney, Lord Lisle, an amiable, cultivated nobleman, who lived in retirement on his estate at Sheen, to 'my Lord Mulgrave's mean Ambition'. There follows a satirical description of the activities of politicians, which was quoted with approval by Lord Chesterfield: 'They who would be great in our little Government, seem as ridiculous to me as School-boys, who with much endeavour, and some danger, climb a Crab-tree, ven-turing their Necks for Fruit which solid Piggs would disdain if they were not starving.' The letter[2] from which these remarks are quoted is that which contains the notorious 'Black Will' passage, already mentioned in connexion with Rochester's quarrel with Dryden.[3]

Between April and August 1676 there is a break in his corres-pondence with Savile and it was possibly in May or June that the 'Alexander Bendo' episode took place (see above p. 82).

Late in June 1676, Rochester was involved in a brawl at Epsom which ended tragically for one member of the 'merry gang'. One Sunday in that month, Rochester and Etherege with a certain Captain Bridges, a Mr. Jephson, and a Mr. Downs, were at the little

---

[1] W., 39.   [2] Ibid., 41; Chesterfield, IV, 1339.   [3] See above, p. 100.

Surrey village, probably to watch the races on the downs, which were already famous. In order to dispel the gloom of a Sunday night in the country they had been drinking, and they wanted some music. The village fiddlers refused to play to them and they proceeded to toss them in a blanket. A local barber, disturbed by the noise, came to see what was the matter. They seized him, but he obtained his release by promising to take them to the handsomest woman in Epsom. He must have been a humorist, for he led them to the house of the village constable. When they found out their mistake, they broke open the door and belaboured the poor constable unmercifully. However, he managed to escape, and called the watch. Then Etherege, who seems to have been the soberest of the party, made a 'submissive oration', and Dogberry dismissed his honest neighbours and prepared to retire. Unfortunately Rochester, who seems to have been very drunk indeed, drew his sword at this point and threatened the constable. Downs held him down, but the constable in his fright had shouted 'murder', and the watch came back to his rescue. In the confusion they mistook Downs for the culprit, and one of them coming behind him gave him a blow on the head with a 'sprittle stave'. There was a scuffle in which the 'merry gang' dispersed, leaving Downs, who had no weapon but a stick, to confront an angry watch, armed with half-pikes. He was severely wounded, and died soon after.[1]

There seems no reason to accuse Rochester of anything worse than drunken folly. Contemporary and later gossip as usual has tried to turn him into the villain of the evening, but the immediate cause of Downs's death was probably the confusion due to the scuffle in the dark, and Etherege and Bridges were quite as much to blame as Rochester for leaving him to his fate. They were probably all too drunk to know what they were doing. The affray was the kind of thing that was bound to happen from time to time when debauchery was considered a normal occupation for a fine gentleman, and when such gentlemen were in the habit of carrying lethal weapons by their sides.

It may have been in a mood that combined recklessness with a touch of remorse for the fate of the unfortunate Downs that Rochester dashed off the following lines, if they are really by him:

---

[1] Hatton, I, 133, 134; H.M.C., 7th Rep., Appendix, 467, J. Verney to E. Verney; Marvell, II, 322.

The Earl of Rochester's Conference with a Post Boy

> Son of a Whore G-d damn thee, canst thou tell
> A Peerless Peer the readiest Way to Hell?
> I've outswilled Bacchus, sworn of my own Make
> Oaths, Frighted Furyes and made Pluto quake:
> Sw-d, Whore[s] more ways than ever Sodoms Walls
> Knew or the Colledge of the Cardinalls,
> Witness Heroic Scars and Wounds: Ne're go!
> Sear Cloths and Ulcers from the top to th'Toe.
> Frightened at my own Mischeifs I am fled
> And basely left my Life's Defender Dead.
> But hang't why do I mention these poor Things?
> I have blasphem'd G-d, and libell'd Kings;
> The readiest way to Hell, Boy; Quick. (Boy) Ne'er stir,
> The readiest way, my Lord's by Rochester.[1]

It is true that the date 1674 is attached to these verses in an old manuscript copy, but this must be a mistake of the copyist if the ninth and tenth lines refer to the Epsom brawl, while the twelfth probably refers to the first stanza of the *History of Insipids* (1676, see above p. 76), which might be described as a combination of blasphemy with *lèse-majesté*. It is difficult to believe that the author of the final couplet had not read Satan's words in *Paradise Lost*:

> Which way I flie is Hell; my self am Hell.

At some time during that summer of 1676 Harry Savile was at Woodstock and we have a glimpse of the two friends with others of the 'merry gang' after a dip in the river leading 'the Coranto' in a state of nudity round Rosamund's fair Fountain, while 'the poor violated Nymph wept' to see 'the strange decay of Manly Parts, since the Days of her dear Harry the Second.'[2] On 15 August Savile writes to the Earl at Adderbury, where he seems for a while to have been leading a quiet life in the bosom of his family, entreating him to come back to London: 'this beeing the criticall time for you to take your fortune, for Monr. Rabell is soe much the favourite of his maj-ty and your Lp of Monr. Rabell, that I do not see you can ever have a better opportunity of doeing your businesse: now, your Chymicall knowledge will give you entrance where Manchester himselfe is kept out for his ignorance'.[3] Charles II, it appears, was at this time

---

[1] P., 147, 229. For another version of this poem, see Appendix, p. 235.
[2] W., 46.   [3] Ibid., 43.

indulging his passion for chemistry with the help of the French apothecary Monsieur Rabell with whom Rochester was on the best of terms. Here, Savile suggests, is a golden opportunity for regaining the royal favour. Who could be better fitted for chemical research (or, at any rate for talking the jargon of contemporary chemistry) than 'Dr. Alexander Bendo', whose recent exploits may be glanced at in the phrase, 'your Chymical knowledge'? There is no record of Rochester's activities in the winter of 1676/7. It seems probable that he was taken into favour at Court again and resumed his duties as Gentleman of the Bedchamber, which appear to have included ministering to the King's pleasures. For some time he had been the friend and adviser of Nell Gwin, Charles's charming, irrepressible 'Protestant mistress'. The King granted her certain disputed lands in Ireland, and in April, 1677, we find Rochester acting as her trustee for this property, and writing on her behalf to the Earl of Essex, then Lord Lieutenant of Ireland.[1] In a letter written to Savile in June 1678[2] he gives his old friend an account of the advice he used to offer to Nelly: 'Take your measures just contrary to your Rivals, live in Peace with all the World, and easily with the King; Never be so Ill-natur'd to stir up his Anger against others, but let him forget the use of a Passion, which is never to do you good: Cherish his Love where-ever it inclines, and be assur'd you can't commit greater folly than pretending to be jealous; but, on the contrary, with Hand, Body, Head, Heart and all the Faculties you have, contribute to his pleasure all you can, and comply with his Desires throughout; And for new Intrigues, so you be at one end 'tis no matter which: Make Sport when you can, at other times help it.' He asks Savile to judge whether he was a good Pimp or no. 'But some thought otherwise; he continues, 'and so truly I have renounc'd Business; let abler Men try it.'

Rochester was often in London in the spring and summer of 1677. He was pretty regular in his attendance at the House of Lords early in the year. The Journal of the House marks him as present four times in February, thirteen in March, seven in April and one in May.[3] His friend Robert Wolseley noted in his Preface to Rochester's *Valentinian* that 'a considerable time before his last Sickness, his Wit began to take a more serious Bent, and to frame and fashion it-self to publick Business; he began to inform himself of the Wisdom

[1] E.P., 123.   [2] W., 57.   [3] J.H.L.

of our Laws, ... and to speak in the House of Peers with general approbation'.[1] Against this testimony can be set a not very well authenticated tradition that Rochester rose to speak in the House on only one occasion. He is said to have begun with the following words: 'My lords, I divide my speech into four parts', then, after a pause of some minutes: 'My lords, if ever I rise to speak again in this house, I give you leave to cut me in pieces.' We are told that he 'then sat down to the astonishment of the assembled peers and kept his promise never to address the house again'.[2] Whatever truth may be in this story, the record of his attendances at the House since he took his seat in July 1667 is by no means a bad one, and he was appointed to several committees, including one to consider a bill against duelling.[3]

On 4 June 1677 Rochester was dining at a restaurant in the Mall with Lord Lumley when a French cook was stabbed by a certain Mr. Floyd in a different room in the same house. Rochester had no connexion whatsoever with the affair but 'the good nature of the town' promptly circulated the story that he was the assassin, and he asks Savile to beg his brother the Marquis of Halifax to stop the rumour from going northward, 'for if it once gets as far as York the truth will not be believed under two or three years'.[4] That summer, Buckingham had been imprisoned in the Tower for insisting that the Parliament which had sat since 1661 was automatically dissolved and was no longer legal. He was released and taken back into favour at the beginning of August, when we hear of the King and the newly enfranchised Duke being 'very merry one evening at Lord Rochester's lodgings'.[5]

In October 1677, Rochester was back at Woodstock, 'almost Blind, utterly Lame, and scarce within reasonable hopes of ever seeing London again'. Yet he is able to write Savile a long and witty letter.[6] He appreciates his old friend's staunchness, and praises him for loving 'a Man whom it is the great Mode to hate'. He protests against a story of his 'hideous Deportment', when he was said to have run naked with some friends in Woodstock Park. All that really happened, according to Rochester, was that they 'went into the River somewhat late in the Year, and had a frisk for forty yards in the meadow, to dry ourselves.' He reminds Savile, who had jestingly professed himself to be 'a grave Man of the number of the Scandaliz'd'

[1] V., Sig. A 4. [2] B.V., XXXVI, 245. [3] J.H.L. [4] S.C., 45–7.
[5] H.M.C., 7th Rep. App., 469. [6] W., 46, 47.

that he himself had taken part in similar sports at Woodstock in the year 1676, when 'two large fat nudities led the Coranto round Rosamund's fair Fountain, while the poor violated Nymph wept to behold the strange decay of Manly Parts, since the Days of her dear Harry the Second'. The story was going all round England apparently. Puritanical young Robert Harley, later to become the great Tory minister and Swift's Earl of Oxford, had heard it and relates it in a letter to his father with the further embellishment that the 'beastly prank' took place on the 'Sabbath day'.[1] Probably much of the gossip about Rochester rests on as slender a foundation as this tale. His free speech and satiric wit made him many enemies, and any story about his wickedness was readily believed. Savile had begged him to come up to London to help to amuse the Dutchmen who had come over with William of Orange for the celebration of his marriage with the Princess Mary. Rochester rejects the proposal with horror: 'To make Dutchman merry', he declares, 'is a thing I would avoid like killing Punaises, the filthy savour of Dutch-Mirth being more terrible.' He excepts the Prince of Orange, however, who is 'exalted above 'em', and wishes himself in Town 'to serve him in some refin'd Pleasures'. This letter is carried to London by Rochester's French servant, Baptiste, who has a fine voice. He sends with him some tunes that the King may hear 'when he is easie and private'. Rochester's unhappiness peeps out at the end of the letter when he describes himself as '*un Bougre lasse qui [s]era toute sa foutue reste de vie*'.[2] Savile replies on 1 November[3] and sends a great deal of amusing Court gossip about the Duke of Buckingham, young William Fanshaw, Nell Gwin, Harry Killigrew and the shabby Earl of Manchester, who has surprised everyone by getting a new suit. He mentions the Prince of Orange's wedding again, and expresses surprise that none of the 'sweet singers' have celebrated it, except 'the old bard Waller' whose verses he promises to send so that Rochester may judge 'whether the old gentleman stinke in the

---

[1] H.M.C., Portland MSS. at Welbeck Abbey, I, 355–7. Hearne gives a highly coloured version of the affair in H.R.C., IX, 78: 'This Lord . . . used sometimes, with others of his companions to run naked and particularly they did so once in Woodstock Park, upon a Sunday in the afternoon, exspecting that several of the female sex would have been spectators but not one appear'd. The Man that stript them, & pull'd off their shirts, kept the shirts, & did not deliver them any more, going off with them before they finish'd the Race.' One must remember that Hearne was a salacious old gossip writing in Jan., 1725/6, nearly half a century after the event.

[2] W., 47.   [3] Ibid., 48.

sockett, or blaze a little yett'. The mention of poetry reminds him to tell Rochester about a 'libell' on the poets 'lately sent by the post to Wills's coffe house'. He has not seen it, but he strongly suspects that it was 'composed att Woodstock' 'especially considering what an assembly either is yett or att least has been there'. The 'libell' in question was probably the squib called *Advice to Apollo*, 1678, published in *Poems on Affairs of State*, 1697.[1] These lines, possibly by Buckingham, certainly reflect the views of the 'merry gang'. The subject is the state of contemporary satire. Car Scroop ('the Knight o' th' wither'd Face'), Mulgrave ('in fee with Dryden to be counted wise') and 'sawcy Sheppard' are all trounced. The god is asked to strike Dryden only 'with a gentle dart' in order that he may drop satire and return to the writing of plays. Dorset and Rochester are both praised, though Rochester's 'delightfull Muse' is urged to keep to love poetry.

Savile reports that the King is pleased with Rochester's gift of music, which consisted of some new pieces by the French composer Paisible. He is longing for Rochester's company to 'dispel the clowdes of dullnesse the Dutchmen have made', and if the Earl does not come to Town 'though upon croutches', he will be thought 'a traytour to King and country'.[2] Rochester is unable to accept this invitation, but he writes a cheerful, witty letter in reply calling himself 'the Grievance of all prudent Persons, the By-word of Statesmen, the Scorn of ugly Ladies, which are very near All, and the Irreconcilable Aversion of fine Gentlemen, who are the Ornamental Part of a Nation'. He is cheerful because he has had 'a fine letter from Mr Savile, which never wants Wit and Good Nature, two Qualities able to transport my Heart with Joy, tho' it were breaking'. He thinks that the royal marriage might be a good opportunity for getting rid of some of the 'old Beauties and young Deformities who swarm', presumably by giving them posts in the Princess's household or marrying them to Dutchmen:

> A Foreign Prince ought to behave himself like a Kite, who is allow'd to take one Royal Chick for his Reward; but then 'tis expected, before he leaves the Country, his Flock shall clear the whole Parish of all the Garbage and Carrion many Miles about. The King had never such an opportunity; for the Dutch are very foul feeders, and what they leave he must never hope to be rid of, unless he set up an Intrigue with the Tartars or Cossacks.

[1] P.O.A.S., 1697, 211. [2] W., 49.

He professes to rejoice in the 'Libel . . . upon that most unwitty Generation the present Poets', and asks Savile to send him a copy.[1]

On 17 December, Savile writes that he has heard strong rumours not contradicted by Rochester's own servants, that he is coming to Town. He speaks with disgust of the prevalence of the jingo spirit at Court, and complains that 'either to doubt of making warr with France or beating them when it is made' is 'an offence against the nation'. He had learnt from the King that Mrs. Barry, Rochester's mistress, had given birth to a daughter. He congratulates him on the birth of the child, but gently reproaches him for the poverty in which Mrs. Barry was living, according to the account given to him by a lady whom he had met in the Mall.[2] This admonition had some effect, if we may judge from the following letter addressed to Mrs. Barry by Rochester: 'Your safe Delivery has deliver'd me too from Fears for your sake, which were, I'll promise you as burthensome to me, as your Great-belly cou'd be to you. Every thing has fallen out to my Wish, for you are out of Danger, and the Child is of the Soft Sex I love. Shortly my Hopes are to see you, and in a little while to look on you with all your Beauty about you. Pray tell no Body, but yourself open the Box I sent you; I did not know, but that in Lying-inn you might have use of those Trifles; sick and in Bed as I am, I cou'd come at no more of 'em; but if you find 'em, or whatever is in my power of use, to you Service, let me know it.'[3]

Mrs. Barry appears to have been a woman of violent and uncertain temper, and, to judge from Rochester's extant letters to her, their liaison must have been a stormy one. 'Dear Madam,' he writes to her on one occasion, 'You are stark Mad, and therefore the fitter for me to love; and that is the reason, I think, I can never leave to be Your Humble Servant'.[4] In other letters we hear of her jealousy, which made her send her neighbour to spy on her lover, her 'Torment of Repentance' and her 'chiding Humour'.[5] We are reminded of Mrs. Loveit in *The Man of Mode* with her violent outbursts of passion against Dorimant, and it is interesting to note that Mrs. Barry probably created this part in the first production of the play.[6]

Rochester seems to have decided, no doubt wisely, to remove from Mrs. Barry's care, at any rate for a time, the child, for whom he clearly had a genuine affection. 'I love Betty so well', he writes,

---

[1] Ibid., 50. [2] Ibid., 52. [3] F.L., II, 10. [4] Ibid., 7. [5] Ibid., 13, 15, 24.
[6] Etherege, II, 38, but cf. A.K.L., III, where Wilson suggests that the part of Mrs. Loveit was actually created by Mary Lee.

'that you need not apprehend any Neglect from those I employ, and I hope very shortly to restore her to you a finer Girl than ever.'[1] This child, 'Betty', was almost certainly the Elizabeth Clerke to whom Rochester left in his will an annuity of forty pounds secured on the Manor of Sutton Malet.[2] If we can trust the evidence of a poem which can be dated c. 1689, she died at the age of about twelve.[3]

In the letter in which he gave Rochester the news about Mrs. Barry, Savile tries to tempt him to come to town with an account of a company of French comedians 'bound for Nimeguen . . . by adverse winds cast into this hospitable port'. Among them is 'a young wench of fifteen, who has more beauty and sweetnesse then ever was seen upon the stage since a friend of ours left it'. Rochester would be 'delighted above all things with her'. The Duchess of Portsmouth, Charles's French mistress, has been ill. Her recovery is said by the King to be due to his famous 'dropps', but by her confessor to the Virgin. She had promised in her name that in case of recovery 'shee should have no more commerce with that known enemy to virginity and chastity the monarke of Great Britain'.[4]

In the winter of 1677–8, Rochester was certainly very ill indeed. This illness was probably that which Burnet describes as having 'brought him so near Death before I first knew him, when his Spirits were so low and spent, that he could not move or stir, and he did not think to live an hour'. During this illness, however, his 'Reason and Judgment were so clear and strong, that from thence he was fully perswaded that Death was not the spending or dissolution of the Soul; but only the separation of it from matter.' It was the old question that had troubled him during the Dutch wars, and now that he was close to death it came back to his mind with redoubled force. In that sickness he had 'great Remorses for his past Life; but . . . They were rather general and dark Horrours, than any Convictions of sinning against God. He was sorry that he had lived so, as to wast his strength so soon, or that he had brought such an ill name upon himself; and had an Agony in his Mind about it, which he knew not well how to express.' He allowed 'Divines to be sent for,' but 'he had no great mind to it', and he only asked them to pray for him out of 'breeding' and 'joyned little himself'.[5]

John Verney, that inveterate gossip, son of Rochester's old guardian, Sir Ralph Verney, wrote to his father on 25 April that

[1] F.L., II, 26.   [2] Prinz, 300.   [3] W., 98.   [4] Ibid., 52, 53.
[5] B.S.P., 21, 22.

'Lord Rochester has been very ill and is very penitent, but is now bettering'.[1]

It was probably in the spring of 1678[2] that Rochester made the acquaintance of John Oldham who was then in his twenty-fifth year. He was a graduate of St. Edmund Hall, Oxford, and was employed as an usher at the Whitgift Grammar School at Croydon. He had published a poem on the marriage of William and Mary in November, 1677,[3] and, we are told that some of his manuscript poems 'coming to the Sight of Lord *Rochester*, raised that witty Nobleman's Curiosity to see the Author'.[4] Anthony à Wood states that Rochester seemed 'much delighted in the mad, ranting and debauch'd specimens'[5] of Oldham's poetry, so it is highly probable that the poem of his which attracted the Earl's attention was his mock Pindaric Ode called *A Satyr against Virtue*, which we know from two extant manuscript copies was actually supposed to be a kind of dramatic monologue spoken by Rochester himself. In one of these copies the poem is headed with the caption, 'suppos'd to be spoken by ye Court Hector who demolised ye Sund-Dial'.[6] It is, perhaps, hardly surprising that Rochester was curious to make the acquaintance with the young poet who made so free with the character given to him by the gossip of the town, but it says a good deal for his tolerance and sense of humour that, instead of being angry, he 'much delighted' in the verses, and went out of his way to befriend their author.

According to Captain Edward Thompson,[7] Oldham's eighteenth-century editor, Rochester, accompanied by his friends Dorset and Sedley went over to Croydon one day to visit Oldham. When they arrived at the Whitgift School, Rochester sent in his servant with 'a verbal compliment to Mr. Oldham', which was delivered by mistake to the headmaster John Shepheard. This old gentleman, we are told, 'immediately dressed himself in his Summer Sabbath Apparel and came to greet the distinguished company from Whitehall, believing that the visit was intended for himself. After 'the tottering Pedagogue' had amused them by 'a stupid dull Preface of the sense of the Honour they had done him', Dorset, 'observing the confusion of the Man, and the laughing Gravity of Lord Rochester', put poor

---

[1] H.M.C., 7th Rep. App. 470 (John Verney to Sir R. Verney).
[2] See D. Vieth in P.Q., XXII, on 'the Wits and A Satyr against Vertue'.
[3] Oldham, III, 98.   [4] Oldham, I, ii.   [5] W.A.O., IV, 120.   [6] Brooks, 14.
[7] Oldham, I, ii, iii.

Shepheard out of his agony 'with a candid assurance that their Invitation was to Mr. Oldham'. The result of this visit seems to have been Oldham's introduction to the literary world of London. There is no doubt that he had an unbounded admiration for Rochester. He copied out in his own hand in a commonplace book *A Letter from Artemisa* and *A Satyr against Mankind*[1] and his poems clearly show Rochester's influence. He proclaims his discipleship in some touching lines in his imitation of Moschus's *Lament for Bion* which he dedicated to Rochester's memory:

> If I am reckon'd not unblest in Song,
> 'Tis what I owe, to thy all-teaching Tongue;
> Some of thy Art, some of thy tuneful Breath
> Thou didst, by Will, to worthless Me bequeath:
> Others, thy Flocks, thy Lands, thy Riches have,
> To me thou didst thy Pipe and Skill vouchsafe.[2]

It has been conjectured that these lines imply that Oldham's poem is founded on an unfinished version of Moschus's poem which Rochester bequeathed to Oldham, and that the melodious rendering of the Greek refrain may be Rochester's own:

> *Come, all ye* Muses, *come, adorn the Shepherd's Herse*
> *With never-fading Garlands, never-dying Verse.*

Even allowing for the conventional adulation of pastoral elegy, the whole poem shows that Oldham's admiration of Rochester's poetry was mingled with genuine affection for him as a man. At the end of his short life Oldham found a congenial home at Holmes-Pierpont in Nottinghamshire in the house of the young Earl of Kingston, and it appears that it was Rochester who introduced him to this hospitable nobleman.

By 4 June Savile has heard from Fanshaw that Rochester has 'recovered beyond all hazzard of a relapse'.[3] Later in the month he sends much Court and parliamentary news. The report that Rochester's cousin, Sir John Talbot, is to be called to the Council Board suggests to him that the Earl may turn his attention to State affairs: 'though you have not yourselfe talents for businesse, you may find them in your owne flesh and blood, and doubtlesse

---

[1] Bodl. MS. Rawl. Eng. Poet., 123; P., XXVI, XLVI.
[2] Oldham, II, 66, 67. See also *The Poems of John Oldham* (Centaur Press), 1960, Introduction by Bonamy Dobrée, pp. 10, 14.
[3] W., 55.

there may some prudent embers lye hidden in your Lordship if you would racke them up which in time might bee of use to your King and country. I beg of your Lordship to take this time of your leasure a little paines to examine yourself on this point.'[1]

By this time Rochester had recovered something of his old joyous spirit and he writes a letter to Savile in his best vein. It begins with his favourite quotation from Shakespeare:

If Sack and Sugar be a Sin, God help the Wicked; Was the Saying of a merry fat Gentleman, who liv'd in Days of Yore, lov'd a glass of Wine, wou'd be merry with a Friend, and sometimes had an unlucky Fancy for a Wench.

The letter ends with some words which are a kind of bantering counterpart to *A Satyr against Mankind*:

For my own part I'm taking pains not to die, without knowing how to live on, when I have brought it about: But most human affairs are carried on at the same nonsensical rate, which makes me (who am now grown Superstitious) think it a Fault to laugh at the Monkey we have here, when I compare his Condition with Mankind![2]

The monkey mentioned in this letter is probably the animal which appears in the well-known portrait of Rochester ascribed to Huys-mans now in the National Portrait Gallery, and he may well be the original of the monkeys mentioned in *A Letter from Artemisa* and *A Satyr against Mankind*. Rochester's love of animals is one of the many traits of his character which links him to Byron.

Savile replies that 'if the good gentleman who loved sack and shugar soe well was soe lucky as to bring mee into your mind I wishe there were more of them'. But he fears that the 'excellent breed' is 'allmost extinguished', and the only one that he can think of 'since poor Sir Simon Fanshaw' died is 'an old cavalier corporall that I believe you have seen begging on St. James's Parke'. Good fellows do not flourish in 'Whitehall Gallery' now. The only talk there is of 'horse, foot, dragoons, cuirassiers, granadeers, guidons, aid-de-camps', and 'whosoever is not drest in this hott season in a *drap de Berry* coate with gold galoon enough to load a mule is not thought affectionate to the government or the army'.[3] Savile's next letter, dated 2 July, is from a 'sweating house' in Leather Lane, Hatton Garden, where he was being treated for the disease which was unhappily so prevalent

[1] Ibid, 58.   [2] Ibid., 60.   [3] Ibid., 61.

at the Court of Charles II. He can joke about his tribulations and is tickled by the fact that Mrs. Roberts,[1] one of the King's mistresses, who had also been a mistress of Rochester's, is undergoing treatment in the same house. William Fanshaw, has also arrived 'and made a third with us, but will have his worse pox than ours passe for the scurvy out of civility to his lady'. This Fanshaw has been described as a 'lean, poverty stricken courtier'. He held the small court office of Master of Requests, and seems to have been on familiar terms with members of the 'merry gang'. He was married to Mary, the daughter of Lucy Walter, Charles II's mistress, probably by Henry Bennett, Earl of Arlington. Rochester was appointed co-trustee with the Earl of Anglesea on 1 December 1679 for an annuity of £600 to be paid to Mrs. Fanshaw out of the Irish Revenue.[2]

The Earl was highly amused by Savile's account of the Leather Lane establishment. He suggests in his reply that if he were in good health he might write 'a small Romance' on the subject making 'the Sun with his dishievel'd Rays guild the Tops of the Palaces in Leather-Lane': 'Then shou'd those vile-Enchanters Barten and Ginman [presumably the physicians in charge of the establishment] lead forth their Illustrious Captives in Chains of Quicksilver, and confining 'em by Charms to the loathsome Banks of a dead Lake of Dyet-Drink; you, as my Friend, shou'd break the horrid Silence, and speak the most passionate fine things that ever Heroick Lover utter'd. . . . Thus wou'd I lead the mournful tale along, 'till the gentle Reader bath'd with the Tribute of his Eyes, the Names of such unfortunate Lovers.' 'It is a miraculous thing', he adds, 'when a Man, half in the Grave, cannot leave off playing the Fool, and the Buffoon.'[3]

On 13 July Savile writes triumphantly from Whitehall that he has been taken back into favour like the Roman general of old 'who was recalled from banishment to command the army', and he is dispatched on a special mission to France with Lord Sunderland, 'who goes Embassadour Extraordinary'. He proposes not to stay in France above three weeks, unless Rochester decides to come over and spend the winter there. He urges that a winter at Montpellier will do him much more good than one at Adderbury,

---

[1] This is Mrs. Jane Roberts see W., 106 and below, p. 195.
[2] W. 63; *Nell Gwin Royal Mistress* by J. H. Wilson, New York, 1952, 205; D.N.B., s.a. Lucy Walter; C.T.B., 1679–80, 284.
[3] Ibid., 65.

and that 'all domestick considerations must be sacrifised to those of health'.[1]

By the following April Rochester was once more in good health and spirits. On the 16th, Savile sends him a letter by a Mr. Hill, a servant of Ralph Montagu, the ambassador of Charles II at the Court of Louis XIV. With the letter he sends Rochester also the first present that he has sent into England since he has been in France: 'a pott of *Aigre de Cedre*, and two bottles of *Syrope de Capilaire*, both great coolers'. Now that Rochester is in such good health he believes that he will return to his 'usuall course of life', 'and in that case this may bee sometimes necessary to refresh you. . . .' With them are 'a bottle of *poudre de cypre* . . . and a bottle of myrtle water . . .' both apparently preparations for ladies' toilets. 'With these conveniences', he writes, 'and good health I shall not bee one of those friends who would advise you to keep your temperance or your virtue longer. They are both excellent in the way to health, but base companions of it'.[2] This is a pithy expression of the cheerful philosophy of the 'merry gang', the belief in

> That *Reason* that distinguishes by sense,
> And gives us *Rules*, of good, and ill from thence;
> That bounds desires, with a reforming Will,
> To keep 'em more in vigour, not to kill.[3]

It is the happy Epicureanism of St. Évremond who wrote that Rochester 'had more wit than any man in England'.[4] Savile has set his heart on seeing Rochester in France and urges that a long vacation will be 'as well past att Paris as at Woodstock'.[5]

On 30 June he had written to Rochester complaining that he had had no acknowledgment of his letter or present from Paris and that he is afraid either that Mr. Hill did not deliver them, or that Rochester did not think them worthy of thanks. There is a touch of reproach in this letter which shows that there was no trace of servility in Savile's relations with Rochester. He expresses the fear that his friend may be ill again.[6] As a matter of fact Rochester had begun to write a letter to Savile on 30th May but he did not finish it till 25 June.[7] He explains that 'neither Pride nor Neglect' caused his delay, 'but Idleness on one side, and not knowing what to say on the other'. He thanks Savile for his letter and present. Now it is

[1] Ibid., 66.   [2] Ibid., 67.   [3] P., 121.   [4] L.S.E., 323.   [5] W., 67.
[6] Ibid., 68.   [7] Ibid., 70, 71.

Rochester's turn to tell his friends the news of Whitehall. The rebellion of the Covenanters has broken out and Lauderdale is said to 'value himself' upon it and to tell the King, solemnly, 'it is very Auspicious and advantageous to the drift of the present Councils'. Monmouth is said to have departed unexpectedly with only two attendants, and so to have left in the lurch all the courtiers who volunteered to served in the expedition to Scotland. His object, according to Rochester, is to 'have the full Glory as well of the Prudential, as the Military part of this Action entire to himself'. Then mention is made of a curious rumour that an informer has promised to reveal 'Priests and Jesuits lands to the value of fourscore and ten thousand pounds a year.' If the King get this money into his hands, 'it is fear'd' that there will be an 'utter interruption of Parliaments'. Savile is informed that his 'high Protestancy at Paris' is greatly approved at home. He has attended the Protestant services at Charenton so often that Rochester suggests that either the Parliament or the Mayor and Common Council might petition the King that he should be 'dignified with the Title of that place, by way of Earldom or Dukedom, as his Majesty shall think most proper to give, or you to accept'. The letter ends delightfully with a reference to Savile's nephew with whom Rochester had dined at Sir William Coventry's: 'I thank God, there is yet a Harry Savile in England, with whom I drank your Health last week at Sir William Coventryes; and who in Features, Proportion, and Pledging, gives me so lively an Idea of yourself, that I am resolved to retire into Oxfordshire, and enjoy him till Shiloe come, or you from France.'

Rochester won the Woodstock Plate at Woodstock races with a grey horse on 16 September 1679.[1] It is not known whether he rode the grey horse himself on this occasion, but it would have been entirely in accordance with contemporary usage if he did. The jockeys in these races were often 'gentleman riders', and the King himself sometimes rode in horse races.

On 1 November he sent Savile a letter[2] by the French singing boy Baptiste whom he calls 'Mr. Baptist'. He describes him as 'this pretty Fool the bearer, whom I heartily recommend to your Favour and Protection, and whose qualities might recommend him more'. He assures Savile that 'the greatest and gravest of this Court of both Sexes have tasted his Beauties', and he profanely suggests

---

[1] Longueville, 247, 248.   [2] W., 72.

that homosexuality is part of the current Romanist propaganda
in England: 'Rome gains upon us here,' he writes, 'in this point
mainly.' This boy, Baptiste de Belle Fasse, remained in Rochester's service until the death of the Earl, who left him in his will all
his 'cloathes, lynnen and other things expressed in an inventorie in
his keeping'. We may perhaps connect him with Lycias the beautiful
singing 'eunuch' beloved by the Emperor in Rochester's *Valentinian*.
Although the evidence is slight, it seems likely that Rochester, like
Byron and some other men of genius, was of the 'bisexual' type that
can find erotic satisfaction in relationships with persons of both
sexes. Baptiste may well have played a part in his life similar to that
which John Edlestone (another singing boy) the subject of the
Thyrza poems, played in Byron's.

On 21 November he wrote to Savile a letter[1] full of disgust at
the condition of contemporary English society. The Utopia of
Gallantry has now turned into a hideous rout of rogues and harlots:

> The Lowsiness of Affairs in this place, is such (forgive the un-
> mannerly Phrase! Expressions must descend to the Nature of Things
> express'd) 'tis not fit to entertain a private Gentleman, much less one
> of a publick Character with the Retaile of them, the General Heads,
> under which this whole Island may be consider'd, are Spies, Beggars
> and Rebels, and the Transpositions and Mixtures of these, make an
> agreeable Variety; Busie Fools, and Cautious Knaves are bred out of
> 'em, and set off wonderfully; tho' of this latter sort, we have fewer now
> than ever, Hypocrisie being the only Vice in decay amongst us; few men
> here dissemble their being Rascals; and no Woman disowns being a
> Whore . . .

This letter, the tone of which recalls that of Swift in his most sardonic moods, concludes with an account of a quarrel arising out of a
recent 'Libel', a copy of which he sends to his friend: 'I have sent
you herewith a Libel, in which my own share is not the least; the
King having perus'd it, is no ways disatisfy'd with his: the Author
is apparently Mr. —; his Patron my — — having a Panegerick in the
midst, upon which happen'd a handsome Quarrel between his L—,
and Mrs. B— at the Dutchess of P—; she call'd him, the Heroe of
the Libel, and Complimented him upon having made more Cuckolds,
than any Man alive; to which he answer'd, She very well knew one
he never made, nor ever car'd to be imploy'd in making—Rogue and

[1] Ibid., 73.

Bitch ensued, till the King, taking his Grandfather's Character upon him, became the Peace-maker.' The 'Libel' in question was undoubtedly the lampoon called *An Essay Upon Satyr*, which was cirlating anonymously in manuscript in the late autumn of 1679.

Rochester's account of this scene at the Duchess of Portsmouth's is corroborated by Colonel Edward Cooke who, in a letter to the Duke of Ormonde dated 22 November 1679 gives the following account of the affair.[1]

> If I may be permitted to play at small game I shall repeat a particular that I was informed part this week at the Dutchess of Portsmouth's, where just before the King came in a most scurrilous libellous copy of verse was read, severe upon all the courtiers save my Lord Mulgrave, whose sole accusation was that he was a cuckold maker. This brought him under suspicion to be (if not guilty of the making, yet) guilty of being privy to the making of them, who just coming in with the King, Mrs. Buckley saluted him (in raillery) by the name of cuckold-maker, who taking it in earnest replied she knew one cuckold he never made, which she took for so great an affront that it seems her husband was entitled to the revenge. But the King, it seems, came to the knowledge of it, and interfered his authority to antidote bloodshed.

An Essay upon Satyr was certainly the work of Mulgrave, who included it, in a revised form, in the collected edition of his works published in 1723, though Dean Lockier, who knew Dryden well, stated that it 'was corrected a good deal by Dryden'.[2] In the original version, as first printed in the *Fourth and Last Collection of Poems, Satyrs, Songs* in 1689, it is a long, loose, sprawling work, the style and versification of which, except in a few passages, are undistinguished. After a rambling introduction in which the Royal mistresses, Shaftesbury and others are attacked, Mulgrave gives a series of verse 'characters' of the Court Wits. Dorset is sneered at for his matrimonial misadventures and described in one of the best lines in the poem as

> Drinking all night and dozing all the day.

It is suggested in an awkward couplet that he is as bad a poet as Ned Howard whom he formerly satirized:

> Dull as Ned Howard, whom his brisker times
> Had fam'd for dullness in malicious rhymes.

[1] H.M.C., Ormonde Papers, N.S., V, 242.
[2] Spence, 48. The text of my quotations from *An Essay upon Satyr* is Dryden, ed. Noyes, 914–16.

Mulgrave is described as 'learn'd in those ill arts that cheat the fair', and the cuckolds whom he has made were, it is implied in a rather obscure passage, disappointed in their hopes of 'sweet revenge', when a plot to involve him in matrimony failed, and

> As his estate, his person too was free.

Sedley is coarsely lampooned, because 'His meat and mistresses are kept too long', and then there follows a long, clumsy 'character' of Rochester.

> *Rochester* I despise for 's want of wit,
> Tho' thought to have a tail and cloven feet:
> For while he mischief means to all mankind,
> Himself alone the ill effects does find;
> And so like witches, justly suffers shame,
> Whose harmless malice is so much the same.
> False are his words, affected is his wit,
> So often does he aim, so seldom hit.
> To every face he cringes while he speaks
> But when the back is turn'd the head he breaks.
> Mean in each Action, lewd in every limb,
> Manners themselves are mischievous in him:
> A proof that chance alone makes every creature;
> A very Killigrew without good nature.

But Rochester's great fault was that he was not a fighting man. Mulgrave was the head of the Jingo party at Court, and Rochester and his friends, as we have seen, had no love for men of war, so the hero of the Knightsbridge duel stigmatizes his opponent as 'a Bessus' (alluding to the coward in Beaumont and Fletcher's tragedy) who is said to have 'contrived' 'his own kicking':

> For (there's the folly that's still mix'd with fear)
> Cowards more blows than any hero bear;
> Of fighting sparks, fame may her pleasure say,
> But 'tis a bolder thing to run away.

Then he turns to Rochester's poetry. He himself was a poetaster and was, doubtless, jealous of Rochester's success in the very kinds of writing in which he had so signally failed.

> I'd like to have left out his poetry,
> Forgot by all almost as well as me.
> Sometimes he has some humour, never wi
> And if it rarely, very rarely hit,

> 'Tis under so much nasty rubbish laid,
> To find it out's the cinder-woman's trade;
> Who for the wretched remnants of a fire,
> Must toil all day in ashes and in mire:
> So lewdly dull his idle works appear,
> The wretched texts deserve no comments here;[1]

That the author of *An Essay upon Satyr* should have attacked the author of *Artemisa's Letter* and the *Allusion to Horace* for lack of wit is surely one of the best jokes in literary history. The 'character' of Rochester in the Essay is full of the hatred of the man with a narrow, conventional mind for the original and courageous thinker. It is worthy of the writer who, after Rochester's death, sneered at

> Such nauseous Songs as the late Convert made,
> Which justly call this censure on his Shade.[2]

The wittiest and best written passage in the poem is, perhaps, that which deals with the King and his mistresses:

> Nor shall the royal mistresses be nam'd.
> Too ugly, or too easy to be blam'd;
> With whom each rhyming fool keeps such a pother,
> They are as common that way as the other
> Yet sauntering Charles between his beastly brace
> Meets with dissembling still in either place,
> Affected humor, or a painted face
> In loyal libels we have often told him,
> How one has jilted him, the other has sold him;
> How that affects to laugh, how this to weep;
> But who can rail so long as he can sleep?
> Was ever prince by two at once misled,
> False, foolish, old, ill natur'd and ill-bred?

The two royal mistresses attacked here are Nell Gwin and the Duchess of Portsmouth. Charles II, as Rochester's letter shows,[3] with his usual easy-going tolerance took no offence at this passage,

---

[2] This couplet is from Sheffield's *Essay on Poetry*, published in 1682 (text, Spingarn, II, 288). This poem must have been written soon after Rochester's death in 1680. In the version published in his collected works (Sheffield, I, 134), the author made the reference slightly less offensive by changing it to:

> Such nauseous Songs as a late Author made
> Call an unwilling Censure in his Shade.

A footnote indicates that person referred to is 'the E. of R.'.

[3] See above, p. 177.

and, Rochester, too, it is clear from the tone of his letter, regarded the whole affair with amused detachment. It is well known that Dryden on the night of 18 December 1679, was waylaid in Rose Alley, Covent Garden, and beaten up by unknown ruffians. The whole town knew that the cudgelling was due to the supposition that he was the author of *An Essay upon Satyr*. Rochester was too shrewd a critic, and, moreover, knew too much about Mulgrave to accept the current version of the authorship of the lampoon. It will be noticed that in his letter to Savile he only writes, 'the Author is *apparently* Mr. [Dryden]' (my italics).[1] We know that the scandalmongers of the town were only too ready to associate Rochester's name with any outrageous act and the facts that he had quarrelled with Dryden and Mulgrave and that he was attacked in *An Essay upon Satyr* were quite enough to start the rumour that he was responsible for the Rose Alley outrage. Gossip of this kind apparently reached the ears of Anthony à Wood at Oxford, perhaps through the medium of his usual informant John Aubrey. In his Life of George Villiers, Second Duke of Buckingham, probably written many years later, he denies a story that Buckingham was responsible for the castigation of Dryden 'at Will's Coffee House in Covent-Garden' but states that 'in Nov. (or before) an. 1679, there being an *Essay upon Satyr* spread about the city in MS. wherein many gross reflections were made on Ludovisa Dutchess of Portsmouth and John Wilmot E. of Rochester, they therefore took it for a truth that Dryden was the author: whereupon one or both hiring three men to cudgel him, they effected their business in the said coffe-house at 8 of the clock on the 16th of Dec. 1679; yet afterwards John, Earl of Mulgrave was generally thought to be the author'.[2] Now that it has been shown that the 'Black Will' letter had nothing to do with the Rose Alley episode, the extremely ambiguous statement of Wood seems to be the only seventeenth-century record that connects Rochester's name with the outrage. Actually it is of no value at all as evidence against Rochester. It was almost certainly written after 1687, the year of Buckingham's death, which is recorded in the Life of Buckingham in which it occurs. It gives the time and the place of the attack on Dryden incorrectly. We know from an advertisement that appeared in the *London Gazette* (18–22 December 1679), that the cudgelling took place on the night of 18 December in Rose Alley,[3]

---

[1] W., 73.   W.A.O., IV, 210.   [2]Dryden, ed. Scott., I, 204.

Covent Garden (not in Will's Coffee House as Wood states). It can be noted also that Wood had only heard vaguely that either the Duchess of Portsmouth or Rochester or both had hired the ruffians who committed the assault. Narcissus Luttrell, a much more reliable witness, in his *Brief Historical Relation of State Affairs* under the date December 1679 records the attack on Dryden. He does not mention Rochester but states the common opinion at the time was that the Duchess of Portsmouth was the real culprit: 'About the same time Mr. John Dryden was sett upon in Covent Garden in the evening by three fellowes, who beat him very severely, and on peoples comeing in they run away: 'tis thought to be done by order of the dutchesse of Portsmouth, she being abused in a late libell called An Essay upon satyr, of which Mr. Dryden is suspected to be the author.'[1]

Rochester, whatever his faults may have been, was never cruel or vindictive. His letter to Savile shows that he regarded the feeble lampooning of Mulgrave quite unemotionally. Louise de Kéroualle, however, who was unacquainted with the niceties of English poetic style, may well have believed that the poem was by Dryden and she must have been furious at being described as

> False, foolish, old, ill natur'd, and ill bred.

The passage on the royal mistresses is one of the few in the poem that have a vigour and a 'bite' worthy of Dryden and it is just possible that Louise may have heard that he had written or corrected this part of the poem. She had an instrument ready to hand in her brother-in-law already mentioned (see above p. 101) Philip Herbert, seventh Earl of Pembroke, the 'boarish' Pembroke, as he is called in a lampoon attributed to Rochester. This nobleman is mentioned in l. 183 of the *Essay*, and, though the allusion to him is fairly innocuous, he probably considered it an insult for his name even to appear in such a lampoon. He had a very black record. He nearly killed a man in a duel in November 1677. In a drunken scuffle in a Haymarket tavern in February 1678 he killed a certain Nathaniel Carey and was tried, condemned for manslaughter and pardoned.

---

[1] Luttrell, I, 30; cf. also the account quoted in T.T., 247 by Terriesi, the well-informed correspondent of the Grand Duke of Florence in London, which records the assault on Dryden but does not mention Rochester. According to Terriesi the assault was due to a satire which attacked the Ministers, the Duchess of Portsmouth and 'the very person of the King', but 'Mr. Dryden', 'protesta sua innocenza'.

On 18 August 1680, he killed an officer of the watch as he was coming out from a drinking bout at Turnham Green. According to Aubrey, he kept '52 mastives, 30 greyhounds, some beares and a lyon and a matter of 60 fellowes more bestiall than they'. It was probably three of these 'bestiall' fellows of Pembroke who cudgelled poor Dryden in Rose Alley on the night of 18 December 1679. A contemporary lampoon actually connects Pembroke with the Rose Alley affair. This anonymous poem called *A Satyr on the Poets in imitation of the Seventh Satyr of Juvenal* was first printed apparently in *Poems on Affairs of State*, 1698,[1] but from internal evidence it can be dated about 1681 or 1682. It contains the following lines in a passage near the end of the poem, where the author is ironically comparing the relationship between patrons and poets in his own age with that which existed between the '*Sydneys*' and '*Spencers*' of the Elizabethan age:

> *Pembrook* lov'd Tragedy, and did provide
> For Butchers Dogs, and for the whole Bank-side:
> The *Bear* was fed; but Dedicating *Lee*
> Was thought to have a larger Paunch than he.
> More could I say; but care not much to meet
> A Crab-Tree Cudgell, in a narrow Street.

The obvious meaning of the last couplet is that the author is going to be careful not to give offence for fear of incurring the same punishment as that which Pembroke inflicted on Dryden. The 'narrow street' is almost certainly Rose Alley.

The old story that Rochester was a malicious persecutor and Dryden a pitiable victim is now seen to be wholly false. They were two gifted men with incompatible temperaments. If Rochester displayed a certain amount of aristocratic haughtiness, Dryden was certainly quick to take offence and impatient of criticism. There is no doubt that Rochester's personality and poetry made a deep impression on him, deeper, perhaps, than he cared to admit. When the younger poet died in 1680, Dryden still had before him twenty years of crowded and creative life. He mentions Rochester several times in his later writings and always with kindness. In his *Discourse Concerning the Original and Progress of Satire* (1693), addressed to Rochester's friend Dorset, he speaks of him as 'an author of your own quality (whose ashes I will not disturb)'. Some sayings of

[1] P.O.A.S., 1698, 57.

Rochester stuck in his mind. On two different occasions[1] he quotes Rochester's profane remark about a certain poet (probably Cowley), 'Not being of God, he could not stand', and in another place he recalls his sardonic comment on a writer of a bad tragedy who boasted that he had written his play in three weeks: 'How the devil could he have been so long over it?'[2] Grave, pious John Evelyn probably heard talk like this when he met Rochester at dinner at the house of Sir Thomas Clifford on 23 November 1670 and noted in his diary that he was 'a very prophane Wit'.[3]

[1] Dryden, ed. Noyes, 515, 744.
[3] E.D., III, 565.

[2] Dryden, ed. Scott, XVII, 332.

Chapter Nine

————⟨⟨◆⟩⟩⟨⟨◆⟩⟩————

DIVINUM ALIQUID

————⟨⟨◆⟩⟩⟨⟨◆⟩⟩————

I

This materialism is a seducing system to young and super-
ficial minds. It allows its disciples to talk and dispenses them
from thinking. But I was discontented with such a view
of things. . . .

SHELLEY, *On Life.*

FROM his youth Rochester had always 'loved to talk and write
of Speculative Matters, and did it with so fine a thread, that even
those who hated the Subjects that his Fancy ran upon, yet could not
but be charmed with his way of treating of them'.[1] He wanted to
know the meaning of life and of death, and after his great sickness
he turned his attention more and more to these ultimate problems.
His mind was essentially dialectical. He was always aware of the
voice of the opponent. Robert Parsons relates an illuminating story
that Rochester told him in the last days of his life:

'One day at an Atheistical Meeting, at a person of Qualities,' I
undertook to manage the Cause, and was the principal Disputant
against God and Piety, and for my performances received the
applause of the whole company; upon which my mind was terribly
struck, and I immediately reply'd thus to myself. Good God! that a
Man, that walks upright, that sees the wonderful works of God, and
has the use of his senses and reason, should use them to the defying
of his Creator!'[2] Rochester was always 'replying to himself'. His

---

[1] B.S.P., 78.   [2] Parsons, 23.

celebrated conversion to religion was no sudden *volte-face*; it was the culminating point of a dialectical process which had been going on in his mind for years.

For a long time the orthodox answers to his questioning were associated in his mind with a narrow and insincere religiosity. Hobbes's materialism had appealed to him at first because of its boldness and the justification that it offered for the life of pleasure. But the *Satyr against Mankind* shows that by the spring of 1675–6 he was outgrowing that 'seducing system', and it was natural that he should turn to the other unorthodox creeds which were current at the time in Western Europe. As he was often in Paris, it is highly probable that he knew something of the works of the French 'libertins', and perhaps had read *Les Quatrains du Déiste*, the notorious anti-Christian poem written about 1622, which circulated in manuscript,[1] and the writings of Théophile de Viau. In the spring of 1675–6 a poem called *Faith and Reason* was being handed round the town in manuscript, and it was commonly attributed to Rochester.[2] It is in the form of an extra canto to Davenant's unfinished epic of *Gondibert* and shows the old sage, Astragon, who is perhaps meant to represent Hobbes, on his death-bed, and grieving at the approach of death. His disciples are troubled and choose one of their number called Thanour to expound their doubts; and most of the poem consists of a long monologue by Thanour on the subject of Faith and Reason, full of powerful arguments against orthodox religious doctrine, bearing some resemblance to those used by the author of *Les Quatrains du Déiste*. The poem was printed as Davenant's in the folio edition of his works in 1673.[3] If it be his, it must, therefore, have been written before his death in April 1668. The association of Rochester's name with *Faith and Reason* may well be due to the supposition that Davenant meant Thanour's arguments to represent Rochester's views. Thanour is Astragon's chief disciple just as Rochester was a leading disciple of Hobbes, and Davenant may have been struck by some of Rochester's brilliant talk on 'Speculative Matters' and embodied it in the speech of Thanour. John Verney, the son of Sir Ralph Verney. Rochester's old guardian, believed *Faith and Reason* to be the work of Rochester and he compares its

[1] Lachère, ii, 105–26.
[2] H.M.C., 7th Rep., App., 467. See also V. de S. Pinto in T.L.S., 22 Nov. and 6 Dec. 1934.
[3] Davenant, 326–35.

'sense' with that of *A Satyr against Mankind.*[1] It is the work of a
mind which is deeply troubled by the apparent irrationality of the
powers that govern human life and the Universe:

> Then hard is Destinie's dark Law; whose Text,
> We are forbid to read, yet must obey;
> And reason with her useless eyes is vext,
> Which strives to guide her where they see no way.

There is, however, much stronger evidence of Rochester's association
with the unorthodox philosophies of his time than the attribution to
him of *Faith and Reason.* When he was in London during the winter
of 1678–9 he seems to have made the acquaintance of a young man
called Charles Blount, the son of Sir Henry Blount, the merry, keen-
witted old philosopher of whom Aubrey tells several good tales.
Blount was twenty-four at this time, and was recognized as one of
the leaders of the English deists or freethinkers who rejected 'revealed religion' and accepted the 'five points' of Lord Herbert of
Cherbury.[2] From a letter of Blount to Rochester dated 'Ludgate-
Hill, Decem. 1678',[3] we learn the Earl and his young friend had
been having '*discourse . . . about the great Changes and Revolutions
that from time to time had happen'd in the Universe*'. Blount undertook to prove to Rochester that '*a Temporal Interest was the great
Machine upon which all human Actions moved; and that the common
and general pretence of Piety and Religion, was but like Grace before
a Meal*'. This sounds very much like the modern 'economic inter-
pretation of history'. In this letter, which is the earliest of three
which he wrote to Rochester, Blount tries to apply his doctrine to the
origin and rise of Christianity. He begins by showing that the sects
of the Pharisees, Sadducees and Essenes were very late develop-
ments in Jewish history, and ascribes their origin to the influence of
Greek philosophy. After the Maccabean rebellion, when Greek
philosophy was 'anathematized', the Sadducees and Pharisees tried
to 'justifie their tenets' by ascribing them 'to Sadoc and Baithos',
and 'the other' (presumably the Essenes) 'to a Cabala derived successively from Ezra and Moses'. It was this 'Cabala' or unwritten
tradition, according to Blount, that was used to interpret the prophecy
of Jacob concerning Shiloh as a prophecy of a Messiah who would
come to rule over Israel. He takes pains to show that the Messianic

---

[1] H.M.C., loc. cit.   [2] D.N.B., s.a. Charles Blount.   [3] Blount, 158–73.

tradition was due entirely to this 'fantastic *Cabala*' and that 'a mysterious promise of a Redeemer was insinuated thereby', and other prophecies in the Old Testament were used for the same purpose. In fact Blount is delivering a shattering attack on the great bulwark of seventeenth-century orthodoxy, the proof of Christ's divine mission by means of the Old Testament prophecies. He goes on to assert that at the time of the birth of Jesus the world was 'big with expectation (rais'd in every Country by the *Jews*, who had received their intelligence from their common Metropolis *Jerusalem*) that the great Prince was coming . . .'. 'These circumstances', he contends, 'made way for the reception of Christ, and the Miracles that he did (for Miracles were the only Demonstrations for the *Jews*) convincing the People that he was the Messiah, they never staid till he should declare himself to be so: (for I think he never directly told any he was so, but the Woman of Samaria).' He ascribes the alienation of the affection of the Jews for Christ (after what he irreverently describes as 'his Cavalcade upon an *Asinego*') to their disappointment that he did not make himself King, and attributes the flight of the disciples and the distrust of the Apostles to the same cause. But after the Resurrection (in which it was not yet safe to express open disbelief), the hope of the temporal Messiahship revived, and Blount finds it an easy task to prove that all the early Christians were 'millenaries', expecting 'the temporal reign of a Messiah together with the Union of *Jews* and *Gentiles* under one most happy monarchy'. He supports this contention by reference to Justin Martyr and Irenaeus, and calls the doctrine of the Second Coming 'a pretence . . . that stopt the Mouths of the unbelieving *Jews*' who 'upon his Death and suffering like other Men, began to doubt very much of the Power of his Messiahship . . . wherefore this *Millenary* Invention of his coming again to reign in Glory salv'd all'. These words are significant; they reveal Blount's true object, which was to show that Christian orthodoxy was based on the deliberate inventions of cunning priests, and the delusions of ignorant and credulous people. He is turning on to the sacred traditions of European religion the dry, hard light of the Enlightenment.

In the following winter Rochester was again in London and was engaged in his famous conversations with Burnet. Early in 1680, however, he saw his friend Blount and had some discussion with him concerning immortality and the soul. On 6 February he sent

Blount[1] a poem on Death suggested by the famous chorus in the *Troades* of Seneca, 'Post mortem nihil est, ipsaque mors nihil':

> After Death nothing is, and nothing Death:
> The utmost limits of a gasp of Breath.
> Let the ambitious Zealot lay aside
> His hopes of Heav'n; (whose Faith is but his Pride)
> Let slavish Souls lay by their Fear,
> Nor be concern'd which way or where,
> After this life they shall be hurl'd:
> Dead, we become the Lumber of the World;
> And to that Mass of Matter shall be swept,
> Where things destroy'd, with things unborn are kept;
> Devouring time swallows us whole,
> Impartial Death confounds Body and Soul.
> For Hell and the foul Fiend that rules
>   The everlasting fiery Goals,
> Devis'd by Rogues, dreaded by Fools,
> With his grim griesly Dog that keeps the Door,
>   Are senseless Stories, idle Tales
> Dreams, Whimseys, and no more.[2]

This is a greater poem even than the fine Latin lyric that suggested it. It cannot be classed as a mere translation. It is an original work based on hints from the lines in the *Troades*. Three laconic verses of Seneca are expanded into six of the most powerful lines in the whole of the English poetry of the seventeenth century:

> Spem ponant avidi; soliciti metum.
> Quaeris quo jaceas post obitum loco?
> Quo non nata jacent.

> Let slavish Souls lay by their Fear,
> Nor be concern'd which way, or where,
> After this life they shall be hurl'd:
> Dead, we become the Lumber of the World;
> And to that Mass of Matter shall be swept,
> Where things destroy'd, with things unborn are
>   kept; . . .

Lucretius, who was one of Rochester's favourite poets,[3] has counted for something here besides Seneca; the poem has a quality similar

---

[1] Ibid.   [2] P., 49, 179, 180.   [3] V. Sig. C 4.

to that of the triumphant arguments against immortality in the third
book of the *De Natura Rerum*. Rochester's mind, like that of Lucretius, is essentially religious in spite of his negative creed. The
external or 'prose', meaning of his poem is that the hope of immortality is a delusion, but its poetic significance is that of a hymn
to the grandeur of the Death which is an annihilation and the vision
of an infinite desolation, a universe of lifeless matter. For Rochester
the poet, the idea of Death is too great to be associated with 'Senseless Stories' and 'Whimseys' about Hell and the Devil. His repu-
diation of them is not the mere denial of the rationalist; it is the de-
mand of a spirit that wants to worship overwhelming greatness and
can only find it in utter annihilation. It is a spirit that is essentially
akin to those of the great poets and preachers of a former generation,
of Ralegh with his address to an 'eloquent, just and mighty Death',
and of Donne with his vision of 'the dust of dead kings . . . blown
into the street, and the dust of the street blown into the river, and the
muddy river tumbled to the sea'. Notice that the metrical movement
of Rochester's poem begins with the stately march of the heroic
couplet, and dies away with the subtler lyric music of an earlier age.
Similarly the style combines the energy and perspicuity of the
Augustans with the spiritual grandeur of the great Metaphysicals.

Blount, in his reply to Rochester dated 7 February 1679–80,[1]
makes the following shrewd comment on the poem on Death. '[I]
must confess, with your Lordship's Pardon, that I cannot but esteem
the Translation to be, in some measure a confutation of the Original;
since what less than a divine and immortal Mind could have produced what you have written? Indeed the Hand that wrote it may
become *Lumber*, but sure the Spirit that dictated it can never be so:
No, my Lord, your mighty Genius is a most sufficient Argument of
its own Immortality; and more prevalent with me, than all the
Harangues of the Parsons, or Sophistry of the Schoolmen.' In the
same letter Blount gives Rochester some account of his own views
on immortality. It is difficult to find out exactly what they are, as he
is extremely guarded. He quotes passages from Ecclesiastes to show
that some of the writers of the Bible did not believe in immortality.
He mentions the Anima Mundi of Pythagoras, and the heretical
opinions of Averroes and Avicenna, which he compares with Monsieur Bernier's account of the opinion of 'some of the Indians of

---

[1] Blount, 117–27.

Indoston' concerning the reunion of the soul after death with the 'common Ocean' of being. He cites Apollonius of Tyana's verses on immortality as recorded by Philostratus, and translates a long passage from Pliny's *Natural History* where the common notions of immortality are described as 'fantastical, foolish and childish Toys, devised by Men that would fain live always'. He then turns to the argument of 'some of our Moderns' that 'if the Soul be not immortal the whole Universe would at this time be deceived, since all our Laws do now suppose it so'. This line of argument impresses him a good deal. Like most seventeenth-century thinkers he seems to feel that there is much to be said for estimating philosophic doctrines according to their 'suasive' value, and he quotes an observation that he ascribes to 'Plato and Aristotle', 'That a Politician is a Physician of Minds, and that his Aim is rather to make Men good than knowing.' He proceeds to insinuate that the popular notions of Heaven and Hell were invented by politicians to frighten the savage and vicious on the one hand, and to encourage the virtuous and the gentle on the other. Such 'Politicians' who 'devise Fables only to regulate the People' (in which Fables according to Averroes cited by Blount 'there is properly neither Truth nor Falsehood') are compared to Nurses who 'bring their children to those things which they know are Good for them after the like manner'. Blount hints that if all men were to be wise and virtuous it might be admitted that the soul was mortal, for such men would still continue to be good without hope of reward or fear of punishment, but, as most men are not capable of this kind of virtue, 'other Expedients' become necessary. Then, as though he feels that he has gone too far, he hastens to declare that immortality (with rewards and punishments) is a necessary corollary to any conception of a rational deity. Unless there is such an immortality, God will be, in Blount's picturesque phrase, only 'a hum-drum Deity chewing his own Nature, a droning God . . . hugging of himself, and hoarding up his Providence from his Creatures'. But it is quite possible that the writer's real meaning is that, as belief in a rational God is necessary for 'suasive' purposes, so the belief in immortality must be accepted as a necessary part of the doctrine. He concludes by referring Rochester to the Italian philosopher Pomponazzi (Pomponatius) and Cardan, the famous medical writer.

Rochester's interest in the nature of the soul, prompted him to ask Blount to let him have the opinions of his father, Sir Henry

Blount, on the subject and on 18 February,[1] in answer to a request from his friend, Charles Blount sent what he calls 'an undigested heap of my Father's Thoughts concerning the Souls acting, as it were in a state of matrimony with the Body'. This fragment by Sir Henry Blount is in Latin, and is an exceedingly interesting and typical product of the seventeenth-century mind. The Spirit in man is said to be like a flame being constantly renewed and always changing, just as his body is always changing. It is suggested that, as the body assimilates the physical part of food, so the soul assimilates the spiritual. We are reminded of the lines spoken by Milton's Raphael:

> Therefore what he gives
> (Whose praise be ever sung) to Man, in part
> Spiritual, may of purest Spirits be found
> No ingrateful food: and food alike those pure
> Intelligential substances require
> As doth your Rational.

Sir Henry Blount's implication, like Milton's, is that 'Spirit' is simply a very refined sort of 'matter'. This view of the soul is combined logically enough with pantheism: 'est Deus in rebus, estque omnia atque omnia agit'. The body and soul of the world are eternal, but are continually changing, and men are 'aeterni Dei apparitiones momentanae'. Charles Blount describes these opinions as 'such twilight Cojectures as our human Reason (whereof we yet so vainly boast can furnish us with'. He admits that the divine element in the world (τὸ θεῖον, or *Divinum Aliquid*) 'is that which does all things; but our capacity not being able to discern it, makes us fasten either upon elementary Qualities, as *Hippocrates* and *Galen* do: Or upon Geometrical Proportions, as our Modern *Descartes* doth; so that (indeed) all Philosophy, excepting Sceptism, is little more than Dotage.' Here indeed was a confession of failure. 'Sceptism' could no longer satisfy Rochester. It was exactly this divine element, this *Divinum Aliquid* that he wanted, not merely to recognize as existing, but to feel and to experience personally. Only through religion could he attain to such an experience, and from religion he had hitherto been cut off by barriers for which the particular form of Christianity practised in his age and country was largely responsible.

It was, perhaps, at about this time that he received a visit from his

---

[1] Ibid., 154-7.

old tutor Francis Giffard, now vicar of Pattishall in Northampton-
shire, of whom, we are told, he 'had always a very good opinion'.
Rochester said to Giffard on this occasion, 'Mr. Giffard, I wonder
you will not come to visit me oftner. I have a great respect for you and
I should be extremely glad of your frequent conversation.' Giffard,
who 'could say anything to him' answered, 'My lord, I am a clergyman. Your lordship has a very ill character of being a debauched man
and an atheist, and 'twill not look well in me to keep company with
your lordship so long as this character lasts, and as long as you continue this course of life.' 'Mr. Giffard,' said Rochester, 'I have been
guilty of extravagances, but I will assure you I am no atheist.' This
incident was related by Giffard to his friend Thomas Hearne, the
antiquary, many years later. He also told Hearne that 'my lord
understood very little Greek, and that he had but little Latin, and
that therefore 'tis a great mistake in making him (as Burnett and
Wood have done) so great a master of classick learning'. However,
Giffard was a scholar and his standards in classical learning were
doubtless high. He told Hearne that Rochester suffered badly from
constipation: 'My lord had a natural distemper upon him, which was
extraordinary, and he thinks might be one occasion of shortening
his days, which was, that sometimes he could not have a stool for
three weeks or a month together. Which distemper his lordship
told him was a very great occasion of that warmth and heat he
always expressed, his braine being heated by the fumes and humours
that ascended and evacuated themselves in this way.'[1]

II

It is true that a little Philosophy inclineth Mans mind to
Atheism, but depth in Philosophy bringeth Mens minds
about to Religion.
BACON, *Of Atheism*.

The last, and in some ways the most interesting, phase of Rochester's life is marked by the establishment of contact between his
proud and fearless spirit, and the one kind of contemporary religion
that could help him, the rationalized latitudinarian Anglicanism of
the Restoration. This kind of religion came to Rochester through the

[1] H.R.H., I, 241-3.

medium of Gilbert Burnet, a man who may be described as his opposite in almost every way. Perhaps the only qualities that Rochester and Burnet had in common were intellectual honesty, courage and literary ability. Burnet was a learned, acute, industrious, keen-witted, upright, conscientious Scot. He was four years older than Rochester, and his life had been as full of hard work as Rochester's had been full of pleasure. The son of a Scottish royalist lawyer and a pious Presbyterian lady, he had gone to Aberdeen University at the age of ten, when he was already 'master of the Latin tongue'! At the University he perfected himself in Greek, Aristotelian logic and philosophy, and graduated as M.A. a year before Rochester went up to Oxford. He resolved to enter the Church, and pursued 'a very hard course of study in theology'. While Rochester was drinking in Oxford taverns and escaping from the proctors with the help of his borrowed gown, the young Scottish student was working for fourteen hours a day amid his great folios of the Fathers, the Schoolmen, and the Reformers. He took orders in the Scottish Episcopal Church in 1661. An important event in his life was his introduction by a Mr. Nairn, 'minister of the Abbey Church at Edinburgh', to John Smith's recently published *Select Discourses*, the great exposition of the new Platonist and Latitudinarian doctrines in the Church of England. Henceforth Burnet became a strong supporter of the Cambridge Platonists and adopted their liberal Christianity with enthusiasm. He visited the English universities in 1663, and met several of the English philosophic divines, Cudworth, Henry More, and Alexander Burnet. In London he made the acquaintance of Whichcote and the younger Latitudinarians, Tillotson and Patrick. He travelled on the Continent, returned to Scotland, and became, first minister of Saltoun, and then Professor of Divinity at Glasgow University, where he worked with amazing energy, 'answering the duty of a Professor with the assiduity of a Schoolmaster'. He refused a Scottish bishopric, but Charles II was so impressed by his preaching that he made him one of his Chaplains. He resigned from his chair at Glasgow, because of a quarrel with the Duke of Lauderdale, and came to London, where in 1675 he was appointed Chaplain to the Rolls and lecturer at St. Clement's.[1] He made a great reputation as a preacher in England and became the friend of many distinguished men. His frankness

---

[1] See Life of Gilbert Burnet by T. Burnet in B.H., VI, 247-335.

and humour endeared him to some of the Court Wits, and particularly to George Savile, Marquis of Halifax, the brother of Rochester's friend.[1] In the summer of 1678 he had attended on a dying
lady, possibly Mrs. Jane Roberts (see above, p. 174), who had been
'engaged in a criminal amour' (to use his own expression) with
Rochester. This seems to have been the first time that Rochester
heard of him.[2] During his convalescence Rochester had read the first
volume of Burnet's *History of the Reformation*, which had appeared
in the spring of 1679, with much pleasure, and after his recovery
he had met the Scottish clergyman 'accidentally in two or three
places'. In October 1679, Burnet heard from a gentleman of his
acquaintance (possibly Halifax) that Rochester would like to see
him.[3] After a few visits a genuine friendship sprang up between
these two curiously different characters. Rochester must have been
biased in favour of Scotsmen because of his pleasant recollections
of his old tutor. In Burnet, too, he probably found a clergyman of a
kind that he had not known before, a seeker after truth with a real
interest in philosophic discussion, not a mere conventional mouth-
piece for musty traditional theology. It must have seemed to him
that he had really found the sort of parson that he sketched in the
epilogue to *A Satyr against Mankind*:

a *Church-Man* who on *God* relyes,
Whose Life, his Faith, and Doctrine Justifies.

Burnet gained his confidence to such an extent that Rochester told
him that he would treat him 'with more freedom than he had ever
used to men of my Profession'. He gave him 'a full view' of his past
life, of which unfortunately Burnet in his *Life and Death of John,
Earl of Rochester*, gives only a brief summary. They agreed then to
enter into a regular debate on the subjects of religion and morality.

Throughout the winter Burnet continued to visit his friend, presumably at his lodgings at Whitehall. Rochester was 'in a low state
of health, and seemed to be slowly recovering of a great Disease'.
He was 'in the Milk-Diet, and apt to fall into Hectical-Fits'. But
he was well enough to go out often, and 'had great Vivacity of
Spirit'. Burnet is certain that he was 'under no such decay, as
either darkened or weakened his Understanding; Nor was he any
way troubled with the Spleen, or Vapours, or under the power of

[1] Marshall, 29.   [2] T. Burnet, op. cit., 269, 270.   [3] B.S.P., Preface, Sig. A 5.

195

Melancholy'. Those who had known him formerly told Burnet that 'they perceived no difference in his parts'. It is to be regretted that no painter has preserved for us the likeness of one of those interviews when the handsome, pale, emaciated English nobleman confronted the burly, broad-shouldered Scottish parson and argued with him about God and the Soul. Their 'freest Conversation' took place when they were alone, but on some occasions others were present, and Burnet learned from them that Rochester took pleasure in the conversations and that the subjects discussed were 'not unacceptable' to him.[1] We can imagine the sensation that must have been caused at Whitehall when it was known that the prince of the 'merry gang', the scoffer at religion and morality was engaged in serious discourse with the learned and pious Dr. Burnet. Burnet did not take notes of these conversations during the winter of 1679–80, but he had a remarkable memory, which had been specially trained in his youth, when, following the practice of the Scottish clergy of his day, he used to memorize the whole of his sermons and deliver them without notes. Therefore, when he came to write his account of Rochester's *Life and Death* about a year later, he was able to give the substance of the conversations pretty accurately, though he admits that he may have enlarged his own part in the discussions somewhat, and this is comprehensible, when we remember that he wrote his book with a definitely didactic aim. 'I am not so sure', he writes, 'of all I set down as said by me, as I am of all said by him to me. But yet the substance of the greatest part, even of that, is the same.' He does not 'pretend to have given the formal words' spoken by Rochester, 'though I have done that where I could remember them'.[2] The frankness of these statements inspires confidence in Burnet's account as accurate in substance, if not always in detail.

What is remarkable in the discussions as Burnet reports them is their fairness and reasonableness and freedom from dogmatizing. Both men, we feel, are true sons of the Enlightenment. Rochester is quite willing to admit the validity of arguments in favour of Christianity, and Burnet never appeals to authority, but always to reason. The temper of the discussion is not that of a medieval priest with a sinner, but of Socrates and his friends searching for truth in a thoroughly disinterested manner. Rochester's starting-point is that of the sceptical deist of the school of Lord Herbert of Cherbury and

Charles Blount, and Burnet's that of the liberal Anglican of the
school of Whichcote and Smith. Burnet's technique in argument is
to make religion appear not as a body of doctrine imposed from
above by a supernatural tyrant, but as an inward spiritual force or
'principle' which grows up in men who lead good lives. He mini-
mizes the dogmatic and historical part of Christianity and lays the
greatest stress on religious experience. It was the technique of
Burnet's masters, the Cambridge Platonists, and it was thoroughly
in harmony with the spirit of the age which had no liking for
'mysteries', but which had the greatest respect for anything that
could be proved by practical experiment.

Burnet records the discussions under three heads,[1] '*Morality,
Natural Religion* and *Revealed Religion, Christianity* in particular'.
Under the first, Rochester disavows the mere immoralism that had
governed much of his life and declares himself to be ashamed of it
'rather because he had made himself a Beast, and had brought pain
and sickness on his Body, and had suffered much in his Reputation,
than from any deep sense of a Supream being, or another State'. In
fact he regarded his faults not as 'sins' in the religious sense, not as
'Offences against God', but 'only as Injuries to himself and to Mankind'. He resolved now to change the course of his life, and thought
that he could effect it by the study of philosophy. Burnet praises
some of these notions as 'no less solid than pleasant', but shrewdly
contends that a morality founded on 'philosophy' alone is not likely
to be able to 'bear down the Propensities of Nature, Appetite or
Passion'. He finds that the Stoic maxim that all passion should be
extirpated is impracticable, as it is contrary to nature. Rochester
told him that the 'two *Maxims* of his *Morality* then were, that he
should do nothing to the hurt of any other, or that might prejudice
his own health'. 'All pleasure, when it did not interfere with these,
was to be indulged as gratification of our natural Appetites', and he
applied these principles especially to 'the free use of Wine and
Women'. This is exactly the cheerful epicurean doctrine of his correspondence with Savile. Burnet replied acutely that, if all natural
appetites were to be satisfied, there were also in some men natural
appetites for murder and stealing, and, if injury to others is admitted
as a cause for restraint, 'the Injury is as great, if a Man's Wife is
defiled, or his Daughter corrupted'. He suggests that appetites exist

[1] The source for the discussions described in the following pages is B.S.P., 35–127.

in men in order that they may be governed by reason, just as wild beasts exist so that they may be 'managed and tamed' by human wisdom. The government of the passions by reason 'Ministers to a higher and more lasting Pleasure to a Man, than to give them their full scope and range'. If Burnet had lived two hundred years later he might have quoted Coventry Patmore:

> Live greatly; so shalt thou acquire
> Unknown capacities for joy.

It is Milton's doctrine in *Paradise Lost*. Passion is justified only when controlled by reason. Burnet then proceeds to argue that the only really valuable kind of virtue is a positive force, and not a mere negation of sin or restraint of appetite. '*Morality* could not be a strong thing, unless a man were determined by a Law within himself.' He must be 'internally regenerated, and changed by a higher Principle'. This is the teaching of the Cambridge Platonists, of Benjamin Whichcote and John Smith, the religion of the good life and the inner light which is 'the Candle of the Lord'.

Rochester replied to this line of argument at first rather sarcastically, in the manner of Hobbes: 'This', he said, 'sounded to him like *Enthusiasme*, or *Canting*: He had no notion of it, and so could not understand it.' Burnet pressed him further, and urged that 'all his Speculations of *Philosophy* would not serve him in any stead, to the reforming of his Nature and Life, till he applied himself to God for inward assistances'. He spoke of the 'disengagement' from sinful 'Impressions' felt by those who 'apply themselves to God by earnest Prayer'. Rochester could only see in this 'the effect of a heat in Nature', and thought that 'if one could turn to a *Problem* in *Euclid*, or to Write a Copy of Verses, it would have the same effect'. Burnet retorted that 'if such Methods did only divert the thoughts, there might be some force in what he said: but if they not only drove out such Inclinations, but begat Impressions contrary to them, and brought men into a new disposition and habit of mind', then his opponent must confess 'there was somewhat more than a diversion in these changes'. It is important to notice that to support these arguments Burnet appeals not to authority but to 'Reason and Experience'. He contends that, if the existence of God be granted, it is reasonable to suppose that he could and would give 'his assistance to such as desired it'. Experience concurred with this 'reasonable' deduction, because good men 'upon their frequent Applications

to God in Prayer' do actually feel a 'freedom from those ill
Impressions that formerly subdued them, an inward love to Vertue
and true Goodness, an easiness and delight in all the parts of Holi-
ness . . . and *had as real a Perception of an inward strength in their
Minds, that did rise and fall with true Devotion, as they perceived the
strength of their Bodies increased or abated according as they had or
wanted good nourishment'*. The words which I have italicized are
significant. Burnet wanted to show that religious experience was
something which could be demonstrated by experiment, something
as real as the growth of the physical body. Rochester was obviously
affected by this argument, which, we are told, was pursued in 'many
Discourses', but he still continued to think that 'all was the effect of
Fancy', though he went so far as to admit that 'he thought they were
very happy whose Fancies were under the Power of such Impressions'. This was an important point gained by Burnet. It was an
admission, not, indeed, of the 'truth' of religious experience, but of
the 'suasive' value of a belief in it, which to seventeenth-century
minds, and especially, as we have seen, to the deists was a kind of
'truth'. It amounts really to admitting that men are happy if they
think that an inward 'principle' comes into their minds as a result
of religion, and this surely is very much the same thing as admitting
that the inward 'principle' is really there. This argument made a
great impression on Rochester. It was showing him the one real way
of escape from the barren world of the materialists and the sceptics.
During his last illness he told Burnet that 'He had another sense of
what we had talked concerning prayer and inward assistances'.

All Burnet's discourses under the other 'Heads' tend to converge
in the same direction. Rochester expounded the deistical view of
'natural religion'. He affirmed his belief in 'a Supream Being' who
had created the universe. He further defined God as 'a vast Power
that wrought every thing by the necessity of its Nature', and he
denied that God could have 'those Affections of Love or Hatred,
which breed perturbation in us'. Hence he deduced that there were
no rewards or punishments after death. These statements recall not
only Charles Blount, but the much greater name of Spinoza, whose
Tractatus Theologico-Politicus had appeared at Amsterdam in 1670,
and had been read by advanced thinkers all over Europe. It is possible, too, that Rochester may have heard of the *Ethics*, which was
completed in 1674, and circulated in manuscript, though it was not
published till after Spinoza's death in 1677. Rochester's conception

of God is very much like the Spinozistic deity of the *Ethics*, who is 'free from passions', and not affected 'by any emotion of pleasure or pain'. As for the 'state after death', Rochester thought that 'the Soul did not dissolve'. Like Sir Henry Blount, he was probably thinking of it as a fine sort of matter which left the body at death. But he 'doubted much of Rewards or Punishments', because 'the one he thought too high for us to attain, by our slight Services; and the other was too extream to be inflicted for Sin'. He has the deist's aversion to ceremonial worship, no doubt strengthened by his own memories of the churchgoing that he had to endure in his boyhood. He suggests that 'there should be no other Religious Worship, but a general Celebration of that Being, in some short Hymn'. Other kinds of religious worship are dismissed in Voltairian fashion as the 'Inventions of Priests, to make the World believe they had a Secret of Incensing and Appeasing God as they pleased', and the notion of Providence is also rejected. It is clear that the old view of worship as the propitiation of an angry deity is particularly revolting to Rochester's essentially modern mind.

Burnet's answer deals with 'natural religion' under four headings: the Nature of God, the State after Death, Providence, and Prayer. He stigmatizes Rochester's God not unjustly as 'nothing but Nature', reminding us of Spinoza's 'Deus sive Natura'. He substitutes for this 'Natural God', one who is 'Wise and Good', or in other words a deification of these concepts. He can thus make the Christian deity appear quite as 'reasonable' as the God of the deists. He declares that it is necessary for a 'Rational Being' not only to love itself but to love all who are like itself. He agrees implicitly that God is passionless, and contends that his love for mankind does not raise 'Passion or Perturbation in him'. Such perturbations in men are not due to love but to weakness, 'want of power, or skill to do what we wish or desire'. 'Rewards and Punishments' are deduced logically from the premises that a reasonable deity will want to reward good men, and that such rewards do not 'appear in this State'. Hence they will appear in the next 'State' together with what seem to Burnet their necessary counterpart of punishments. It is noticeable that in speaking of 'Rewards and Punishments' Burnet is careful to avoid the 'superstitious' pictorial views of them. In the words of Whichcote he shows them as '*first* a Temper, and then a *Place*'. The punishment of the damned is no longer hell fire but 'a total exclusion from him, with all the horrour and darkness that must follow that'. Notice that the conceptual word 'horrour' is given the first place, while the pictorial word 'darkness' may also be taken in a psychological sense. Moreover, the 'Rewards and Punishments' are explained rationally as states of mind due to the memory of their past lives that may reasonably be supposed to persist in disembodied spirits, whose existence Rochester had admitted. According as departed souls have good or ill dispositions, so they 'either rise up to a higher Perfection, or sink to a more depraved, and miserable State'. Providence is deduced logically from the existence and power of God. The only argument against it is the complexity of the Universe and 'the distraction which that Infinite Variety of Second Causes, and the care of their Concernments, must give to the first, if it inspects them all'; but this objection is judged to be invalid in the case of a 'Divine Understanding . . . far above ours'. Worship and prayer are defended on thoroughly modernist lines. The notion of propitiation is firmly rejected: 'if we imagine Our Worship as a thing that adds to his happiness, or gives him such a fond Pleasure as weak people have to hear themselves commended, or that our repeated Addresses do overcome Him through our meer Importunity, We have certainly very unworthy thoughts of him'. Prayer in fact is to be used rather for its effect on the worshipper than for its effect on God. It is conceived as 'Meditations of God', which will bring into existence that 'new Principle' in the mind on which Burnet insists so strongly. In fact prayer is to be regarded less as a petition than as a spiritual exercise, and any 'Returns' that may appear are not to be considered as 'Favours extracted by meer Importunity, but as Rewards conferred on men so well disposed, and prepared for them'. To the objection that men 'cannot have suitable Notions of the Divine Essence' and so cannot meditate on it, Burnet replies by turning the tables on the sceptics and arguing that 'we have no just *Idea* of any Essence whatsoever', but we can form some notion of God from the 'Discoveries' he 'has made of Himself', and 'when we say we love God, the meaning is, We love that Being that is Holy, Just, Good, Wise and infinitely Perfect'. Burnet is almost paraphrasing his master John Smith: 'wheresoever we may find true *Beauty, Love and Goodness*, we may say, Here or there is *God*'.[1] He is presenting to Rochester not the tribal deity of Sinai, but a deification of the Platonic Idea of the Good. The final object of religion is 'to beget in us a

---

[1] Smith, 136.

Conformity to [God's] Nature'. Religion is thus to have the practical psychological task set before it by the Cambridge Platonists of making men 'deiform', to use their favourite phrase. Burnet admits that there has been corruption and cheating in religion and draws a parallel between deceitful priests and '*Mountebanks*' who 'Corrupt Physick' (perhaps with a sly glance at 'Alexander Bendo') and '*Petty-foggers*' in law.

Rochester was not 'equally satisfied' with all these arguments. He admitted the 'suasive' effect of such 'Impressions of God' as 'a powerful means to reform the World'. He did not deny the possibility of Providence, but was inclined to think that the soul 'began anew' after death, and lost all memory of its former life. Burnet replied that 'this was at best a conjecture', and countered it with the 'reasonableness' of supposing that the soul remembers as well as thinks in a future life either 'by its own strength, or by the means of some subtiler Organs'. He 'pressed' Rochester 'with the secret Joys that a good Man felt, particularly as he drew near Death, and the Horrours of ill Men especially at that time'. Rochester, however, ascribed such feelings to the 'Impressions they had from their Education', though he admitted that men who believed in God and 'had the hope of an endless Blessedness in another State' were 'the happiest Men in the World', and he said 'He would give all that he was Master of, to be under those Perswasions, and to have the Supports and Joys that must needs flow from them'. These are very significant words. We can recognize in them the longing of his inner being for the religious experience which had hitherto been denied to him.

Burnet's most difficult task came under the heading of 'Revealed Religion'. Here Rochester opened fire with the usual batteries of sceptical argument. He 'believed that the Pen-men of the Scriptures had heats and honesty', but the Bible was full of difficulties. He could not 'comprehend how God should reveal his Secrets to Mankind'. How could there be 'any corruption in the Nature of Man, or a Lapse derived from *Adam*'? As for 'Prophecies and Miracles' 'the World had been always full of strange Stories', and they might be due to the 'boldness and cunning of Contrivers meeting with the Simplicity and Credulity of the People'. He criticized the Scriptures for their 'odd Transitions', their 'seeming Contradictions, chiefly about the Order of time', and the 'Cruelties enjoyned the *Israelites* in destroying the *Canaanites*, Circumcision, and many other Rites of

the *Jewish* Worship' which 'seem'd to him insutable to the Divine
Nature'. Finally he could not believe the first three chapters of
Genesis, 'unless they were Parables'.

As the historical criticism of the Bible was still in its infancy,
Burnet had to answer these arguments 'rationally', and his replies,
though ingenious, are the weakest part of his defence of religion. He
answers the argument against the miracles in the New Testament by
appealing to the number of trustworthy witnesses, and accuses the
deists of making up their minds not to believe, '*let the Evidence be
what it will*'. Rochester at once answers acutely that a man may not
be able to believe, and that 'believing was at highest, but a probable
Opinion'. Burnet replies that a man who had only taken 'a slight
view' of the matter and had lived 'an ill course of Life' was not
'fitly qualified to examine the matter aright'. To form an opinion he
should grow 'calm and vertuous, and upon due application examine
things fairly'. This is the poorest argument that Burnet had used,
and it shows that he felt that this was the weakest part of his case.
His great endeavour now was to overcome the strong prejudice against
traditional beliefs which he perceived to exist in Rochester's mind.
His technique is to connect the 'revealed religion' of the Bible with
the practical argument concerning religious experience, where he
feels himself to be on firm ground. He says that there are two kinds
of belief in Divine Matters. One is belief 'wrought in us by comparing all the evidences of matter of Fact'. Under this heading he
just mentions the fulfiment of the Old Testament prophecies but
lays greater stress on 'the excellent Rule and Design of the Scriptures
in matters of *Morality*'. But this sort of belief is 'only a general
perswasion in the Mind'. The more important kind of belief comes
when 'a Man applying himself to the Directions set down in the
Scriptures . . . finds a power entring within him, that forces him from
the slavery of his Appetites and Passions; that exalts his Mind above
the accidents of life, and spreads an inward purity in his Heart,
from which a serene and calm Joy arises within him'. Belief in the
Bible in fact, like prayer, is to be regarded mainly as a spiritual
exercise that will bring valuable religious experience to the believer.
John Smith himself might well have written this fine passage.
Rochester replied with his old objection that 'all this might be
fancy'. Burnet retorted that those who had this experience were
'neither hot nor *Enthusiastical*, but under the power of calm
and clear Principles'. Rochester remained unconvinced, and not

P

unreasonably protested that to argue thus was 'to assert or beg the thing in Question'. Burnet then proceeded to defend Revelation as a 'power' awakened by God 'in some mens Minds, to apprehend and know some things, in such a manner, that others were not capable of it'. Miracles are to be regarded as 'a divine Credential to warrant such Persons in what they deliver to the World'. Little stress is laid on 'the business of the Fall of Man' (Burnet's own rather disrespectful phrase) and 'other things of which we cannot perhaps give our selves a perfect account'. It is suggested that it is unreasonable to reject 'an excellent Systeme of good and holy Rules' because of a few difficulties like these. The corruption of human nature is said to be apparent in the struggle that all men feel between 'Reason' and 'Nature', so that it is plain, 'there is a Lapse of the high powers of the Soul'. Pressed further by Rochester, who asks why some 'plain Rules' could not be given and why 'men must come and shew a trick to perswade the World they speak to them in the Name of God', Burnet now uses a favourite method of the Cambridge Platonists when they tried to explain away difficulties in the Bible. Religion has to deal not with philosophers but with simple-minded men. It is therefore necessary to equip the 'Messengers sent from Heaven' with 'such allarming Evidences, as might awaken the World, and prepare them by some astonishing Signs, to listen to the Doctrine they were to deliver'. As John Smith puts it, the deity speaks 'with the most *Idiotical* sort of men in the most *Idiotical* way'.[1] This might not be necessary for philosophers, but philosophers are rare. Religion has to rouse common men up' with 'great and sensible excitation'. Burnet reproved Rochester for using such phrases as '*the shewing of trick*', which he calls an 'ill use' of 'his Wit', and which, he contends also 'did really keep him from examining' the gravest things, 'with that care which such things required'. The criticism of the historicity of the Old Testament is answered by the argument that our knowledge of the Language in which it is written and the 'History of those Ages' is so imperfect that 'it is rather a wonder We should understand so much of it, than that many Passages in it should be so dark to us'. For Christians it is chiefly valuable because of its prophecies of a Messiah. Burnet makes a valiant effort to rationalize the barbarous command of Jahweh to the Hebrews to destroy the Canaanites. He compares it to a plague sent to destroy them and

[1] Ibid., 172.

even suggests that the 'taking away People by the Sword' is a 'gentler way' than by 'a Plague or a Famine'. As for 'the Children who were Innocent of the Fathers faults', God 'could in another State make that up to them'! It is interesting to find Burnet hinting at the possibility of salvation for the innocent children of Canaanitish idolaters. Finally the massacre was 'no Precedent, for future Times', but was done by 'special Warrant and Commission from Heaven . . . evidenced . . . by . . . mighty . . . Miracles'. Jewish rites could not be judged except by comparison with the idolatries around them. They were to be defended as 'Indulgences . . . given to a People naturally fond of a visible splendor in Religious Worship'. Burnet's defence of the story of the Creation is half-hearted. He admits that it is much disputed 'how far some things in it may be Parabolical, and how far Historical'. The seventeenth-century belief that 'Spirits can form Voices in the Air' is used as an argument to show that Eve may have thought 'that a *Serpent* spake to her, when the Evil Spirit framed the Voice'.

But Burnet cares little for such things. The man who examines 'the business of Religion, by some dark parts of Scripture' he emphatically declares to be 'in the wrong way'. Christianity is judged 'by the Rules it gives, and the Methods it prescribes'. Its moral code is praised as best both for society and for the individual. It is 'Generous and Great' to 'supply the Necessities of the Poor, and to forgive Injuries'. Everything in it is made to depend on the Golden Rule of the Gospel '*Of doing as we would have others do to us, and loving our Neighbours as our selves*'. Its ceremonies are described as 'plain and simple', 'the admission to it by a washing with Water, and the Memorial of our Savour's Death in *Bread* and *Wine*'. In fact Burnet describes the Church as it would have been if the latitudinarians could have had their way. Its ritual is stripped of all mystic significance. To quote the title of Toland's famous pamphlet it is 'Christianity not Mysterious'. Finally great stress is laid on the historical fact that Christ and the disciples had no worldly motives. 'Interest appears in all Humane Contrivances', 'Our Saviour plainly had none'. The prominence given to this argument suggests that Rochester had made use of Blount's contention that '*a Temporal Interest was the great Machine upon which all human Actions moved; and that the common and general pretence of* Piety *and* Religion *was but like a Graec before a Meal*'. Pliny, Lucian and Julian the Apostate are invoked as unwilling witnesses to the purity and disinterestedness

205

of the early Christians. All these arguments are to be laid in the balance with 'some Cavils about some Passages in the *New Testament*, or the *Old*'. The 'right method' according to Burnet was to take a general unprejudiced view of the whole matter first, and then 'to descend to more particular Enquiries'. The deists 'suffered their Minds to be forestalled with Prejudices; so that they never examined the matter impartially'.

Rochester was powerfully affected by these arguments. He accepted Burnet's conclusions generally, but made three final objections to Christianity. One was the belief in 'Mysteries', which a man could not believe if he could not understand them, and which opened the way to 'the Juglings of Priests'. The second was the Christian morality which forbade 'the use of Women, Except one in the way of Marriage', and denied 'the remedy of Divorce'. The third was the 'business of the Clergy and their Maintenance with the belief of some Authority and Power, conveyed in their Orders' which 'lookt, as he thought, like a piece of Contrivance'. 'Why must a man tell me', he asked, 'I cannot be saved, unless I believe things against my Reason, and then I must pay him for telling me of them?' These words are certainly Rochester's own; they have the exact ring of the direct, hard-hitting English of the great satires.

Burnet replied to these three objections in turn as well as he could. The mysteries of religion are compared with the mysteries of nature, and nothing in them is more unaccountable than the mystery of the union of the Soul with the Body, which caused such trouble to seventeenth-century philosophers. The Trinity is explained on rational lines as 'three different Principles of Operation', 'in one Essence'. 'Father', 'Son', 'Holy Ghost', and 'Persons' are, it is hinted, mere popular pictorial names used 'for want of terms fit to express them by'. The second 'person' is said to have united himself with 'the Humane Nature of Jesus Christ', and to have undergone sufferings which 'were accepted of God as a Sacrifice for our Sins', and power was then given to him to grant 'Eternal Life' to 'all that submit to the Terms on which He offers it'. The resurrection of the body is explained as the reunion with our souls of the 'Matter of which our Bodies once consisted', 'being refined and made more spiritual' so that it can become 'a fit Instrument for them in a more perfect Estate'. In fact the Apostles' Creed is restated in terms of the Enlightenment and the mysterious element in Christianity minimized. Burnet admits that 'too many Niceties' have been 'brought

in indeed, rather to darken then explain' the 'mysteries', that they
have been injured by the use of 'weak Arguments', and 'illustrated
by Similies not always so very apt and pertinent' and that 'new
subtilties' were added by the Fathers and the Schoolman. In fact
'mysteries' were to be treated with a firm hand and kept in their
place and 'the descantings of fanciful men upon them' were to be
ignored. If this line was taken, there need be no fear that more
mysteries could be added by priests. A sharp distinction was to be
drawn between 'Truths about the Divine Essence, of which the
manner is not understood', and such an alleged 'mystery' as transub-
stantiation, of which Burnet speaks as contemptuously as any deist.
'No Mystery is to be admitted, but upon very 'clear and express
Authorities from Scripture, which could not reasonably be understood in any other sense'. We feel that Burnet regards the 'Mysteries'
as rather a nuisance, and he is determined that the few respectable
'mysteries' of Protestantism shall not be confused with the vast,
spurious brood of Popery, just as a contemporary Englishman would
have drawn a distinction between the constitutional monarchy of
his country and the arbitrary despotisms of the Continent.

Burnet has to defend Christian sexual ethics on the ground that
they are laws given by a wise law-giver. But he tries to give reasons
for them as well. His chief argument is not a very lofty one. It is the
view that women are property: 'Men have a property in their Wives
and Daughters, so that to defile the one, or corrupt the other, is an
injust and injurious thing.' Women are possessions and to damage
them is an attack on the sacredness of property. We may remember
that Burnet was becoming a leading light in the Whig party, the
great party of 'liberty and property'. The waste of estates, time and
health, the unfairness of polygamy to women (who are apparently
not always to be regarded as mere chattels) and the encouragement
given to matrimonial quarrels by freedom of divorce are among
Burnet's replies to this difficulty. Finally Christianity is said to offer
'high Rewards' and therefore has a right to 'exact difficult Performances'. To this Rochester answered drily: 'We are sure the terms are
difficult, but are not so sure of the Rewards'. Burnet replies that
we have assurances of those rewards in 'the Promises of God made
to us by Christ, confirmed by many Miracles' and we have 'Earnests'
of them 'in the quiet and peace which follows a good Conscience'
as well as in Christ's resurrection. Difficulties just as great are
to be found in the 'learning of some Trades or Sciences', and 'the

governing our Health and Affairs'. The blame should be placed not on Christianity but on our 'corrupt Natures' and 'vitious habits'. Christian ethics will be easy when we are 'renew'd and in a good measure restor'd to our Primitive Integrity'. Here Burnet reveals that unorthodox belief in the possibility of overcoming 'original sin' by personal effort, which was typical of his age and his church.

He defends the maintenance of the Clergy as necessary to preserve them from 'the Contempt that follows Poverty, and the Distractions which the providing against it might otherways involve them in'. He will have nothing to do with a superstitious sacerdotalism. 'The Priests of the true *Christian Religion* have no secrets among them, which the World must not know'. They are only 'an Order of Men dedicated to God, to attend on Sacred things', and there is no 'mystery' about them. They must have 'due Esteem paid them, and a fit Maintenance appointed for them', just as 'in the Order of the World, it was necessary for the support of Magistracy and Government, . . . that some state be used (though it is a happiness when Great Men have Philosophical Minds, to despise the Pageantry of it)'. He admits that there are abuses by some who use 'Ambition or Covetousness' and 'indirect Means, or servile Compliances to aspire to such Dignities, and being possessed of them, applied their Wealth either to Luxury or Vain Pomp, or made great Fortunes out of it for their Families'. Rochester interposed the remark that nothing had encouraged him and many others 'in their ill ways' more than the behaviour of some of the Clergy at Court. He spoke of their 'aspirings', 'the servile ways they took to attain to Preferment', and 'the Animosities among those of several Parties, about trifles', that 'made him often think they suspected those things were not true, which in their Sermons or Discourses they so earnestly recommended'. He gave many instances, some of which Burnet was able to deny as 'Mistakes and Calumnies', but 'something of them' he had to admit 'might be too true'. He argued, however, that because some men had certain failings, it was unjust to conclude that they were wholly insincere, and also that Rochester should set over against such instances the example of the good lives led by many of the clergy and religious laity. The conference ended with an admission by Rochester of the anti-social character of libertinism; 'Vice and Impiety', he said, 'were as contrary to Humane Society as wild Beasts let loose would be.' He announced his firm resolution to 'change the whole method of his Life; to become strictly just and true, to be

Chast and Temperate, to forbear Swearing and Irreligious Discourse, to Worship and Pray to his Maker'. Rationally he was convinced by Burnet's arguments in favour of Christian ethics. He had not yet 'arrived at a full perswasion of *Christianity*', but he promised 'he would never employ his Wit more to run it down, or to corrupt others'. Burnet's rejoinder was to point out that a virtuous life led under these conditions would be 'very uneasie to him, unless Vicious Inclinations were removed'. He repeated his conviction that what was wanted was the establishment of 'an inward Principle', and advised him to try to obtain it by means of 'frequent and earnest Prayers'. Such a mind as Rochester's, when 'cleared of these Disorders', and 'cured of those Distempers, which Vice brought on it', would 'soon see through all those flights of Wit, that do feed Atheism and Irreligion'.

The conversations ended in the spring of 1680. Rochester left London 'about the beginning of April', intending, no doubt, to spend the summer in the country according to his usual custom. He had a premonition that he would never return and he told Burnet that 'he believed he would never come to Town more'.[1] He went first to Newmarket, where the King and the Court were attending the races.[2] This was the last glimpse that he had of the Vanity Fair of fashion and high politics. The talk at Court was certainly of the preparations for the projected military expedition to Tangiers, which had begun as early as January,[3] and it is possible that he may have heard that his old enemy Mulgrave was likely to be appointed to command the expeditionary force. On his way back from Newmarket to Oxfordshire, he stopped at Bishop's Stortford, and wrote a note there on 5 April to Harry Savile, acknowledging the receipt of a 'Pacquet' in which apparently Savile gave him information about the machinations of a certain 'Mr P', who appears to have been spreading false reports about him in Paris, either with a view to blackmail or because he had been paid to do this dirty work. 'Misery', Rochester writes, 'makes all Men more or less dishonest; and I am not astonish'd to see Villany industrious for Bread; especially, living in a place where it is often so *de gayeté de Coeur*.' The last words of the letter seem to imply that he had imagined that there had been a cooling of Savile's feelings towards him, but he was now convinced that he retained his old friend's affection: 'In the

[1] B.S.P., 33, 127.   [2] W., 74, 116.   [3] C.S.P.D., 1679–80, 1, 31, 38.

mean time you have made my Heart glad in giving one such a Proof of your Friendship, and I am now sensible, that it is natural for you to be kind to me, and can never more despair of it.'[1]

This was the last letter he is known to have written to Savile, and it ends a correspondence which gives expression to some of Rochester's best qualities, his gaiety and wit, his shrewd observation and understanding of human nature and his capacity for sincere and warmhearted friendship. We have no definite knowledge of his movements till about the middle of May, but it is almost certain that he spent the next few weeks at the High Lodge in Woodstock Park. It was here that he was accustomed to retire to write his satires and lampoons, and now that he was going to make a break with his old life, it seems likely that he began to sketch a final satiric outburst in the form of a Farewell to the Court.

A poem called *Rochester's Farewell*, containing passages of great power, but remarkably uneven in style and in parts somewhat incoherent, was first printed in the *Third Part of Poems on Affairs of State* in 1689, and is ascribed to Rochester in a number of the eighteenth-century editions. It is also found in a slightly extended form in a manuscript now in the Houghton Library at Harvard.[2] Samuel Woodforde in his *Ode to the Memory of Rochester* seems to deny his authorship of this poem when he speaks of the dishonest editors who 'vex his Happy Ghost' with 'Farewells, Droll, and Shredds of Verse.'

Yet Farwells such as those He never took.[3]

However, it must be remembered that Woodforde was a pious author who wanted to make all the capital he could out of Rochester's conversion, and would be only too anxious to discredit the ascription to him of a profane 'libel' written shortly before that event. It has been pointed out that this poem, as printed in 1689 and in the form found in the Harvard manuscript, contains allusions to events that happened when Rochester was no longer in a state to write satiric verse, and that it includes a violent attack on Buckingham, with whom Rochester always seems to have been on friendly terms. A French scholar, in a recent careful analysis of *Rochester's Farewell*, has found traces in it of at least two different hands.[4] However that may be, commentators have generally agreed that parts at least of

---

[1] W., 74. [2] P., 149–55, 230, 231. [3] Rochesteriana, 67.
[4] J. Auffret, 'Rochester's *Farewell*', E. A. Avril-Juin, 1959, 142–50.

the poem show unmistakable signs of Rochester's characteristic thought and style. We know it was his custom to write 'libels' when he retired to the country, and what could be more natural than that he should plan a final 'libel' in the form of a Farewell to the court life which he had now resolved to abandon for ever? It is true that before leaving London he had promised Burnet that he would never 'employ his Wit more to run . . . down' Christianity, 'or to corrupt others',[1] but a fierce denunciation of court life could hardly be reckoned under either of these headings.

I suggest that he started to make a rough draft of the *Farewell* when he returned to the High Lodge after his last glimpse of Charles II and his Court at Newmarket in April 1680. This draft was doubtless similar to the rough drafts of his poems preserved in the Portland manuscript. After his death it was probably edited and expanded to form the work printed in 1689 under the title of *Rochester's Farewell*. The opening lines are undoubtedly Rochester's. They are in his best manner, the work of the indignant and disillusioned moralist of *A Satyr against Mankind*:

> Tir'd with the noysom Follies of the Age,
> And weary of my Part, I quit the Stage;
> For who in Life's dull Farce a Part would bear,
> Where Rogues, Whores, Bawds, all the head Actors are?
> Long I with Charitable Malice strove,
> Lashing the Court, those Vermin to remove,
> But thriving Vice under the rod still grew,
> As aged Letchers whipp'd, their Lust renew;
> What though my Life hath unsuccessful been,
> (For who can this *Augean* Stable clean)
> My gen'rous end I will pursue in Death,
> And at Mankind rail with my parting breath.[2]

III

> Si l'homme n'est pas fait pour Dieu, pourquoi n'est il heureux qu'en Dieu? Si l'homme est fait pour Dieu, pourquoi est il si contraire à Dieu?
>
> Pascal, *Pensées*, II. i. iv.

The country air and quiet life at Woodstock brought about a

---

[1] B.S.P., 125. [2] P., 149.

temporary improvement in his health, and he felt so well that some-where about the middle of May he decided to visit his wife's estates in Somerset and 'rode thither Post'.[1] The exertion proved too much for him, and he reached Enmore in a state of collapse. According to Burnet, 'this heat and violent motion did so inflame an Ulcer that was in his Bladder, that it raised a very great pain in those parts', and he was brought back by coach 'with much difficulty' to the High Lodge. There 'the Ulcer broke and vast quantities of purulent matter past with his Urine'.[2] His physical agony was combined with mental anguish. He seems to have been overcome now by a frenzy of re-morse for his past life and of disgust with all connected with it, 'not only a general dark Melancholy over his Mind, such as he had formerly felt; but a most penetrating cutting Sorrow'. He may have thought of his old friend Harry Savile at this time. He told Burnet later 'to tell it to one for whom he was much concern'd, that though there was nothing to come after this life, Yet all the Pleasures he had ever known in Sin, were not worth that torture he had felt in his Mind'.[3] He was passing through what the mystics have called the dark night of the soul, and it was probably only by means of this experience that he was able to attain to illumination at last.

On 26 May,[4] just after his return from the west, he was visited by his mother's chaplain, Robert Parsons. This clergyman, afterwards Archdeacon of Gloucester, was a man of the same age as Rochester, and had taken his M.A. degree at University College, Oxford, in 1670. In the same year Rochester had used his influence to procure for him the small academic office of Esquire Bedell,[5] and it is pos-sible that he may have introduced him to his mother. He received Parsons kindly, and, according to the chaplain's account, 'shewed me extraordinary respects upon the score of mine Office, thank'd God, who had in mercy and good providence sent me to him, who so much needed my prayers and counsels; acknowledging how un-worthily he had treated that order of men, reproaching them that they were proud and prophesied only for rewards; but now he had learnt how to value them; that he esteem'd them the servants of the most High God, who were to shew him the way to everlasting life'. This account is perhaps not to be taken too literally; its style is that of the conventional rhetoric of the funeral sermon in which it occurs, but we can well believe Parsons when he tells us that he found

[1] B.S.P., 127.　　　[2] Ibid., 128.　　　[3] Ibid., 129.　　　[4] Parsons, 22.
[5] D.N.B., s.a. Robert Parsons; C.S.P.D., 1670, 637.

Rochester at this time 'labouring under strange trouble and conflicts of mind, and his conscience full of terrors'. The dialogue in his soul now seems to have reached a pitch of frenzy. 'Upon his journey', he told Parsons, 'he had been arguing with greater vigor against God and Religion than ever he had done in his life time before, and that he was resolved to run 'em down with all the argument and spite, in the world, but, like the great Convert St. Paul, he found it hard to kick against the pricks.'[1]

On the very day that Parsons visited Rochester (26 May 1680), Narcissus Luttrell noted in his Diary that 'the troops that are design'd for Tangier will be commanded by the earl of Mulgrave, who will also be accompanied by the earl of Plymouth, lord Mordant and lord Lumley as volunteers'.[2] Two days later the Earl of Sunderland in a letter from Windsor to Sir Leoline Jenkins wrote that 'Lord Mulgrave is named by the King to go with the men he now sends to Tangier'.[3] The Court was at Windsor at this time, and we know that Rochester had an excellent intelligence service. There can be little doubt that the news of the appointment of his old enemy Mulgrave to command the Tangiers force would have reached him by the end of May. Though he was very ill and his mind was in a disturbed state he may well have amused himself sometimes by turning to the unfinished draft of the *Farewell* and adding some verses to it. We know from Burnet that he had great powers of recuperation and that, during his previous period of sickness in London, he 'went often abroad and had great Vivacity of Spirit'.[4] The obvious plan for a poem like the *Farewell* would be to follow the powerful exordium with a procession of the 'Rogues, Whores, Bawds' who were the chief actors in the 'dull farce' of court life. The procession naturally starts with Rochester's *bête noire* Mulgrave, the newly appointed leader of the '*Tangier* Bullies'. The following lines are full of Rochester's contempt for the man and his hatred of the jingoism fashionable at court:

> First then the *Tangier* Bullies must appear
> With open Brav'ry and dissembled Fear:
> *Mulgrave* their Head, but Gen'ral have a care,
> Though skill'd in all those Arts that cheat the Fair,
> The Undiscerning and Impartial Moor,
> Spares not the Lover on the Ladies score.

[1] Parsons, 22.   [2] Luttrell, I, 46.   [3] C.S.P.D., 1679–80, 494.   [4] B.S.P., 34.

> Think how many perish by one fatal shot,
> The Conquests all thy goggling every got.
> Think then (as I presume you do) how all
> The English Ladies will lament your fall;
> Scarce will there greater Grief pierce every heart,
> Should Sir George *Hewitt* or Sir *Car* depart.
> Had it not better been than thus to roam,
> To stay and play the Cravat-string at home?
> To shut, look big, shake Pantaloon, and swear
> With *Hewitt, Damme*, there's no action there.

Rochester never wrote better satiric verse than this; the allusions to Donne's *Second Anniversary* and Milton's *Lycidas* in these lines are brilliant examples of his favourite device of parody.[1] Of the rest of the *Farewell*, as the text has come down to us, the lines that betray most clearly Rochester's hand are those which contain the superb denunciation of the 'Imperial Whore', Hortense Mancini, Duchess of Mazarin:

> Nor does Cold Age, which now rides on so fast,
> Make thee come short of all thy lewdness past:
> Though on thy Head, Grey-hairs, like *Etna's* Snow
> Are shed, thou'rt Fire and Brimstone all below.
> Thou monstrous thing, in whom at once doth rage
> The Flames of Youth, and impotence of Age.[2]

It may be urged that such lines as these are hardly consonant with the penitential mood in which Parsons alleges that he found the Earl on 26 May. However, we know that he was a man of rapidly changing moods and, before the religious experience which brought about his final conversion, he may well have had some unregenerate moments when the urge to write satiric verse was irresistible. The *Farewell* ends with a contemptuous fling at the Duchess of Portmouth and her cully Charles II in a couplet which is very much in Rochester's manner:

> But what must we expect, who daily see
> Unthinking *Charles*, Rul'd by Unthinking thee?[3]

The grotesque pageant of the *Farewell* is an image of the company of rogues and harlots among whom the poet had spent some of the

---

[1] P., 149, 150. Cf. Donne, *The Second Anniversary*, ll. 85–92 and Milton, *Lycidas*, ll. 67–9.
[2] P., 153.   [3] Ibid., 145.

best years of his life. Now, like a magician forsaking his art, he conjured up the evil spirits once more to bid them farewell.

Two distinguished physicians, Doctors Short of London and Radcliffe of Oxford came to attend him at the High Lodge and his pious mother and long-suffering wife arrived to nurse him. John Cary, a friendly neighbouring squire, wrote on 2 June that Rochester 'is now very weak, God Almighty restore him if it be his will, for he is grown to be the most altered person, the most devout & pious, & would certainly make a most worthy brave man, if it would please God to spare his life'.[1] There seems to have been a crisis in his condition on the night of 6 June. His mother and wife sat up with him all night and he was delirious 'he was disordered in his head' on this occasion, his mother writes, 'but then he said no hurt, but only some little *ribble-rabble* with no hurt in it'. However, the two ladies both noticed that 'whenever he spoke of God, that night he spoke well and with good sense', and since then, according to the old countess 'he never had a minute of disorder in his head'. In the letter in which she gives these details to her sister[2] she mentions that a lampoon was circulating under Rochester's name in Court circles at Windsor: 'they are fine people at Windsor, God forgive them! Sure there never was so great a malice performed, as to entitle my poor son to a lampoon, at this time, when for aught they know, he lies upon his death-bed.' It is possible that the lampoon referred to here is some garbled version of *Rochester's Farewell* which may have already been circulating at Court, though it is equally possible that it is some other work. Whether the 'lampoon' in question was really Rochester's or not, we can be sure that the pious countess would want to discredit the attribution to him of such a work at this time.

On 15 June Cary reports that the patient has rallied: 'My lord Rochester we hope is on the mending hand, but many changes he meets withall, pretty good dayes succeed ill nights, which help to keep upp his spirits, but he is very weake, and expresses himself very good.'[3] 'Many messages and complements' came 'from his old acquaintance', but he received them with disgust and said, 'let me see none of them; & I would to God, I had never conversed with some of them'. One of the physicians, 'thinking to please him, told him the King drank his health the other day'. Rochester 'look'd

[1] V.M., III, 244, 245.
[2] Hayward, 322. (Anne, Dowager Countess of Rochester to Lady St. John.)
[3] V.M., III, 245.

earnestly upon him, and said never a word, but turn'd his face from him'.[1]

He was visited by several clergymen including the Bishop of Oxford, and Dr. Marshall, rector of Lincoln College, his parish priest'[2] But he took most pleasure in the ministrations of Robert Parsons. His deliverance from his mental agony came to him one day when Parsons was reading to him the noble poetry of the 'Second Isaiah'. It was the strange and beautiful passage in the fifty-third chapter describing the ordeal of the 'Suffering Servant' of Jahweh that the chaplain had chosen on this occasion in order to convince the Earl that it was a prophecy of the sufferings of Christ.[3]

> . . . he shall grow up before him as a tender plant,
> and as a root out of a drie ground:
> hee hath no forme nor comelinesse:
> and when wee shall see him, there is no beautie that
>   we should desire him.
> He is despised and rejected of men,
> a man of sorrows, and acquainted with griefe:
> And we hid as it were our faces from him;
> he was despised, and wee esteemed him not.
> Surely he hath borne our griefes, and caried our
>   sorrowes:
> yet we did esteeme him striken, smitten of God,
>   and afflicted.
> But he was wounded for our transgressions,
> he was bruised for our iniquities:
> the chastisement of our peace was upon him,
> and with his stripes we are healed.
> All we like sheepe have gone astray:
> we have turned every one to his own way,
> and the Lord hath layd on him the iniquitie of us all.
> He was oppressed, and he was afflicted,
> yet he openeth not his mouth.
> He was taken from prison, and from judgement:
> and who shall declare his generation?
> For he was cut off from the land of the living,
> for the transgression of my people was he stricken.
> And he made his grave with the wicked,
> And with the rich in his death,

---

[1] Hayward, 322.　　　[2] B.S.P., 131.　　　[3] Ibid., 140; Parsons, 24.

because he has done no violence
neither was there any deceit in his mouth.

.   .   .   .   .

He shall see of the travell of his soule, and shalbe
    satisfied;
by his knowledge shall my righteous servant justifie
    many:
for hee shall bear their iniquities . . .

As he heard these words of the Hebrew prophet in the majestic
English of the King James Bible, Rochester felt at last that spiritual
exaltation which he had once affected to despise as mere 'fancy', but
for which the subconscious part of his mind had really been longing.
In a flash he knew that 'divinum aliqud' which he had vainly sought
among the deists. His experience must be described in his words as
reported by Burnet, to whom he said that,

> *as he heard it* [the chapter of Isaiah] *read, he felt an inward force upon
> him, which did so enlighten his Mind, and convince him, that he could
> resist it no longer : For the words had an authority which did shoot like
> Rays or Beams in his Mind; so he was not only satisfied in his Under-
> standing, but by a power which did so effectually constrain him, that he
> did ever after firmly believe in his Saviour, as if he had seen him in the
> clouds.*[1]

There can be no doubt that this is the record of a genuine and
memorable religious experience. The language is exactly of the kind
used by the great mystics on similar occasions and many parallels
could be quoted from their works. It is interesting to compare it
with the experience of Rochester's elder contemporary, John
Bunyan, as described in *Grace Abounding* when he writes that 'I . . .
was, as if I had with the eyes of my Understanding, seen the Lord
Jesus looking down upon me.' Bunyan's naïve mind received the
illumination in pictorial form. Rochester only adds the pictorial
reference at the end of his statement as an illustration. For him the
only way of describing his experience was by means of the metaphor
of an energizing light, the image which is commonly used by intellectual mystics whose minds do not work in the pictorial way.
Notice too that, as Rochester was a poet and a man of letters, so it was
through poetry that his great moment of vision came to him. Now
religion was not a matter of intellectual conviction, the result of a

[1] Ibid., 141.

philosophic comparison between deism and Christianity. Rochester
had felt religion at first hand as an inward force: he had found in an
overwhelming degree that significant emotion for which he had been
seeking all through his life.

This event probably happened on 19 June. On that day we know
that he made a kind of public recantation, calling in all his servants,
including even the 'piggard boy', or lad who looked after the swine.[1]
Before them all he read and signed a declaration expressing detesta-
tion and abhorrence of his past life and warning all against denying
the 'Being' or 'Providence' of God, or making a mock of Sin or
'contemning' religion. This strange document was witnessed by his
mother and Robert Parsons.[2] Then he took the sacrament in company with his wife, who, to his great joy had renounced Roman
Catholicism, to which, he had been 'not a little Instrumental in
procuring' her 'perversion'. Now 'it was one of the joyfullest things
that befel him in his Sickness, that he had seen that Mischief removed, in which he had so great a Hand'. His love for his wife came
back to him now too, and 'he expressed so much tenderness and
true kindness' to her 'that as it easily defaced the remembrance of
every thing wherein he had been at fault formerly, so it drew from
her the most passionate care and concern for him that was possible'.[3]
It was probably on this day too that he gave strict orders to burn 'all
his profane and lewd writings, as being only fit to promote Vice and
Immorality, by which he had so highly offended God, and shamed
and blasphemed that Holy Religion into which he was Baptiz'd; and
all his obscene and filthy Pictures, which were so notoriously
scandalous'.[4] When this holocaust took place, a manuscript 'History
of the Intrigues of the Court of Charles II, in a series of letters to his
friend Henry Savile' was apparently overlooked, but unfortunately
this work, which must have been one of the most fascinating of his
writings, was burned by his mother after his death.[5] Rochester did
nothing by halves. Just as he had flung himself recklessly into the
vortex of pleasure and libertinism at Whitehall, so now he would
throw himself with passionate ardour into the life of religion.

A curious incident occurred on the very day of his conversion.
William Fanshaw, his old friend of the 'merry gang', came to see
him, probably with the object of cheering him up with some lively
gossip from Court. But it was a different Rochester from his old

[1] Aubrey, II, 304. [2] Parsons, 32. [3] B.S.P., 143, 144.
[4] Parsons, 28, 29. [5] See below, p. 229.
218

companion that Fanshaw found now. He must have been amazed
and terrified to stand by the Earl's bedside, and to hear him say,
'Fanshaw, think of a God, let me advise you; & repent you of your
former life, and amend your ways. Believe what I say to you; there
is a God, a powerful God, & he is a terrible God to unrepenting
sinners; the time draws near, that he will come to judgment, with
great terrour to the wicked; therefore delay not your repentance; his
displeasure will thunder against you, if you do. You & I have long
been acquainted, done ill together. I love the man & speak to him out
of conscience, for the good of his soul.' Fanshaw stood, we are told,
and 'said never a word to him, but stole away out of the room'.
When Rochester saw him go, 'Is a gone,' says he, 'poor wretch! I
fear his heart is harden'd.' It is impossible not to feel some sympathy
with poor Fanshaw. Here was his old friend changed in a twinkling
from the prince of good fellows into the likeness of some terrible
figure from the Bible. No wonder he told some of the people of the
house that the Earl should 'be kept out of melancholy fancies', and
then spread the report that he was mad.[1] Judged by the standards of
Whitehall and the Rose, he *was* mad, but so also were all the great
saints and mystics. He had passed into regions of the spirit where
such men as Savile and Fanshaw could not follow him.

In the five weeks that elapsed between his conversion and his
death his mind seems to have been comparatively clear and un-
troubled. On 2 July his mother reported that 'he sleeps much; his
head, for the most part, is very well. He was this day taken up, & set
up in a chair, for an hour; and was not very faint, when he went to
bed.' She noted that he did not 'care to talk much; but when he does,
speaks for the most part, well.' She told him that Fanshaw had said
'he hop'd he wou'd recover, and leave those principles he now
profess'd'. He replied 'Wretch! I wish I had convers'd, all my life
with link-boys, rather than with him, & that crew; such, I mean, as
Fanshaw is. Indeed, I wou'd not live, to return to what I was, for
all the world.'[2] Parsons states that he 'never dictated or spoke more
composed in his life' than he did at this time. These words are
significant as they imply that during this period he sometimes
dictated. We are told that he promised Parsons that, if he lived, he
would make it his business to produce 'an Idea of Divine Poetry'.[3]

[1] Hayward, 323, 324. See also the more detached account of the interview with Fanshaw by William Thomas in *Rochesteriana*, 57, 58.
[2] Hayward, 325.   [3] Parsons, 33, 7.

Two poems ascribed to him in a collection published shortly after
his death seem to represent a first attempt to carry out this resolution, and I believe they are his last compositions in verse, dictated
at some time between 19 June and 26 July 1680. The two poems
are called *Consideratus Considerandus* and *Plain Dealing's Downfall*.[1]
The central image of both is that of virtue conceived as poor, home-
less, outcast and rejected, yet possessing the secret of true happiness. It seems to me obvious that both these poems are closely connected with the description of the suffering servant in Isaiah liii,
which Parsons states that Rochester 'got by heart'. *Consideratus
Considerandus* begins with a powerful indictment of the pleasures
of the senses and worldly success:

> What pleasures, can this gaudy World afford?
> What true delights do's teeming Nature hoard?
> In her great Store-house, where she lays her treasure,
> Alas, 'tis all the shaddow of a pleasure;
> No true Content in all her works are found
> No sollid Joys in all Earth's spacious round:
> For Labouring Man, who toils himself in vain,
> Eagerly grasping, what creates his pain.
> How false and feeble, nay scarce worth a Name,
> Are Riches, Honour, Pow'r and babling Fame.
> Yet 'tis, for these Men wade through Seas of Blood
> And bold in *Mischief*, Storm to be withstood;
> Which when obtain'd, breed but Stupendious Fear,
> Strife, Jelousies, and sleep disturbing care,
> No beam of comfort, not a Ray of light
> Shines thence, to guide us through Fates Gloomy Night;
> But lost in devious Darkness, there we stay,
> Bereft of Reason in an endless way.

This picture of human misery is worthy of the author of *A Satyr
against Mankind*. It is tempting to conjecture that Dryden may have
seen a manuscript copy of these lines and remembered them when
he wrote the magnificent opening of *Religio Laici* (1682):

> Dim as the borrow'd beams of moon and stars
> To lonely, weary, wand'ring travelers
> Is Reason to the soul; and, as on high
> Those rolling fires discover but the sky,
> Not light us here, so Reason's glimmering ray

[1] P., 125–7.

Was lent, not to assure our doubtful way,
But guide us upward to a better day.

The poet of *Consideratus Considerandus* goes on to describe 'Vertue' as 'the sollid good, if any be' which 'Creates our true Felicitie'. This may be the work of a mind convinced by the arguments on the side of the angels but it is abstract and lacking in vitality and imaginative power. The poem only comes to life again when it proceeds to show 'Vertue' as despised and rejected like the Man of Sorrows:

Therefore in Garments poor, it still appears,
And sometimes (naked) it no Garment wears;
Shun'd by the Great, and worthless thought by most,
Urg'd to be gone, or wish'd for ever lost;
Yet is it loath to leave our Wretched Coast
But in disguise do's here and there intrude,
Striving to conquer base Ingratitude
And boldly ventures now and then to Shine,
So to make known it is of Birth divine;
But Clouded oft, it like the Lightning plays,
Loosing as oft as seen, its pointed Rays.

The 'pointed Rays' will recall the 'Rays or Beams' to which Rochester compared the 'Authority' of the Second Isaiah's words in his description of his conversion (see above p. 217).

Plain Dealing's Downfall is much more satisfying as a work of art; it is, indeed, a little masterpiece of terseness and irony, recalling the work of George Herbert in its directness, simplicity and homely realism: 'Vertue' in this poem is no abstraction, but is represented most effectively as *Plain Dealing*, a betrayed country girl, an image which clearly springs directly from the poet's own experience:

Long time plain dealing in the Hauty town,
Wandring about, though in thread-bare Gown.
At last unanimously was cry'd down.

When almost starv'd, she to the Countrey fled,
In hopes, though meanly she shou'd there be fed,
And tumble Nightly on a Pea-straw Bed.

But Knav'ry knowing her intent, took post,
And Rumour'd her approach through every Coast,
Vowing his Ruin that shou'd be her host.

Frighted at this, each *Rustick* shut his door,
Bid her begone, and trouble him no more,
For he that entertain'd her must be poor.

At this grief seiz'd her, grief too great to tell,
When weeping, sighing, fainting, down she fell,
Whil's Knavery Laughing, Rung her passing Bell.

In these powerful lines we seem to see the transition from satire to religious poetry. They may be well compared with the story of Corinna in *A Letter from Artemisa in the Town to Cloe in the Country* (see above pp. 125). There the emphasis is upon the 'Hauty town'; here it is on the sorrow of the dying country girl, who becomes a tragic figure putting a mean and heartless world to shame.

On 25 June he wrote to Burnet to inform him of his conversion and to suggest that he should visit him, so that in his 'Conversation' he might be 'exalted to that degree of Piety, that the World may See how much I abhorr what I Soe long lovd, & how much I Glory in repentance in Gods Service'.[1] Burnet did not answer this appeal at once. He thought that it might be considered a presumption by the clergymen attending on Rochester, if he hastened to his friend's bed-side. Not realizing the seriousness of Rochester's condition he de-layed for nearly a month, and finally reached Woodstock on 20 July. When he arrived, Rochester's French valet gave his name incorrectly, and he was mistaken for a physician who had worried Rochester with offers to undertake his cure. Some hours passed before the mistake was cleared up. On the previous night Rochester had been on the verge of death. Opiates were administered, and he slept for some hours. When he awoke, he was feeling better, and was transported with delight to find Burnet by his side. His friend was shocked at the change which had taken place in his appearance. 'The whole substance of his Body was drained by the Ulcer, and nothing left but Skin and Bone, and by lying much on his Back, the parts there began to mortifie.' He was not able to speak for long at a time, but he expressed himself very strongly on the subject of 'Apprehensions and Perswasions of his admittance to Heaven' which he believed that he

---

[1] B.S.P., 133–5. The text of Rochester's letter to Burnet, which is not transcribed very accurately in B.S.P., was printed in a limited edition from the original manuscript at Cambridge, Mass., in 1950. My quotation is from that edition.

felt. Burnet noticed the extraordinary passion with which he spoke on the subject. This 'was the only Time', he writes, 'that he spake with any great warmth to me'. He was most anxious to have Burnet's opinion concerning the value of a death-bed repentance. Burnet would not give a direct answer until he had heard the story of the change that had come over the penitent. Rochester then told him of his experience when he had heard Mr. Parsons reading the fifty-third chapter of Isaiah on 19 June. He said that since then he 'made it be read so often to him, that he had got it by heart'. He quoted much of it from memory 'with a sort of heavenly Pleasure', and commented upon some of the phrases. He laid particular stress on the second verse:

> He hath no Form nor Comliness, and when we see Him, there is no beauty that we should desire him.

Rochester paraphrased the passage as follows:

> The meanness of his appearance and Person has made vain and foolish People disparage Him, because he came not in such a Fool's-Coat as they delight in.[1]

Observe the contempt in the phrase 'a Fool's-Coat'. The life of sensuous pleasure which once meant so much for Rochester was now utterly hateful to him. He had reached a stage of mental development when only the naked spirit could satisfy him. Unfortunately he was too weak for any kind of exertion, otherwise he might have written great religious poetry in these last days of his life.

He told Burnet that 'he had overcome all his Resentments to all the World; so that he bore ill will to no Person, nor hated any upon personal accounts'. He had also made arrangements for the payment of all his debts. He made no complaint of the pain that he was enduring, but 'in one of the sharpest Fits', he said he *did willingly submit; . . . God's holy Will be done, I bless him for all he does to me*. It now seemed indifferent to him whether he should live or die, but on the whole he preferred to die. He knew that he would never be well enough to enjoy life again, and he feared that he might relapse into his old way of living: nevertheless he resolved, if he should live, *'to avoid all those Temptations, that Course of Life, and Company that was likely to ensnare him, and he desired to live on no other account, but that he might by the change of his Manners, some*

----
[1] B.S.P., 142.

way take off the high Scandal his former Behaviour had given'. He urged Burnet to give certain messages to his old friends, 'which very well became a dying Penitent', and gave him also 'a Charge to publish any thing concerning him, that might be a mean to reclaim others'.

He questioned Burnet again about his 'Eternal State', and Burnet replied honestly and frankly that the only repentance that had any value in religion was one that involved 'a real change of Heart and Life', and that a death-bed repentance due to fear had no more significance than the 'howlings of condemned Prisoners for Pardon'. Nevertheless there was a hope for a sinner even on his death-bed if his mind was 'truly renewed and turned to God'. Rochester assured him that *'his Mind was entirely turned; and though Horrour had given him his first Awaking, yet that was now grown up into a settled Faith and Conversion'*. Burnet strongly repudiates the suggestion that Rochester's wits were affected by his illness, and vehemently denies the report spread by Fanshaw that his friend died mad. Only on one occasion apparently (probably the night of 20 July) was he delirious, but at all other times, in Burnet's words, he was 'not only without Ravings, but had a clearness in his Thoughts, in his Memory, in his Reflections on Things and Persons, far beyond what I ever saw in a Person so low in his strength'.

He lived for six more days after Burnet's arrival, and during four of them Burnet was by his side. Sometimes his thoughts went back to the past, and once he spoke with great affection of his old tutor, Sir Andrew Balfour, whom Burnet's Scottish accent may have brought back to his mind. As he lay exhausted in the great bed, he may have taken pleasure in recalling the happy days spent in the sunny French and Italian towns when he drank wine with the kind Scottish physician, and explored churches and galleries and bookshops. One day he was in 'unexpressible torment: Yet he bore it decently without breaking into Repinings, or impatient Complaints'. Once only he had 'a full and sweet Nights rest', but it was the result of a dose of laudanum given to him without his knowledge. When he awoke, he thought that his sleep had been a natural one, and that he was recovering. He said 'he had nothing ailing him but an extream weakness, which might go off in time', and then he began with something of his own sanguine spirit to make plans for a future life, 'how retired, how strict, and how studious he intended to be'.

He could not speak for long at a time, but for a half or a quarter of an hour would talk with a 'Vivacity in his Discourse that was extraordinary in all things like himself'. He often sent for his children, the boy Charles now ten years old and his three sisters; he spoke to them 'with a sense and Feeling that cannot be expressed in Writing'. Once he called Burnet in to look at them, and said, '*See how Good God has been to me in giving me so many Blessings, and I have carried my self to him like an ungracious and unthankful Dog.*' At another time he spoke a great deal about public affairs, and many things and persons with his normal clearness and good sense.[1] He praised Halifax particularly, and, later, Halifax was touched when he heard that Rochester had spoken well of him on his death-bed.[2] Burnet observed one change in his conversation. He had given up his old habit of swearing entirely. During the previous winter, Burnet had noticed that he could not speak with any warmth without 'repeated Oaths, which upon almost any sort of Provocation, came almost naturally from him'. Now, 'by a resolute and constant Watchfulness the Habit of it was perfectly master'd. Once only he relapsed, and in a moment of impatience spoke of someone who kept him waiting as '*that damn'd Fellow*'. When Burnet gently protested, he answered, '*O that Language of Fiends, which was so familiar to me, hangs yet about me: Sure none has deserved more to be damned than I have done.*' He 'humbly asked God Pardon for it', and wanted to call the man back and ask his forgiveness too, but Burnet 'told him that was needless, for he has said it of one that did not hear it, and so could not be offended by it'.[3]

On Friday 23rd, Burnet wanted to depart, but Rochester begged him to remain for that day at least. He complied with this request, but left the house early on Saturday morning without taking leave of his host, as he feared that he might be troubled, since he had expressed great unwillingness to part with him the day before. Some hours later Rochester asked for him, but was told that he had gone. 'He seem'd to be troubled, and said, *Has my friend left me, then I shall die shortly.*' After that he spoke only once or twice more, but lay for the most part in silence. Once he was heard praying very devoutly. At two o'clock in the morning of Monday, 26 July, when the great trees in Woodstock forest were still in the dark hours before the summer dawn, the last flicker of life went out in the poor, wasted body. His

[1] B.S.P., 150–1. [2] Marshall, 29. [3] B.S.P., 153, 154.

death was peaceful, 'without any *Convulsion*, or so much as a groan'.[1]

'Thus', writes Burnet, 'he lived and thus he died in the Three and Thirtieth Year of his Age. Nature had fitted him for great things, and his Knowledge and Observation qualify'd him to have been one of the most extraordinary Men, not only of this Nation, but of the Age he lived in: And I do verily believe, that if God had thought fit to have continued him longer in the World, he had been the Wonder and Delight of all that knew him.'[2] Burnet was an honest man and a good friend to Rochester, but he was prevented by his character and education from fully understanding the poet's much more complex mind. Rochester was a great artist ('grand poète et homme de génie',[3] as Voltaire rightly called him), who had the misfortune to be born an English nobleman in the middle of the seventeenth century. After voyaging through many strange seas of thought, he found in his experience of 19 July 1680 the 'felicity and glory' which he had been seeking all his life. That experience is the culmination of his career, and all his work must be read in the light of it. At last he escaped from the irrelevant world of time and space, and he might well have repeated then with a new and deeper conviction the words of his most memorable lyric, 'All my past Life is mine no more.' His conversion was at once his glory and his tragedy: his glory because his courage and intellectual honesty had carried him to his goal in spite of almost insuperable difficulties, his tragedy because his body was too wasted by disease to allow him to express in poetic form his supreme experience.

He is the Byron of the Restoration, one of those fiery souls whose intensity of passion and terrible directness of speech frighten their contemporaries and succeeding generations, and surround their memories with clouds of mistrust and scandal. Now it is time that the clouds that have hidden the true Rochester should be dispelled. He was called 'mad Rochester' by his contemporaries as Blake and Shelley were called mad. Like them and like Marlowe, Byron and D. H. Lawrence, he should be recognized as one of the great English 'thought-adventurers', the Dionysian explorers of areas of experience that lie outside the boundaries of rationality, harnessing the powers derived from those areas to artistic creation and using them to cleanse and invigorate the human spirit.

[1] Ibid., 157, 158.   [2] B.S.P. 159.   [3] Voltaire, II, 24.

EPILOGUE

———⟪◆⟫⟪◆⟫———

Rochester's will was opened and read on 27 July 1680, the day after his death, in the presence of his wife, his mother, John Cary, Francis Warre, Isabella Wheate and Martha Gey.[1] It is a sensible and humane document. He leaves to his wife and son all his estates: 'lands, tenements and hereditaments heretofore at any time by mee settled upon them respectively, to have to them according to the limitations in the settlements thereof contained.' To each of his three daughters, Anne, Elizabeth and Mallet, he leaves a portion of four thousand pounds. Ann, the eldest, is to have hers on attaining the age of eighteen, the other two on attaining the age of sixteen. Provision is also made for their maintenance until they receive their portions. All his 'debtes upon bond, book debtes or otherwise whereunto I have subscribed my name' are to be paid out of his personal estate, and 'what shall be overplus' is to be paid out of the arrears of five thousand pounds, due to him 'upon several grants or patents out of his Majesties Court of the Exchequer'. A certain Mrs. Patience Russell is to have a hundred and fifty pounds to be charged on these arrears. Every servant with him at the time of his death is to receive a year's wages and a mourning suit to be paid out of his personal estate. Edward Jacob and William Moore are to have 'ten pounds apiece in lieu of pretended arreres'. His French servant Baptiste de Belle Fasse is to have 'all his cloathes, lynnen and other things expressed in an inventarie in his keeping signed by my owne signe manual'.

The will shows that, when it was made, Rochester still felt anxiety about the relationship between his wife and his mother:[2] 'For the better assurance of a happy correspondencie between my deare

---

[1] Prinz, 298–302. Rochester's Will is printed in *Wills from Doctor's Commons etc.*, ed. Nichols and Bruce, Camden Society, 1863, 138–41.

[2] See above, p. 140.

227

mother and my deare wife', he appoints these ladies joint guardians
of his son, the young Charles Wilmot, now aged ten, 'till he attaine
the age of one and twentie'. but this joint guardianship is only to last
'so long as my wife shall remaine unmarried and friendlily live with
my mother'. If she 'shall marrie or wilfully seperate herself from
my mother, her guardianship shall determine'. In case of the decease of his mother his 'verie good Uncle Sir John St. John' is to
take her place as the boy's joint guardian. An annuity of forty pounds
secured on the manor of Sutton Mallet is bequeathed to 'the infant
child by the name of Elizabeth Clerke', who is probably 'Betty' his
natural child by Elizabeth Barry.[1] His mother, his wife, his uncle
Sir John St. John, Sir Allen Apsley, Sir Richard How and John
Cary of Woodstock Esq.[2] are appointed his executors. His funeral
is to be the first charge on his personal estate. On 22 June, four days
before his death, he added a codicil to his will. This provides that if
any of his three daughters should die before attaining the ages when
they become eligible for their portions, their portions were not to
go to the executors or to 'the administrators of them' but to 'remaine and be with my son Charles Wilmot'. He also remembered
his friend Robert Parsons and wills that 'Mr. Rob[1] Parsons, Clerke,
have the next presentation to my parsonage of Charlench after the
decease, forfeiture or surrender of Mr. Bourne now incumbent
there'. The will was proved in London on 23 February 1680–1 'by
oath of John Cary esq'.

On 8 August 1680 the Earl was buried at Spelsbury Church and
Robert Parsons preached the funeral sermon. This duty was en-
joined upon him by Rochester's own 'particular Commands'.[3] He
took as his text the verse from St. Luke's Gospel: 'I say unto you,
that likewise joy shall be in heaven over one sinner that repenteth,
more than over ninety and nine just persons that need no repentance.' The sermon was printed at Oxford with a brief Preface by
Parsons, which informs the reader that it was published at the request of Rochester's mother and wife,[4] who, doubtless, paid for the
printing. Parsons was no genius and his task was not an easy one,
but he acquitted himself pretty well, and his sermon is a passable
piece of seventeenth-century pulpit oratory, valuable still for some

[1] See above, p. 170, Curll, 127; Davies, III, 210.
[2] John Cary appears to have been a highly respected Oxfordshire squire. See R.
Gould's eulogy of him, Gould, I, 275.
[3] Parsons, sigg. A1, A2.   [4] Ibid., sigg. A2, A2v.

vivid biographical details and for preserving some of Rochester's own words spoken during his last illness.

Rochester was buried beside his father in the north aisle of Spelsbury Church,[1] and, probably by his own order, no inscription or monument was placed on his tomb.

Like Byron, Rochester left behind him Memoirs in manuscript which filled the surviving members of his family with such horror that they destroyed them. According to Horace Walpole, Rochester's Memoirs took the form of 'a History of the Intrigues of the Court of Charles II in a series of letters to his friend Henry Savile'.[2] These were probably the 'whole trunk of letters', which, we are told, his mother burned shortly after his death.[3] For this conflagration Richard Bentley, Walpole's friend, wittily suggested that she is now 'burning in heaven'.[4] The loss of Rochester's Memoirs and those of Byron are, perhaps, the two greatest disasters that English literature has sustained through the misplaced scruples of well-meaning people. If only Rochester's family and Byron's executors had had the sense to put the manuscripts away with directions that they should be printed after a lapse of a hundred years! It is true that Rochester's mother might have justified her action by her son's own alleged strict orders given before his death 'to burn all his profane and lewd writings, as being only fit to promote Vice and Immorality, by which he had so highly offended God and blasphemed that Holy Religion into which he had been Baptiz'd and all his obscene and filthy Pictures, which were so notoriously scandalous'.[5] Nevertheless there is something ghoulish about the vision of the old countess, doubtless accompanied by the zealous Mr. Parsons, going round the High Lodge and burning every picture, book and manuscript, which appeared 'profane' or 'lewd' to their heated imaginations.

In spite of all the precautions of his family, however, some of Rochester's 'profane and lewd writings' appeared in print immediately after his death. According to Anthony à Wood, 'no sooner was his (Rochester's) breath out of his body, but some person or persons, who had made a collection of his poetry in manuscript, did, meerly for lucre sake (as 'twas conceiv'd) publish them under this title, *Poems on Several Occasions* Antwerp (alias Lond.) October 1680.'[6] In the early autumn of 1680 badly printed little

---

[1] W.L.T., II, 492, 493. [2] Walpole, C.R.N.A., II, 48.
[3] Walpole, Letters, IX, 308. [4] Ibid. [5] Parsons, 28, 29.
[6] W.A.O., III, 1230.

octavo volumes, claiming on their title pages to be *Poems on Several Occasions by the Rt. Hon. the E. of R.* appear to have been circulating in London and by 2 November Samuel Pepys had bought one of them and mastered its contents. He kept it in a drawer 'on the right hand of his scriptor with his flutes and music books', explaining in a letter to his clerk Will Hewer that the book contained Rochester's poems' 'written before his penitence, in a style I thought unfit to mix with my other books'. 'However,' he adds, 'pray let it remain there for as he is past writing any more so bad in one sense, so I despair of any man surviving him to write so good in another.'[1] Later Pepys had it bound up with some other poems of a porno-graphic kind and copy of Burnet's *Some Passages of the Life and Death of the Right Honourable John Earl of Rochester.* The volume was innocently lettered on the spine 'Rochester's Life'.[2] Pepys's treatment of his copy, the spurious 'Antwerp' imprint and the ab-sence from the title page of the name of a printer or publisher show that the book was regarded as a pornographic and clandestine pub-lication. Its popularity is proved by the fact that no less than ten editions of it have been traced and there is reason to believe that there were others.[3] Rochester's friends were understandably indig-nant. They inserted in the London Gazette of 22–25 November 1680 the following advertisement: 'Whereas there is a Libel of lewd scandalous Poems lately Printed, under the name of the Earl of Rochesters, Whoever shall discover the Printer to Mr. *Thom L Cary* at the Sign of the *Blew Bore* in *Cheap-Side, London*, or to Mr. *Will Richards* at his house in Bow-street Covent-Garden, shall have 5 l reward.'[4] Will Richards has been identified as a publisher. Thom. L. Cary was probably a relative of John Cary, Rochester's executor, and it seems likely that the Earl's family was trying to find and prosecute the printer of the book through his agency and that of a publisher employed by him.

The 'Antwerp' editions contain sixty-one poems. Besides authen-tic works of Rochester they include verses by Aphra Behn, Oldham, Car Scroop, Alexander Radcliffe, Lord Dorset, Thomas D'Urfey and possibly others. Some of the verses in the collection are bawdy trifles which might have been written by any of the Court Wits, who were all addicted to this form of amusement. In 1685 Andrew Thorncome, a publisher who may have been responsible for one of

---

[1] Bryant., 340.   [2] Thorpe, xii.   [3] Ibid., xi.   [4] Prinz., 350, 351.

the 'Antwerp' editions, produced a little volume entitled *Poems on Several Occasions Written by a Late Person of Honour* with a London imprint and the publisher's name on the title page. This collection contains much of the same material as the 'Antwerp' editions, but omits nine poems included in them and adds five others. The last named, it is interesting to notice, include *Plain Dealing's Downfall* and *Consideratus Considerandus*, the two poems which seem to be connected with Rochester's conversion, and which were, I believe, written during his last illness. In the same year as that of the publication of Thorncome's collection, two editions of Rochester's *Valentinian*, which had been produced at Drury Lane on 11 February 1683–4 with Sarah Cooke and Elizabeth Barry on the cast, were published. They included an extremely able and interesting Preface by Rochester's friend Robert Wolseley,[1] defending his poetry and eulogizing him as one in whose company no man could stay 'unentertain'd or leave it uninstructed'. 'Never', Wolseley continues, 'did he laugh in the wrong place, or prostitute his Sence to serve his Luxury; never did he stab into the Wounds of fallen Virtue with a base and cowardly Insult, or smooth the face of prosperous Villany with the Paint and Washes of a mercenary Wit; never did he spare a Fop for being rich, or flatter a Knave for being great. . . . Never was his Talk thought too much, or his Visit too long; Enjoyment did but increase Appetite, and the more men had of his Company, the less willing they were to part with it. He had a Wit that cou'd make even his Spleen and Ill-humour pleasant to his Friends; and the publick chiding of his Servants, which would have been Ill-breeding and intolerable in any other Man, became not only civil and inoffensive, but agreeable and entertaining in him.'

In the latter end of February, 1690 (i.e. 1690–91), Jacob Tonson printed a neat octavo volume entitled *Poems &c on Several Occasions with Valentinian a Tragedy Written by the Right Honourable John Late Earl of Rochester*. It includes 137 pages of Rochester's non-dramatic poems, Alexander Bendo's Bill and *Valentinian*, together with an unsigned Preface (ascribed to Thomas Rymer on the reprint of 1714) and Oldham's Pastoral Elegy on Rochester. The Tonson edition contains thirty-nine poems, sixteen of which had not appeared either in the 'Antwerp' or in Thorncome's edition. Rymer states in his Preface to the Reader that the Publisher 'has been diligent

---

[1] V. sigg. A1–C2v, reprinted in Spingarn, III, 1–31.

out of Measure, and has taken exceeding Care that every Block of Offence shou'd be removed. So that this Book is a Collection of such Pieces only, as may be received in a vertuous Court, and not unbecome the Cabinet of the Severest Matron'.[1] These words are ambiguous. They may refer to the fact that Tonson omitted a number of the more bawdy pieces that had appeared in other collections; they may also signify that a certain amount of expurgation had taken place in the texts that he printed. Actually, as compared with the versions in the 'Antwerp' editions, the texts printed by Tonson omit several bawdy passages, but, as we know nothing of the origins of either edition, it is impossible to tell which is the more authentic. Tonson was, doubtless, capable of bowdlerization, but the pornographers who produced the 'Antwerp' editions were probably also capable of inserting bawdy phrases or even passages.

No less than seven elegies are known to have been written on Rochester's death by contemporary poets and several of them were probably hawked in the London streets in the autumn of 1680. The authors included Aphra Behn, Thomas Flatman, Anne Wharton, Samuel Holland, Samuel Woodford and John Oldham.[2] Oldham's pastoral elegy quoted above[3] is the only one that has any real literary merit. A touching tribute was paid to his memory (under the name of Count Rosidore) by Nathaniel Lee in his comedy *The Princess of Cleve* produced at the Dorset Garden Theatre in September 1681.[4] This passage alone would be sufficient to refute the old story that Rochester was regarded by contemporary men of letters as a malicious tyrant. Lee had nothing to gain by eulogizing him in 1681, and, like Wolseley's Preface, his 'character' of Count Rosidore is clearly the product of genuine affection and admiration. It is reprinted here because it preserves a vivid personal impression of the man, worthy to be set by those of Burnet and Wolseley. The Vidame of Chartres is speaking to the Count Nemours (as, for example, the Earl of Dorset might be speaking to the Duke of Buckingham):

VIDAME: He that was the Life, the Soul of Pleasure,
           Count *Rosidore* is dead.
NEMOURS: Then may we say
           Wit was and Satyr is a Carcass now.
           I thought his last Debauch would be his Death—
           But is it certain?

[1] 1691, sig. A 6v.   [2] Prinz, 239.   [3] Oldham, III, vi, vii, 59–69.
[4] Nichol, 437.

VID: Yes I saw him dust.
I saw the mighty thing a nothing made
Huddled with Worms, and swept to that cold Den
Where Kings lye crumbled just like other Men.

NEM: Nay then let's Rave and Elegize together,
Where Rosidore is now but Common Clay,
Whom every wiser Emmet bears away,
And lays him up against a Winter's day.

He was the Spirit of Wit—and had such an Art in guilding his Failures, that it was hard not to love his Faults: He never spoke a witty thing twice, tho' to different Persons. His Imperfections were catching, and his Genius was so Luxuriant, that he was forc'd to tame it with a Hesitation in his Speech to keep in it view—But, oh! how awkward, how Insipid, how poor and wretchedly dull is the Imitation of those that have all the affectation of his Verse and none of his Wit.[1]

It is interesting to notice the references to Rochester's lines *Upon Nothing* and his poem adapted from Seneca on Death, and to see that the dramatist seems to assume a knowledge of these poems on the part of his audience. The allusion to the hesitation in his speech seems to be the only record of this personal detail.

Rochester's title and estates were inherited by his son the boy Charles Wilmot. He only survived his father by a little over a year, dying at the age of eleven on 30 November 1681.[2] His mother died 'of an apoplexy' shortly afterwards. The old countess seems to have survived till 1687.[3] In 1682 Charles II bestowed the Earldom of Rochester on his faithful supporter Laurence Hyde, younger son of the great Earl of Clarendon.[4]

Rochester's three daughters all married well. The eldest, Anne, 'a tall handsome body' according to Hearne[5] married first a Wiltshire gentleman, Henry Baynton of Spy Park, and secondly Francis Greville, by whom she became ancestress of the Earls of Warwick.[6] It was for Lady Anne Baynton that Thomas Alcock wrote his account of the Alexander Bendo frolic. She appears to have written verses[7]

---

[1] L.P.C., 7.   [2] Prinz, 239; G.E.C., XI, 49.   [3] Luttrell, I, 399.
[4] G.E.C. XI, 49.
[5] H.R.C., IX, 79. Lady Anne's beauty and intelligence are celebrated in a poem on her marriage by 'Placidia' printed in P.O.A.S., 1698, 112–14.
[6] G.E.C., II, 334.
[7] Gould, I, 275: 'To Madam B occasioned by a Copy of Verses of my Lady Ann Bayntons.'

and was praised by the poet Robert Gould who called her '*the Poet's Friend*' and declared that

> in her conduct we see fairly writ
> Her Mother's Heavenly Modesty, her Father's Pow'rful Wit.[1]

Elizabeth, described by Hearne as 'a pretty little Body'[2] married Edward Montague, third Earl of Sandwich, son of that Lord Hinchinbrooke who had once been her mother's suitor. The third daughter, Mallet married John Vaughan, Viscount Lisburne.[3]

Of all Rochester's children Lady Sandwich is said to have resembled him most. We are told that she had 'all the fire and vivacity of her father'.[4] She was the friend of Saint Évremond in her youth and Chesterfield in her old age. Saint Évremond, in a letter to Ninon de L'Enclos, wrote in 1698[5] that Rochester 'had more Wit than any man in England', and that 'my Lady Sandwich has more Wit than her father had: she is as generous as she is witty; and as lovely as witty and generous'. Over half a century later Lord Chesterfield in a letter to his son describes her as one who, 'old as she was, when I saw her last, had the strongest parts of any women I ever knew in my life . . .'.[6] She died in the Rue de Vaugirard, Paris, on 1 July 1757,[7] and may be regarded as the last link with the Wits of the Restoration, that intellectual aristocracy of which her father's genius was the finest flower.

---

[1] Gould, I, 116.   [2] H.R.C., IX, 79.   [3] G.E.C., VIII, 34.   [4] Ibid.
[5] L.S.E., 323.   [6] Chesterfield, 1763.   [7] G.C.E., XI, 434.

APPENDIX

ROCHESTER AND THE POST-BOY (see p. 111)

SOTHEBY'S in a catalogue issued in April 1958 advertised for sale a Poetical Commonplace Book, 304 pp. + 3 pp. index, with contemporary ownership inscription (deleted) of a member of Trinity Hall, Cambridge, dated 1684. I was enabled to inspect this manuscript book by the courtesy of Messrs. Sotheby, before it was purchased by the Seven Gables bookshop, New York, for £360. Among other poems ascribed to Rochester in it, there appeared on p. 254 the following version of the poem quoted on p. 164 of the present work:

> Roch: to a post boy
> Son of a whore G. Dam yee can you tell
> A Peerless Peer ye ready way to hell
> Ive outswill'd Bacchus, sworn of mine own make
> Oaths wou'd ffright ffuries & make Pluto shake
> Ive swiv'd more whores more ways yn Sodom walls
> Ere knew or ye College of Cardinalls
> Witness Heroick scars look here I goe
> Seare & Cloath'd; & ulcered from top to toe
> Broke houses to break Chastity & dy'd
> That flower with murder that my lust deny'd
> Pox ont why doe I mention those poor things
> I have blasphem'd ye Gods & libell'd Kings
> The readiest way to Hell boy quick, ne'r stir,
>
> Boy: The readiest way my Lord's by Rochester

INDEX

237

Van Tromp, M. H., 42
Vanbrugh, Sir J., 106
Vaughan, H., xix
Vaughan, J., Lord, afterwards 3rd
  Earl of Carbery, 73
Vaughan, J. 2nd Viscount Lisburne,
  234
Vaughan, Mallet (Mallet Wilmot),
  Viscountess Lisburne, 139, 234
Vaughan, R., 2nd Earl of Carbery,
  73
Verney, J., 151n., 170, 186
Verney, Sir R., 4, 44, 151n., 170,
  186
Viau, T. de, xiv, 186
Vieth, D., 75n., 141n., 171n.
Villiers, G., 2nd Duke of Bucking-
  ham, 34, 45, 92, 127, 136, 148,
  166, 167, 181, 210, 232
Virgil, 19, 46
Voltaire, F. M. A. de, xvii, 226
Vyner, Sir R., 78

Wadham College, 5, 6
Waller, E., 61, 167
Walpole, H., viii, xvii, 229
Walter, Lucy, 174
Walter, Mary, 174
Warre, F., 227
Warre, Lady, 35, 141
Warre, Sir J., 35, 43
Watteau, A., 46, 47, 49
Wharton, Anne, 232
Wheate, Isabella, 227
Whibley, C., 120
Whichcote, B., 194, 197, 198
Whitehall, R., xiii, 7, 24, 45
Whitfield, F., xvii, 120n.
Wilkins, Dr. J., 6
Wilkinson, H., 11
Willey, B., xvii, 26n., 29
William, Prince of Orange, after-
  wards William III, viii, 167
Williams, C., xvii, 145n.

Williamson, Sir J. (Secretary
  Williamson), 161
Wilmot, Anne, see Baynton, Lady
  Anne
Wilmot, Anne (Anne St. John),
  Countess of Rochester, 2, 4, 25n.,
  39, 40, 55, 140, 145, 154, 215,
  218, 227–9, 233
Wilmot, Charles, Viscount Wilmot,
  afterwards 3rd Earl of Rochester,
  24, 72, 139, 143–5, 225, 228, 233
Wilmot, Elizabeth (Elizabeth
  Malet), Countess of Rochester,
  viii, 35–8, 43, 44, 48, 49, 52, 54,
  107, 139–46, 215, 218, 227, 228,
  233
Wilmot, Elizabeth, see Montagu,
  Elizabeth, Countess of Sandwich
Wilmot, H., 1st Earl of Rochester,
  2–4, 9, 229
Wilmot, John, 2nd Earl of Rochester: portraits, viii; reputation,
  xx–xxii; birth, 2, 3; education,
  4–11; travels, 12–21; enters
  Padua University, 20; influence
  of Hobbes, 22–9; at Court, 32ff.;
  attempted abduction of Elizabeth
  Malet, 35, 36; imprisoned, 37;
  service in Dutch war, 38–42; at
  Bergen, 39, 40; marriage, 44;
  Gentleman of the Bedchamber,
  44; as Dorimant, 61–3; Miss
  Hobart and Miss Temple, 65–9;
  boxes Killigrew's ears, 71; in
  Paris, 72; 'Generall' of the Ballers,
  73; satirizes Charles II, 74–9;
  smashes the King's dials, 80;
  practises medicine as 'Alexander
  Bendo', 81–90; relations with
  Dryden, 91–3, 96–102, 181–4;
  'Black Will' letter, 100, 101;
  Quarrels with Mulgrave, 93–6;
  Rochester as patron, 102–4; trains
  Elizabeth Barry, 104–6; Oxford-

DATE DUE